HUMAN TYPES
Essence and the Enneagram

HUMAN TYPES
Essence and the Enneagram

SUSAN ZANNOS

SAMUEL WEISER, INC.

York Beach, Maine

First published in 1997 by
Samuel Weiser, Inc.
P.O. Box 612
York Beach, ME 03910-0612

Library of Congress Cataloging-in-Publication Data

   Zannos, Susan
     Human types essence and the enneagram / Susan Zannos.
        p. cm.
     Includes index.
     ISBN 0-87728-883-6 (pbk. : alk. paper)
     1. Enneagram. 2. Typology (Psychology) I. Title.
   BF698.35.E54Z36 1997
   155.2′6—dc21   97-9193
                                                    CIP

ISBN 0-87728-883-6
EB

Typeset in 11 point Bembo

Photographs of human types © 1997 Frederic Choisel

Cover design by Ray Rue

Playing card illustrations reproduced by permission of U.S. Games Systems,
Inc./Carta Mundi. Further reproduction prohibited.

Printed in the United States of America

05 04 03 02 01 00 99 98 97
10 9 8 7 6 5 4 3 2 1

The paper used in this publication meets the minimum requirements of the
American National Standard for Permanence of Paper for Printed Library
Materials Z39.48-1984.

*To Kathryn Tate, my mother, who has always
believed in the highest possibilities, and to
Robert Burton, my teacher, who has realized them.*

CONTENTS

LIST OF FIGURES

Photographs of the Types

PREFACE

It is reasonable for the reader of any book to want to know something about the person who had the temerity to write it. This is particularly so in the present instance, since the subject matter of this book is a system which has as its object the development of consciousness. I begin with the contention that we are all asleep and subjective, unable to understand the truth about our condition because of the limitations of being a specific type.

Have I escaped from this condition? I have not. I have worked with the ideas of this system for over twenty years and, in the process, have verified that my understanding is partial and limited. The system itself, as far as I can tell, does not seem to be either partial or limited, but reveals more, becomes richer and deeper, the more it is used as a tool with which to increase the understanding of human experience.

This Fourth Way system, which was brought to the West from Russia in the early years of this century, is currently used in many different ways in many different groups and organizations all over the world. The particular organization with which I have had the good fortune to work is the Fellowship of Friends, a school that has its center of operations in the Sierra Foothills of Northern California, and other centers, some seventy or eighty of them, in most of the major cities of the world. The Fellowship has as its leader and teacher Robert Burton, a man who has developed certain of the aspects of the Gurdjieff-Ouspensky tradition into a teaching that is uniquely his own. Always practical in his approach, Robert Burton has held to a single clear method which he has spoken of and demonstrated for the twenty-five years his school has been in existence. This method is described in his book, *Self-Remembering*.

This method of self-study and development begins with Ouspensky's observation that functions are not consciousness and consciousness is not functions. In other words, our real identity is not in the body that bears our name, that was born on a particular day and will die on a particular day, that has nerves and muscles and heart and mind programmed with the language and customs of a particular culture and the memories of specific experiences. Rather, our identity is, or could be, in the consciousness that can observe and understand these beings we take to be ourselves.

This book is not primarily about the process of observation and separation from the manifestations of "the machine"—a Fourth Way term traditionally used to describe the physical body and its programming. For that there are many excellent books available. This book speaks to a beginning level and attempts to describe the considerable variety of human beings, using the system of classification developed in Robert Burton's teaching.

This system of classification developed gradually through the work of Gurdjieff, Ouspensky, Rodney Collin, and other Fourth Way teachers. It has been refined and further developed by Robert Burton as a tool to help his students understand what they see when they try to observe themselves. Only when this understanding of human types has penetrated deeply will the student become serious about developing the inner unity, the "self" or soul, which may become strong enough to exist independently of the body and control its many different manifestations.

Although this book does not focus directly on the process of observation and separation, it has little meaning outside of that context. Without the possibility of developing something other than the naturally occurring creatures that we are, the information in this book is horrible. We are born, act in certain predetermined ways, have certain inevitable kinds of experiences as a result of the type of human animal we happen to be, and die, our lives no more significant than those of sheep or flatworms, regardless of what we may achieve in the world of material existence and time.

As to why I have undertaken to write this book, since I, too, am a beginner, and very much involved in the world of material existence, I am not entirely sure. I can, however, recount briefly the experiences which motivated me. I was in St. Petersburg, where I had the chance to work with a center of the Fellowship which had opened there after the renewed availability of these ideas in Russia. The Russian students had access to the classic Fourth Way books of Gurdjieff and Ouspensky (many of them clandestinely printed on mimeograph machines and hand-bound to be owned and read secretly during the Soviet period when they were banned). They did not, however, have access to the Fourth Way material which has been published in the West during the past seventy-five years. A Russian publisher expressed his interest in producing a book on body types, and, since I had some previous writing experience and had worked with these ideas in an attempt to observe myself and others for the past twenty years, some friends suggested that I might be the person to write such a book. One thing, as we say, led to another, and I returned from Russia with a contract to write a book on human types. This is that book.

As to my own qualifications, they have certainly been called into question during the writing process. In their defense, I can say that I have been singularly fortunate in that, in addition to being a member of the Fellowship and having a teacher of the stature of Robert Burton, I have had a career as a college teacher all my adult life. This has given me the opportunity to observe, and observe quite closely over extended periods, thousands of college students. (Assuming an average of about fifty students per quarter and three quarters per year for thirty years—which is a conservative estimate since I usually have more students than that and nearly always teach summer classes—that would be 4,500 students. Whew!) Since I am an English teacher and my students do a lot of writing for my classes, my observations have not been limited to my students' external manifestations, but have included glimpses into their thoughts and attitudes as well.

When I have been present, and awake enough to do so, I have applied information about body types to my observations of students, to observations of and discussions with members of the Fellowship with whom I have worked closely over the last twenty years, and to observations of professional colleagues, friends, and family members. This has resulted in my personal verification of the accuracy of this information.

My personal opportunities and experiences constitute my qualifications. But of course I have brought to those opportunities and experiences the limitations of my own subjectivity, the biases and prejudices of my own type. It cannot be otherwise. Certain of my mechanical proclivities have been useful in the process of writing this book. Others have not.

I am an emotionally centered Mars-Jovial woman. For those who have made observations about human types using this system of classification, the previous sentence is a complete autobiography. It is also an explanation of the way I see the world. Even when I intentionally apply the information of the Fourth Way system, I cannot change the distortions made by the equipment I have for perceiving, for understanding, and for expressing what I perceive and understand, any more than I can see the ultra-violet spectrum with my unaided eyesight. I am attracted more to some types than to others. I understand those people who have mechanics similar to my own better than I understand those whose mechanics are very dissimilar. Furthermore, the Mars-Jovial type has a discernible tendency to consider its own subjectivity to be divinely revealed objective truth, so there is always the danger that misunderstandings will be presented in tones of ringing conviction.

On the other hand, each type has its own subjectivity, and that subjectivity persists (although it is certainly mitigated) even though the level of consciousness and understanding increases through work and persistent effort over time. Therefore the limitations of my particular type make me no less qualified than other types would be. The vanity of the Jovial encouraged me to embark upon the project, and the cussedness of the Martial enabled me to complete it.

CHAPTER 1

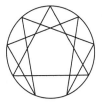

ORIGINS

No question has consistently baffled and preoccupied human beings more than that of what we are and how we got to be what we are. No answers have satisfied us completely for long. The attempt to define a species that has included, in this century alone, Albert Einstein, Mother Theresa, Adolf Hitler, the assistant manager of the supermarket on the corner, and the victims of famine in Africa has produced theories that fall into distinct categories. Over centuries of recorded history, the most popular category postulates a divine origin—our creation by some form of higher being. Recently these theories have fallen into disfavor, although certainly they have not disappeared.

Replacing theories of divine creation have been theories of evolution, such as Lamarck's and Darwin's, which consider human beings as just another kind of living organism which has developed on this planet according to certain natural laws governing the development of species. These theories have been bolstered by increasingly sophisticated technologies that enable researchers to see smaller and smaller particles with electron microscopes. They have discovered the strands of DNA molecules that carry genetic coding. This revelation has so entranced them that they have been willing to abandon most previous conjecture in favor of definitions of humankind that emphasize genetic development.

At the same time the theories of genetic evolution have thrived, the psychological differences so obvious between one human and another have been attributed to differences in the conditions under which particular persons come into the world and grow to adulthood. Which of these two factors, nature or nurture, genetic endowment or social conditioning, is the most important is a question that has received much attention during the last century. Like most either-or postulates, this one has had the effect of organizing observations and data into diametric positions, and has prevented serious consideration of any other possibilities.

During the past fifty years, however, observers have been suggesting that there is another factor that needs to be considered: human types. William Sheldon's categories of human physique, which he correlated with psychological tendencies, achieved prominence in the early 1940s. Sheldon's endomorphs, ectomorphs, and mesomorphs have, as we will see, been followed by other theories that describe distinct human types. The existence of types of human beings is no longer so hotly debated as it was at midcentury (the generation that had just survived a war to establish the master race was understandably leery of any such classification), but neither is any system of types widely accepted. Furthermore, it is assumed even by most of those who are convinced that definite human types exist, that these types are determined by either genetic endowment or social conditioning. In other words, the issue is assumed to fall within the nature/nurture controversy. That there might be other factors operating to determine human types has not been investigated by the scientific community, at least as far as I know.

Which of the systems of classifying humans is correct? Only your observations will enable you to verify the accuracy of any system. The problem of determining human types is so difficult and confusing because human beings are the most complex and intricately organized life form on this planet. And the earth abounds with different life forms of amazing complexity. Humans, who have not even begun to understand all the mysteries of plant and animal life, have nonetheless created marvelous machines, incredible technologies, global electronic communications systems using artificial satellites, computer networks and databases that can make all of human knowledge available and any fact retrievable in seconds. Yet humans are immeasurably more complex organisms than any cellular or electronic creation that they either study or use.

Because there are so many speculative theories about human types, it seems reasonable to begin with a brief discussion of where the information presented in this book comes from. In looking at the recent history of this particular way of classifying humans, it is important to remember that the people who use, and have used, this system have never claimed that these ideas were developed by them. What they have claimed is that there is objective truth, that this truth has always been available to people willing to learn it, but that the way to understanding the truth requires a higher level of consciousness than humans habitually function with.

This description of human types, and the use of an ancient symbol called the enneagram to explain the types and their relationships to each other, is a part of a system of spiritual development known as the Fourth Way. The description of human types in the Fourth Way system is only part of a much larger whole. The practical study of these physical and psychological types is, however, a good place to begin to verify some of the ideas of the larger system. And this information can help anyone who understands it—and uses it for self observation and observation of others—to save a lot of the effort and grief that results from trying to change people.

The human propensity to think that things could be other than they are in human relationships is one of our most pervasive illusions. We think that if only we had behaved differently, such and such a situation would never have happened. If only our husbands or wives would behave differently, we would be so much happier. If only our children behaved differently. . . . If only our employer would behave differently. . . . If, instead of trying to change ourselves and others, we put the same amount of effort into trying to understand why people behave as they do, and why they could not possibly behave in any other way, we probably would not change much of what happens. We might, however, change the way we react to what happens.

If you are not going to change what happens, what good is all this anyway? We are trapped in our belief that if our lives were somehow different—if we had more, if we had better, if we had someone else or something else—we would be happier. The potential gain from this effort to understand human beings and why we behave the way we do is not toward any exterior, material good. This effort may produce, after very long sustained observations, greater understanding. And when we understand, truly understand, we begin to love.

There is no need to offer any arguments on behalf of love. Anyone who has had even a fragmentary glimpse, the most partial experience, of loving others knows that it is the ultimate value. It is the pearl of great price, the kingdom of heaven within, nirvana. None of the words that have tried to describe love have come close to describing the experience, but St. Paul made a very moving attempt in his first letter to the Corinthians:

> If I speak in the tongues of men and of angels, but have not love, I am a noisy gong or a clanging cymbal. And if I have prophetic powers, and understand all mysteries and all knowledge, and if I have all faith, so as to remove mountains, but have not love, I am nothing. If I give away all that I have, and if I deliver my body to be burned, but have not love, I gain nothing.

> Love is patient and kind; love is not jealous or boastful; it is not arrogant or rude. Love does not insist on its own way; it is not irritable or resentful; it does not rejoice at wrong, but rejoices in the right. Love bears all things, believes all things, hopes all things, endures all things. (I Corinthians, xiii, 1–7).[1]

---

[1] All biblical references are from *The Holy Bible*, Revised Standard Version, New York: Nelson & Sons, 1951.

If understanding human types and human relationships doesn't change much in the outer world, and it probably won't, it can cause changes in the inner world that qualify as miracles. You probably won't get a big house and a new car and a wonderful job, but you may come to realize that those are very small gifts compared to true understanding.

The Fourth Way system of describing human types is believed to be very old, but the recent history of its transmission can be traced. In the early years of this century, a Russian journalist returned to St. Petersburg from his travels in the East. He had been in search of a school in which he might learn about the reality which he felt must underlie the surface absurdity of life. His trip had been cut short by some of the social, economic, and political aspects of that absurdity in the form of the beginning of the First World War. The journalist was Peter Demianovitch Ouspensky, a mathematician who had already published several important works, such as *Tertium Organum*, which had been translated into several Western languages and had won acclaim abroad.

Ouspensky lectured about his experiences in the East, both in St. Petersburg and in Moscow. While in Moscow in 1915, he met a Greek-Armenian from the Caucasus who had also made trips to the East, but with somewhat better results. This man, George Ivanovitch Gurdjieff, was teaching a system which Ouspensky became convinced would enable him to find the reality he was seeking. Gurdjieff was already working with groups in Moscow. When Ouspensky returned to St. Petersburg, he helped to organize a group there which worked with the ideas Gurdjieff explained to them in his talks and demonstrations.

Gurdjieff's work with groups, his dance movements, his music, his relocations and travels, and his associations with his students have been well documented from 1915 until his death in 1949. Prior to his meeting with Ouspensky in Moscow, however, the record is not at all clear. As a result, we do not know the exact sources of the system he taught. Gurdjieff's own account of his early life, his travels, and his supposed membership in a group which called itself "The Seekers of the Truth," is presented in his book, *Meetings with Remarkable Men*. (The Peter Brooks film of the same name is based on Gurdjieff's book.)

Gurdjieff was a teacher, not a historian. His books were written with a purpose, and that purpose was not factual accuracy. *Meetings with Remarkable Men* is a great read. It is lively, entertaining, wise, and well written. It contains reminiscences, particularly about his father and early home life, which are deeply emotional and certainly seem genuine. It contains adventurous narratives which are wonderfully interesting and may or may not be based on events which actually occurred. And it contains delightful spoofs and parodies that only the most hopelessly credulous could believe really happened. Ultimately, it seems that we can do no better than Gurdjieff's own version of his early life, although certainly many biographers have tried to ferret out the facts.[2]

Gurdjieff was born in Alexandropol in the Russian Caucasus region. His father was Greek and his mother Armenian. His exact date of birth is not known—the date on his passport was November 28, 1877, but he was probably born at least five or six years earlier than that. His family moved to nearby Kars where he studied with the dean of the Russian military cathedral. This area at this time was a place of great cultural mixing and intermingling of religions and traditions. The young Gurdjieff had many direct experiences of inexplicable events—miracle cures, occult phenomena, evidence of telepathic and clairvoyant abilities. His teachers and priests were unable to explain these occurrences satisfactorily, so Gurdjieff determined to find some answers on his own.

He gathered much material in his native area. The region between the Black Sea and the Caspian Sea had long been a migratory route where the traditions of Europe and Asia mingled. Gurdjieff learned much from the Orthodox Christian monastic sources of his family's religion. Indeed, one of his contemporaries, Boris Mouravieff, contends that Gurdjieff's system is taken entirely from esoteric Orthodox Christianity.

---

[2]See particularly James Webb, *The Harmonious Circle* (New York: G. P. Putnam's Sons 1980).

It is almost certain that the famed Gurdjieff dance movements were taken from, or at least very strongly influenced by, the Islamic Sufi tradition in Afghanistan. Gurdjieff joined various Sufi orders and stayed for a while in an isolated monastery. The enneagram, a central symbol in Gurdjieff's work, is probably of Sufi origin, perhaps used in the movements of the dervishes in their whirling dance.

It has been suggested that Gurdjieff's activities at this time, the years near the turn of the century, included being a secret agent for Russia. At any rate, he crossed many borders with ease. His presence in Tibet may have been arranged by the Tsarist government in response to the Dalai Lama's request for protection from Britain and China. It is almost certain that Gurdjieff had access to monasteries in Tibet that would have been closed to anyone without official connections. In later years, he attributed a few of his dance movements to Buddhist sources within Tibet.

Other places Gurdjieff is assumed to have traveled in search of esoteric knowledge and possibly also as a secret agent include Egypt, Crete, Sumeria, Assyria, the Holy Land, Ethiopia, and the Sudan. The facts are few, the rumors exotic and romantic. Gurdjieff seems to have been many things to many people, but he seems consistently to have been a very practical man. As a practical man, he was aware of how much his fellow humans love romance and mystery and wondrous tales. He seems not to have been above using our natural credulity for his own purposes.

Gurdjieff returned to Russia and evidently found a place at the court of Tsar Nicholas II. Certainly what we know of the fascination with the occult at Nicholas's court makes Gurdjieff's presence there plausible. He married a Polish lady-of-the-court, Countess Ostrofska, during this period, and is rumored to have had a friendly relationship with Rasputin.

After the meeting of Ouspensky and Gurdjieff in 1915, Gurdjieff worked with groups of students in both Moscow and St. Petersburg until it became increasingly apparent that the chaos of war and revolution was so disrupting life in Russia that their work would soon be impossible. A determined group fled on foot over the mountains to Essentuki and later to Tiflis. But even there, the effects of the revolution made their efforts impossible. They moved on to Constantinople, then Berlin, and finally to Paris. Gurdjieff was able to raise enough money to purchase a château near Fontainebleu outside of Paris, and it was there that he founded the institute known as the Prieure. There his students worked together, practiced the dance movements, and concentrated on their development of consciousness.

Gurdjieff's ideas spread among the intellectuals and artists of Western Europe during the 1920s. Ouspensky had parted from Gurdjieff, for reasons that remain obscure, and was working with groups in London that included such writers and J. G. Bennett, A. R. Orage, and Maurice Nicoll, each of whom was to produce many volumes about the Fourth Way. After Ouspensky's death in 1947, his students went their various ways. Some joined the groups working with Gurdjieff. Others began their own groups. Rodney Collin led a small group in Mexico where he lived and taught until his death on a trip to Cuzco in 1956. By then Rodney Collin's groups had spread to many South American cities. He had been visiting a group in Lima, Peru when he took the fatal sidetrip to Cuzco.

Gurdjieff's work has now spread to all parts of the world. Before he died in Paris in 1949, Gurdjieff spent hours with Mme. de Salzmann who had been his student since the early days in Tiflis and Constantinople. She became the head of the Gurdjieff Foundation, which has groups working throughout the world. Outside of the official institution of the Foundation, many other groups exist which work with Gurdjieff's system, or some version of it.

In beginning to discuss his system in five lectures titled *The Psychology of Man's Possible Evolution*,[3] Ouspensky distinguished between two quite different types of psychology. The first type studies man as he is; the second type studies man as he might become. It is the second type, an evolutionary psychology, with

---

[3]P. D. Ouspensky, *The Psychology of Man's Possible Evolution* (New York: Alfred A. Knopf, 1974), p. 6.

which the Fourth Way is primarily concerned. Nonetheless, this system of spiritual development begins with the observation of man as he is. In other words, there is considerable overlap in the two kinds of psychological study. In order for a person to develop a higher level of being, it is first necessary to understand what sort of being that person is now. That was the injunction carved at the entrance to the Delphic Oracle: "Know Thyself."

One of the central ideas of Ouspensky's system is that most human beings have many illusions and erroneous ideas about themselves, and that it is exactly these imaginary notions that prevent them from changing, from reaching a higher level of existence. People dream their lives rather than living them. Whether lost in memories and regrets about the past, or planning for and dreaming of the future, men and women bypass the only life that they can have, the life existing in the present moment. But because their dreams create the illusion that they are awake, that they are leading real lives, few notice that they actually do not exist—that is, they are not aware of themselves or their surroundings—most of the time.

One illusion we have relates to our individuality and unity. When we refer to ourselves we say "I", and we believe that there is an "I" that is consistent and responsible for our actions. There is, however, no such "I." Instead, there is a rapidly fluctuating and alternating stream of "I's," a different one appearing about every three seconds. Because we have the same body from one day to the next, the same name, the same habits, we are able to sustain the illusion that we have unity. There may be different moods, different desires, different thoughts, different appetites, different aims, but surely there must be something that unites them all, or so we think when we think about it at all.

According to Gurdjieff, a person is nothing but a stimulus-response machine—"Machines we are born and machines we die," he said.[4] A human in the usual condition is nothing but a

---

[4]P. D. Ouspensky, *In Search of the Miraculous* (New York: Harcourt Brace, 1949), p. 19.

sort of automaton that reacts to whatever is occurring in the environment but has no control over those reactions. Such a thing has no unity because it only responds to whatever impressions and experiences accidentally come its way.

Not only do we not have the unity that we imagine ourselves to have, but we also do not have the ability to "do" anything, and for the same reason. The idea that we can "do," that we make decisions, formulate plans, set goals, and achieve the things we set out to do is one of the most cherished illusions we have. According to Gurdjieff, however, people are only intricately designed and programmed robots with particular functions. When one of our buttons is pushed and a function is activated, it performs as it was designed to perform. If a piece of bread is put into a toaster and the lever is pushed down, the wires heat up and toast the bread. If a friend tells you that you look good in what you are wearing, the wires heat up and produce a little glow in the solar plexus so that you feel warm and good. In both cases, it is just the response of a machine to a particular stimulus. You are not "doing" any more than the toaster is.

Of course we are very much more complex than toasters. We have more possible functions, and respond to a much greater variety of stimuli. We are so well designed that we can perform very intricate activities in sleep, while we are dreaming that we are awake and actually deciding to do what we are "doing." We believe that we have will and can determine our future circumstances.

Yet another imaginary attribute that we humans ascribe to ourselves is consciousness. When we are not stretched out in our beds completely oblivious to what is around us, we consider that we are awake, and that we know what is going on. In fact, however, people very seldom notice what is going on around them. Either they are totally absorbed in one small part of their environment, such as a newspaper they are reading or a person with whom they are conversing, or they are equally absorbed in their own inner worlds, thinking about something that they read in the newspaper that morning, or replaying a conversation they had with a friend the previous night. Whether the awareness is directed outward or inward, it is both partial and dim.

The irony of our situation is that our illusions, the lies we tell ourselves about our actual condition, are what prevent us from attaining the very qualities that we believe we already have. As long as we are satisfied with dreams and imaginings about our lives, we won't make the effort necessary to actually live our lives. If we think we are conscious, we won't have to struggle to wake up. If we believe that we are unified individuals, we won't even notice the chaotic shifting "I's" that pull us aimlessly around in circles. If we are convinced that we already have will, that we can do whatever we set out to do, there is no reason to make the large efforts required to actually develop will.

Gurdjieff used the metaphor that we own a splendid mansion, but we only live in the cellar and the kitchen. We are not aware that there are other stories to our dwelling. There are magnificently furnished rooms of beautiful furniture we have never seen. We live in squalor on the lower levels, never venturing beyond the kitchen door. Our birthright is a palace more splendid than any ever built by tsar or emperor, but we live like serfs in the scullery.

There are four states of consciousness possible for human beings, but most experience only the two lowest states. Each of these states is added onto the state below it, as a house is built on its foundations, the second story upon the first, and so forth. The lowest state of consciousness is called the first state, the state called sleep. The next state, the second state, is actually a kind of waking sleep in which we rise from our beds, dress, eat, work, write books, build bridges, fight wars, contribute to charities, and carry out all the work of the world, believing that we are conscious and that this is all there is to consciousness.

The third state of consciousness is as different from the second as the second is from the first. In the third state of consciousness, we can know the truth about ourselves and our condition. We are aware of our surroundings and of ourselves in our surroundings. We remember ourselves. This term, "self-remembering," is a very important concept—indeed, it is the central concept of this system. Ouspensky emphasized that all of our problems occur because we do not remember ourselves. Even if we are aware of our surroundings, of where we are and who we are with, we do not remember ourselves, that we are there.

Most people have brief experiences of the third state of consciousness at times during their lives, but they do not recognize these states for what they are; they do not value them or realize the possibilities that are suggested by them. The third state can be evoked by danger, by intense suffering, by sudden shocks, and sometimes by great beauty. Sometimes being in new and unfamiliar surroundings can cause the third state to appear. One is suddenly aware not only of the environment, but of oneself in the new setting. It is as though a fog had cleared and everything is seen clearly.

Beyond, or above, this state is yet another. The fourth state of consciousness is a state in which objective truth can be known. Paradoxically, there is probably more information about this highest state than there is about the third state which must precede it. Religious literature, accounts of mystical visions, describe a reality beyond day-to-day experience. But only by first becoming consistently aware of what our day-to-day experience actually is, as opposed to what we imagine it to be, can we have any chance of penetrating this higher reality.

The Gurdjieff Work, as it is known, consists of exercises designed to help students work directly on increasing their level of consciousness. Our mechanicality, our sleep, is a very well-constructed prison in which we are trapped. Once we realize that we are imprisoned, we may want to escape. Of course, not everyone wants to escape. Some may be satisfied with making the prison as comfortable as possible, bribing the guards to provide a television and VCR, having pizza delivered, and buying a more comfortable mattress and some big pillows. That is entirely their right.

But for those who want to escape and find out what sort of life might be possible outside of the prison, a lot of work is required. Nature only brings the development of human beings to a certain level. To progress beyond that point is left to the efforts of the person who wishes a higher level of being. The prison break, getting the tools, digging the tunnel to the light, requires help from both those who have escaped before—that is, people who have achieved consciousness and all it implies—and from others who are also trying to escape. Because of the strength and durability of the prison—that is, the depth and soundness of our sleep—it is virtually impossible for one person working alone to escape. But a group of people working together can try to keep each other awake, can take turns digging, can share the tools, and may have a chance. The person on the outside, the one who has already escaped, is essential to the effort. The work is not likely to succeed without the guidance of a conscious teacher.

The tools the prisoners are given will depend to a certain extent on the expertise of the particular teacher. Teachers must of necessity work from their own being. If they have achieved consciousness, this implies that they are unique individuals, no longer stimulus-response machines. They will not copy the methods of another. Gurdjieff increased his students' level of awareness by teaching them the dances and movements he had learned from Sufi and Buddhist traditions. To be executed correctly, these movements cannot be performed mechanically, but require constant sustained attention. As soon as students lose control of their attention, it is apparent to them and to everyone else involved.

Ouspensky and his direct circle used lectures and questions and answers to examine the mental processes and the observations that they were making. Rodney Collin used still other methods, combining the principles of the Fourth Way with the ideas of charitable service and the Catholic religion. Other teachers use still other forms to help their students raise their level of consciousness. But whatever the method, the increase of consciousness is the reason for the exercise. When a method begins to be used for its own sake, as though the value were in the preservation of the method itself, then it is quite likely that the organization is no longer a Fourth Way school in the sense that Gurdjieff and Ouspensky intended, but is just an ordinary human institution.

Although the tools, the forms, the techniques used by one conscious teacher may be very different than those used by another, there are certain characteristics of the Fourth Way that are not likely to be very different. Whatever the form, it will require controlled attention. Students who are beginning to work on themselves do not have much in the way of consciousness, but they do have some ability to control attention (if not, they will be unable to continue and will wander off and spend their time and energies on something else). This is the beginning.

The attention of an ordinary person—someone who is not attempting to control attention—flows in one direction. The attention is either going outward to some object or person in the exterior world, or it is directed inward to the person's own thoughts and feelings. This is the natural condition of human beings, the state of waking sleep, and is called "identification." The term indicates that there is no distinction between the person and the object or thought or emotion that has captured the attention. The person has ceased to exist and has become entirely the words in the newspaper, the decision of what to cook for dinner, the words spoken to a friend. The basic technique that a teacher assists a student in developing is to divide the attention. This means that the student tries to have his or her attention divided between two, or more, things at once. The student may be attempting an intricate dance movement, but at the same time he is observing himself trying to execute the movement. The student may be trying to understand one of the diagrams in a book by Ouspensky, but at the same time she is trying to be aware of herself holding the book, sitting at a desk with a mug of tea beside her. In other words, whatever the activity, the student is simultaneously trying to perform the activity and observe himself performing the activity.

This system is called the "Fourth Way" precisely because of these techniques and the fact that they can be applied anywhere at any time. The three traditional ways of spiritual development—the way of the yogi, the way of the monk, and the way of the fakir—require that practitioners be removed from the everyday life of the world, from jobs, families, hobbies, entertainment, whatever their lives formerly involved. The way of the yogi, for example, requires disciplining the mind, meditating on intellectual problems in a monastic setting. The way of the monk, the religious way, requires control of the emotions in an effort to have a constant attitude of thankful obedience. This also is typically in a monastic setting. The way of the fakir also requires control, this time control of the body as the practitioner endures physical suffering. The three traditional ways, as they work on the mind, the emotions, and the physical body, require the control of attention and can lead to higher levels of consciousness. The Fourth Way concentrates from the beginning on the development of consciousness. Since the effort to divide attention can be made no matter what activity is being experienced, there is no need for the student of the Fourth Way to retire from the world. He can observe himself whatever else he is doing, having dinner with his wife and children, programming a computer, mowing the lawn, watching a movie. Whether he has the inner discipline to do so is another matter.

This aspect of the Gurdjieff Work, the self observation, the self remembering, is, as mentioned before, the core of this system. Only through self observation can these ideas be verified. But as soon as the student begins to try to control his attention, it becomes apparent how very difficult this is. No sooner has an observation been made than the inner voices begin to comment on it, and observation ceases. Identification with the associations that start piling up captures the attention, and the former observer is asleep again. For example, a man is reading his morning newspaper at the kitchen table before leaving for work. He is attempting to divide his attention. As he turns the page, and readjusts the paper, his left hand goes to his face and he pushes his glasses up the bridge of his nose with his thumb. Suddenly the image of his father reading occurs to him. He remembers that his father used to make exactly that movement of pushing his glasses back into position when they slipped down his nose. Then he remembers a recent article on behaviorism that contended all of human movement patterns were learned by imitation. The newspaper, the table he is sitting at, the room he is in all disappear from his awareness as he sinks into the associative dream that was started by his observation of a simple gesture he had not formerly realized he made. Because sustained observation is so difficult, we would have little chance of piecing together our glimpses of reality into a coherent whole without assistance.

The assistance the Fourth Way system gives is a series of schematics, descriptions of what sort of beings we are. It is important to remember that these descriptions—be they diagrams or explanations or complicated tables of numbers or metaphors—are not intended to form a belief system. Of course, it is much easier to believe than to observe. But to use the system in this way is only to incorporate it into our dreams, not to use it to wake up. On the other hand, having these explanations of what the human machine is like can assist observers in classifying and organizing observations.

I remember dissecting a frog in a biology lab. I had a diagram of an open frog in my biology book, and the book was open on the lab table beside my frog. The inside of my frog did not look much like the diagram. It was a mess. Gradually, however, I was able to find the frog's circulatory system. It was all mixed up and hidden in muscle and bone and organs and other stuff, but it was there. It was not clear and well defined and colored in clear red lines like the picture in my book, but it was there. Left to my own devices without the diagram, I don't believe I would have been able to dissect out the arteries and veins.

Having the explanations of what we will probably observe when we begin work on ourselves can help us to understand what we see. If learning the descriptions replaces observation rather than assisting it, there is no purpose served.

The most important distinction to be made when observing human behavior is between essence and false personality. To put it as simply as possible, essence contains the qualities inherent in a person at birth, while false personality is all the learned behaviors and psychological mechanisms which develop in response to pressure on the child to behave in ways which parents and other members of the culture find acceptable. Gradually people become convinced that these learned behaviors of false personality actually are who they are, and they accept these identities as real. Eventually this false personality completely dominates the lives of most people, even though the learned attitudes and patterns of behavior may be very unlike their true natures in essence. The schematics presented in this discussion of human types refer to human essences, that is, what is most genuine in us.

Before looking at these schematics, it is useful to set them in the context both of the long history of such descriptions of human types and of the scientific research in this century which has turned up some interesting and relevant data.

CHAPTER 2

ANCIENT WISDOM

There is every reason to believe that more was known about human beings 1,000 years, 2,000 years, even 4,000 years ago than is known today. The illusions harbored about human progress are based on increasingly sophisticated technologies, not on increased understanding. No one, for example, has improved on the Sermon on the Mount. Indeed, as technology has increased our ability to interact with each other, either in person by supersonic travel or electronically with various media, it has become very much more apparent that we miscommunicate. We do not understand. And since technology has increased our ability to destroy each other, the need for understanding and compassion has become more than just important. It has become crucial.

The study of human types is very ancient, far older than recorded history. A good way to begin an investigation of human types is to look briefly at some of the systems of classifying humans that existed in the ancient world. Some of these, such as the astrological systems of Egypt and Mesopotamia, and the descriptions of the Olympian gods known to the ancient Greeks, predate the use of writing. We cannot know where or when these systems actually originated, or how long they existed in an oral tradition before their first appearance in written form. We also have no way of knowing how much or how little distortion of the original system may have taken place before it took a set form in written literature.

By the time of Homer, who probably lived in the eighth century B.C., the description of types that was included in the stories about the Olympian gods was already well developed. This compelling mythology, which fascinates us today as it fascinated the Greeks four millennia ago, contains wonderfully accurate depictions of human psychological types. It provides us with archetypes of the human essences which exist today as they have always existed. Indeed, the names of the Greek gods, in the form given them by the Romans who adopted the Greek religion as their own, are the names given to the planets of the solar system, and to the human types that those planets govern.

In the eighth century B.C. both Homer and Hesiod produced works of epic poetry that contain many tales of the gods. Later the Greek tragic poets Aeschylus, Sophocles, and Euripedes revealed more material about the gods. Roman poets like Ovid also used the Greek gods as material in their narratives. Sometimes the gods were the central focus of a work, but more often their stories were told in passing, sometimes as embellishment, sometimes to establish the lineage of a hero, sometimes to call upon traditional wisdom. It is clear from the contexts in which they appear that these stories were already known to the audience, or were at least set in the familiar context of the life of the gods on Mount Olympus.

Many writers since Greek and Roman times have worked at reconstructing the tales of gods and heros, and many volumes about Greek and Roman mythology are available to us. We can, therefore, see at least the rough outlines of this ancient system, and what we see looks very much like a description of human types and their interactions. There are twelve gods who reside on Mount Olympus. There is some discrepancy in the various sources regarding exactly which twelve these are, but there is agreement that there were twelve and not eleven or thirteen or some other random number. (You will notice that this number comes up frequently in ancient sources, whether it is the twelve tribes of Israel, the twelve signs of the zodiac, the twelve clans among American Indian tribes, the twelve disciples of Jesus, or whatever the system may be.)

All of the gods and goddesses had their particular attributes and particular spheres of human activity over which they presided. And to each there accrued many stories of their exploits and the exploits of their mortal favorites. Although the gods each had clearly defined spheres of influence, Olympus was not an egalitarian society but a definite hierarchy. Jupiter was the unquestioned and unquestionable authority. On the rare occasions when this authority was questioned, his power was equal to the combined efforts of all the others together. He was called "Father of the Gods." Although some, including his wife Juno, were his siblings, he ruled them all. Next in rank came his favorite children, and of course his powerful brother, Neptune, god of the sea. His other brother, Pluto, was god of the underworld and did not live on Olympus. The lesser Olympian gods, such as Vulcan, the smith and ingenious craftsman who built the palaces of the gods, seemed to occupy positions of lesser power, or were not as interested in power as were their more active relatives.

Since it was the Roman names for the gods that were given to the planets, and since the human types are named for the planets of the solar system, I use the Roman rather than the Greek names for the gods. I will not attempt to show that each of the Olympians corresponds to a particular type in the Fourth Way system. In the first place, I don't think this can be done without wrenching the material, or lopping off parts of it like Cinderella's sisters' heels and toes as they tried to fit into her slipper. In the second place, my purpose is not to demonstrate that these ancient systems were exactly the same as this system, but merely to suggest that such systems of human types did exist thousands of years ago. And that they present realities of human life to which we would do well to pay attention.

I will consider only a few of the Olympians, choosing some whose attributes seem most like those of classic human types. Mercury, whose Greek name was Hermes, is one of the gods about whose exploits and attributes we know a great deal since he is mentioned more times in ancient literature than any of the other gods. Of all the gods, Mercury was the quickest, the most cunning, and the most perceptive. These attributes gave him his reputation as master thief and patron of thieves, and he achieved this reputation early. Before nightfall on the day of his birth, he stole Apollo's cattle. Jupiter made him give them back, and to appease his anger, Mercury created the lyre from a tortoise shell and gave it to his delighted brother, beginning Apollo's career as god of music. Portrayed with wings on his heels and hat, Mercury soon won his position as messenger of the gods and carried Jupiter's messages to the far corners of the Earth. It was Mercury who guided the dead to the underworld where Pluto reigned, and, on those rare occasions when one of the dead was allowed to return, it was Mercury who was sent to retrieve him or her. Jupiter sent him to the underworld to tell Pluto that he had to return Proserpine, Ceres' daughter, after Pluto had abducted the girl to be his consort in the land of the dead. Ceres, goddess of grain and harvest, had grieved so that nothing would grow upon the Earth. So Jupiter took pity on the starving humans and sent Mercury to bring the goddess's daughter back.

Mercury's cleverness included talents as an entertainer as well as a thief. When Jupiter needed assistance in rescuing the unfortunate Io who had attracted Jupiter's affections with her beauty, Mercury was equal to the task. The jealous Juno had placed Io under the guard of Argus, a monster with a hundred eyes, some of which continued to keep watch while the others slept. Mercury caught Argus's attention by telling him stories, and continued with tale after inventive tale, allowing his voice to become more and more monotonous until finally all of Argus's hundred eyes fell asleep at once and Mercury was able to slay the monster and rescue Io.

When we discuss the seven classical human types, it will become apparent that there are many similarities between the characteristics of the Mercurial type and the attributes of the Olympian whose name the type still carries. Mercury is not the only god from Greek and Roman mythology who bears a remarkable similarity to the type of the same name, a type considered to be influenced by the planet which also has that name.

The lovely Venus, goddess of sensual love, is both one of the most powerful and one of the most passive of the immortals. It is her voluptuous beauty that gives her power, not force or persuasion. She cannot refuse when asked a favor, even when the one asking is an enemy. During the seige of Troy, Venus was a protector of the Trojans who were being attacked by the Greeks, and Juno was the implacable persecutor of Troy. Nonetheless, when Juno asked Venus for the use of her magic girdle which made the wearer irresistible, Venus gladly granted the favor even though she knew Juno's purpose. Juno, Jupiters wife, used the magic to seduce her own husband so that the rest of the gods could help the Greeks attack Troy while Jupiter slept. Even though Venus was one of the Olympians, and even though she was sworn to protect the Trojans and their city, she was of little use in battle. In one battle scene when Jupiter allows the other gods to join the fighting in defense of their favorites, Venus is wounded in the hand by a mere mortal, and goes weeping from the field of battle to seek the comfort of Jupiter, who reminds her that hers are the works of love, not war.

The lovely languorous goddess, the slow-moving planet, and the warm, sensual, passive human type seem connected by more than just a name. The same intriguing similarities emerge again when god and planet and type share both characteristics and name: Mars. This implacable god of war, the fiery-tempered Mars, was the lover of the tender, passionate Venus. Nor was this the only gentle and mild woman that he attracted. He also was loved by the peace-loving nymph, Harmony. With her, Mars fathered the Amazons, a fierce race of warrior women. Mars was not a complex god about whom many stories were told. Aside from his sexual exploits, he has only one province, battle. He was single-minded in his ruthless and blood-thirsty nature. He was accompanied on the battle field by two companions, Phobos (Dread) and Deimos (Terror), which are also the two small moons which orbit the planet Mars.

Other gods in the Greek and Roman pantheon, although they do not give their names to specific human types, nonetheless seem to exemplify them. Diana, cool and solitary goddess of the moon, does not frequent the palaces on Mount Olympus with the other gods and goddesses, although Olympus is considered her home. She is the virgin protector of women and of wild animals. Those who intrude upon her, even accidentally, find how zealously she guards her solitude. One unfortunate, Acteon, came upon Diana as she was bathing in a forest pool he had approached to drink from on a hot day while hunting. Diana turned him into a stag, and he was torn to pieces by his own hounds—rather severe punishment for an accidental encounter. She was relentless in protecting the creatures sacred to her, as Agamemnon, leader of the Greek forces, found when his men killed a deer in her sacred grove. Diana demanded the sacrifice of Agamemnon's daughter, Iphigenia, before she would allow the wind to blow that would carry the Greek forces to Troy. Her preference for solitude, her cold unfeeling treatment of anyone who attempted to disturb her or the creatures she protected, can be seen in the characteristics of the Lunar type.

Like the tales of the Greek gods, the study of astrology began long before the development of writing, so its origins are lost to us. It can be traced back to the great cities of Mesopotamia where it was used to predict the fates of rulers and nations on the basis of *omina*, celestial events considered to presage human events. One of the first known examples of writing, a cuneiform text from the First Dynasty of Babylon about the 18th to 16th century B.C., is devoted to celestial *omina*. Astrology is predicated on the theory that celestial bodies affect what happens on the Earth, and most particularly what happens in the lives of men. This theory has strongly influenced many civilizations both ancient and modern. The names given to the planets, and the gods associated with them by the Chaldeans, gave way to Egyptian names that in turn gave way to the names used in the Sanskrit holy books of India, and, in the West, to the names the Romans gave to the Greek gods. Hermes Trismegistus, for instance, was the Greek name given to the Egyptian god, Thoth (which is the name still used in Arabic astrology and by the Qabalists of the Hebrew mystical tradition).

In the ancient world, the Earth was understood to be the center of the universe. The Sun and Moon, the planets and the fixed stars, were thought to revolve around the Earth in various celestial spheres. In Egypt under the rule of the Ptolemies, the Greek ruling dynasty in the centuries immediately preceeding the Christian era, a correspondence was believed to exist between the macrocosm, or universe, and the microcosm man. This correspondence was mathematized. The orbital circle of the Sun was divided into twelve equal parts, visualized as stripes across the sky. Each of these divisions occupied 30 degrees of the complete circle. Each also was considered to be the location, or house, of one of the signs of the zodiac pictured among the fixed stars. The more rapidly moving spheres, those of the Sun and Moon and the five planets recognized at that time, appeared to pass through these houses of the zodiac. At the precise moment of a particular person's birth at some location on the Earth's surface, various areas of the zodiac contained the particular celestial bodies. By determining exactly what this configuration was, and by studying it, astrologers claimed to know the characteristics and attributes of the individual. The complex chart thereby obtained is called a horoscope. Since the first century B.C., this has been the basic procedure.

In addition to the twelve signs of the zodiac, astrology also considered the influence of the four elements: earth, air, fire, and water. Each of the elements is associated with three of the twelve signs of the zodiac. This of course adds more complexity to an already very complicated system, but it is far from being the only system where both the numbers twelve and four are significant.

At various times and in different civilizations, there have been very different attitudes toward the relationship between the astrological fate of the individual and his higher possibilities for spiritual development. In India the spiritual life is considered predicted by the horoscope to the same degree that the physical life is determined. The Christian Gnostics of the second and third centuries A.D., on the other hand, thought that the motions of celestial bodies govern the elemental world but that the soul is free to choose. Later Christians, having declared the Gnostics heretical, rejected astrology entirely as the work of the devil. This made its practice hazardous since it was grounds for trial and punishment as an aspect of witchcraft. During the Middle Ages, astrology found a haven among alchemists. Whatever else arcane alchemical studies might have been, they were the precursors of modern scientific inquiry. Alchemists also seem to have kept alive much of the knowledge of the ancient world that the Catholic Church attempted to suppress.

Today astrology is relegated to the status of pseudoscience and the study of planets and stars is called by another name, astronomy. Since Galileo demonstrated that the Earth was not, in fact, the center of the universe but revolved around the Sun (the Catholic Church didn't care for that idea, either), our whole conception of the solar system and the rest of the universe has changed radically. It is no wonder, perhaps, that the precepts of astrology were entirely discredited along with the concept of a geocentric universe. In our time popularized and trivialized versions of astrology have been relegated to newspaper columns and cultist enthusiasms among the lunatic fringe. But even though the original system is lost to us and the remaining fragments have been debased, there seem to be in the characteristics attributed to those born under certain planetary influences, intriguing indications of a system for describing human types.

A person's Sun sign is considered one of the most, if not the most, significant factors affecting that person's characteristics. The Sun sign is that house of the zodiac which the Sun's orbit passed at the moment of the person's birth. Discussions of the zodiac signs traditionally begin at the vernal equinox, around March 21. On this date the Sun enters that part of the heavens designated as belonging to Aries. Astrologists attribute a specific set of characteristics to those born under the sign of Aries. To begin with, this sign of the zodiac is ruled by the planet Mars. (In fact, the name of the sign is very similar to that of the Greek god of war, Ares.) The symbol of this sign is the Ram, an animal known for butting its head obstinately into any opposition, and the element associated with Aries is fire. Some of the words used to describe people born with the Sun in Aries—between March 21 and April 20—

are "energetic, impulsive, enthusiastic, enterprising." This type enjoys overcoming obstacles and will go out of the way to challenge opposition. Aries is very direct, open, and honest—frequently to the point of bluntness. Those born with the Sun in Aries are likely to indulge in rash behavior to the point of causing themselves injury, and are as loyal to their friends as they are brutal to those who oppose them.

All of the above characteristics, as we will see when the type is discussed, are typical of the Martial body type. Whether they are also typical of people born during the last week of March and the first three weeks of April, I am unable to hazard a guess. There are, however, several other Sun signs which seem similar to the Fourth Way essence types. Cancer, represented by the Crab, is a water sign ruled by the Moon. Some of the words used to describe those born under this sign are "tenacious, patient, sensitive." This type never confides in strangers, and even their best friends don't know certain things about them. The Cancer native can be subject to melancholy moods, and may be extremely cautious, even timid. These are the characteristics of the Lunar essence type. Again, as was noted about the pantheon of gods from Greek and Roman mythology, there are striking similarities between some of the astrological types and those of the Fourth Way system.

Another system that is based on the movements of celestial bodies, particularly on the cycles of the Moon, is found among the North American Indians. The Medicine Wheel divides the year into twelve segments using one moon for each unit, beginning at the Winter Solstice. The first group, the Snow Goose people, are those born in this first, or Earth Renewal Moon. Like their totem, these people are cautious and unobtrusive. They are cool and reserved, but their imaginations soar like the great flocks of white geese who follow the snow. Each of the moons has an animal totem, and the characteristics of the animal are used in describing the essential nature of the person born at that time.

The twelve moons are in turn grouped into three moons for each season, each group of three assigned to one of the four directions, north for winter moons, east for spring, south for summer, and west for autumn. There are, in addition, four clans, into one of which each of the moons will fall in sequence. The Thunderbird clan is related to the element of fire, the Turtle clan to earth, the Frog clan to water, and the Butterfly clan to air. The Snow Goose people mentioned above are members of the Turtle clan and have the stability of this most stable of the elements:

> Because of the Turtle clan traits—stability bordering on stubbornness and a fear of anything except very gradual change—added to the persistence that is inherent in their natures, it is very difficult for Snow Goose people to turn themselves around when they are on an unbalanced course.[1]

Once again the Lunar type is described here with accuracy. The Medicine Wheel system of describing human types is closely tied to the natural cycles of the Earth and its seasons, reflecting the closeness and harmony with nature that the native peoples consider necessary for human well-being.

Another intriguing ancient esoteric tradition is that of the Qabalah. The Jewish mysticism in which the system (if it can legitimately be called a system) originated has roots going far back in time through an oral tradition, so it is not possible to say much about its beginnings. Furthermore, a basic assumption of this tradition is that it does not operate in a way that can be understood by the mind. The Tree of Life, the central symbol for Qabalists, is a complex image to be meditated upon rather than understood. Qabalists say that

> They do not try to explain to the mind that which the mind is not equipped to deal with; they give it a series of symbols to meditate upon, and these enable it to build the stairway of realisation step by step and to

---

[1] Sun Bear and Wabun Wind, *The Medicine Wheel* (Englewood Cliffs, NJ: Prentice Hall, 1986), p. 127.

climb where it cannot fly. The mind can no more grasp transcendent philosophy than the eye can see music.[2]

There does seem to be, in one of the several traditions of Jewish mysticism, a system of archetypes. It is said that both angels and demons can know human fate by knowing this "deepest source of the soul's hidden activity." Furthermore, certain prophets are able to develop the same understanding and thus have a fore-knowledge of a person's future.

I would not venture into waters this murky were it not for one unavoidable connection between the Fourth Way system and the Qabalah. The Qabalah, and its central symbol the Tree of Life, is the content of the tarot, and the tarot deck is the forerun-ner of our modern deck of playing cards. In the tarot deck the four suits represent the four elements: Wands represent fire; Cups represent water; Swords represent air; and Disks represent earth. Whatever the historical process through which Disks became the modern club suit, Cups became spades, Swords became dia-monds, and Wands became hearts, the cards are still used as a shorthand method of referring to the four functions and to the divisions within each function. Peter Ouspensky was interested in the tarot, studied it, and wrote about it. In other words, there is a very clear linear descent from this esoteric Jewish mystical tradi-tion to a current symbol used in the Gurdjieff Work.[3]

In chapters 4 through 8, the four lower functions are dis-cussed. These four types of human intelligence—the instinctive, the moving, the intellectual, and the emotional—are represented by the four suits in the deck of playing cards. The instinctive cen-ter is represented by clubs, the moving center by spades, the intel-lectual center by diamonds, and the emotional center by hearts.

---

[2]Dion Fortune, *The Mystical Qabalah* (York Beach, ME: Samuel Weiser, 1984), p. 29.

[3]P. D. Ouspensky, *A New Model of the Universe* (New York: Vintage Books, 1971), Chapter V, "The Symbolism of the Tarot," pp. 185–215.

Each of the suits, then corresponds to one of the four functions or types of human intelligence. The face cards, or court cards as they were called in the tarot, of each suit indicate a particular part of a center. The jacks stand for the mechanical part of each center. In this part, the function operates without any attention on the part of the person who is acting. To understand the operation of the moving center, consider the example of your ability to walk, which is learned movement. You can walk without being aware that you are walking, and usually do. In terms of the cards as shorthand symbols for the parts of centers, you can say that you walk with the jack of spades, the part of the moving center that functions without any attention, the mechanical part.

The queens of each suit represent the emotional part of each of the functions. In the emotional parts there is some level of attention, but the attention is attracted and held by the object. The queen of diamonds, therefore, would be that part of the intellectual center that becomes emotional about facts and ideas and concepts. Suppose that a boy is just learning to play chess and has become very involved in the game and excited about it. He might take his allowance to a bookstore and spend it all on a book about chess manuevers. Instead of saying that *he* bought the book, it would be more accurate to say that his queen of diamonds bought the book since the "I" that bought the book was an "I" from the emotional part of his intellectual center. Another part of him, the emotional part of his instinctive center—or the queen of clubs—would be emotional about food and would have spent the allowance on a pizza. Since in the queens, the emotional parts of centers, the attention is held by an object of some sort, it is fair to say that the queens do most of the spending for the whole person.

The kings of the suits represent the intellectual parts of each center. In the intellectual parts of centers the attention is held by the person's efforts. It requires the intellectual part of the intellectual center, the king of diamonds, to study for a test or to learn the word forms and vocabulary of a foreign language. It requires the intellectual part of the moving center, the king of spades, to figure out how to assemble a tricycle that comes with its parts in a small box with an instruction sheet. In both of these instances the activity is neither automatic nor fun, so the attention has to be controlled.

This is not intended to be an exhaustive listing of ancient systems which present ways of classifying human beings, any more than it has been a complete description of any of the systems that were mentioned. There are other systems of which I am aware, and no doubt still others about which I know nothing. Those that have been discussed here have many areas in common, both in their general approaches and in the specifics of the way they describe certain types. In the stories told of Diana, solitary goddess of the Moon, in the tendencies attributed to those born under the astrological sign Cancer, in the characteristics of the Snow Goose people, and in the Lunar type as described in the Fourth Way essence types there are many similarities.

When we find such similarities in different traditions, religions, or philosophical systems, they can be explained in different ways. One of these, of course, is to assume that there were contacts between the peoples who had these ancient beliefs, and as a result of this contact their ideas influenced each other. Another assumption might be that this knowledge comes from divine sources and that whenever the gods, in whatever form, reveal the truth to men, it is the same truth but recorded differently by different peoples in different cultures. Yet another possibility is that whenever people are observed carefully, and studied objectively without judgment and without attempting to change them, it becomes apparent that there is a pattern to behavior. In other words, there are similarities shared by certain people that indicate they are of a similar type. The description of the Lunar type then becomes considerably more than a theory. It becomes a reliable prediction of the behavior of your youngest child, the computer programmer at your office, the woman who lives in the apartment next door, your sister's new husband. It can become the understanding that persons who are of the same type behave the way they do because that is the way they must behave, as lions must hunt and rabbits must run. Indeed, all of the above explanations may be true to some extent.

There are several passages in Ouspensky's *In Search of the Miraculous*[4] in which he discusses such systems as astrology or alchemy or the tarot with Gurdjieff. Each time Gurdjieff's response is similar. Each time he explains that, while these systems contain accurate esoteric knowledge, they are different ways of presenting truth and there is no use in studying the systems until you have studied yourself. No one, no teacher, no book, no system, can give people something they have not first made the effort to get for themselves. You cannot have what you have not paid for.

Esoteric knowledge is "esoteric," that is "hidden," only because many do not make the effort to find it. It is not hidden in the sense that a powerful and secret group is trying to keep it away from other people. Anyone who genuinely has esoteric knowledge will do anything possible to try to give it to others, but he will not be able to. If others want this knowledge, and are willing to work for it, they will have access to it. But this knowledge cannot be given away.

---

[4]P. D. Ouspensky, *In Search of the Miraculous* (New York: Harcourt, Brace and Co., 1949), pp. 282–283.

CHAPTER 3

MODERN RESEARCH

The myth of the modern age is science, the belief that measurable and repeatable experiments will lead to ultimate meaning. Ironically, of course, the scientific method has led to a technological nightmare on the one hand and a metaphysical quandary on the other. Releasing the awesome energies of the atom and its nucleus gave us the ability to destroy life on this planet; pushing on into subatomic worlds of pure energy brought us to a realm—quantum physics—where science not only can't find answers but doesn't know what questions to ask.

On our blithe and merry way along the perceived horizontal timeline called history, we have learned some quaint and curious things. The second half of the twentieth century has produced an explosion of factual data about the planet Earth, about the solar system, and about ourselves. As a species we know so much that no single member of the species can assimilate even a fraction of it. We can have access to all the factual data available through computer networks that put us in the fast lane on the information superhighway. Anyone with a computer and the money to pay for a modem and sundry communication services can find out any fact that is known or has ever been known, can have access to any book extant on the Earth. Most of us have gotten so excited about this, so intoxicated with what we can know and do, that we forget to ask the most important question: So, what?

The ancient systems which have been briefly considered above were very much concerned with questions of ultimate meaning and value. What is a good man? What is justice? Are there beings higher than human beings? If so, what is their nature? Do human beings have any relationship with or duty to such beings if they exist? In the ancient world knowledge was conceived of as coming from higher beings; now knowledge is thought to result exclusively from investigation and experiment.

Rodney Collin, in his remarkable book *The Theory of Celestial Influence*, says in his introduction:

> Man has two ways of studying the universe. The first is by induction: he examines phenomena, classifies them, and attempts to infer laws and principles from them. This is the method generally used by science. The second is by deduction: having perceived or had revealed or discovered certain laws and general principles, he attempts to deduce the application of these laws in various specialized studies and in life. This is the method generally used by religion. This first method begins with "facts" and attempts to reach "laws." The second method begins with "laws" and attempts to reach "facts."[1]

Since the spring of 1948, when Collin's work was published, developments in many areas of the sciences and the social sciences have given researchers much more information about some of the components of the Fourth Way system of body types. The data brought back by space probes, manned and unmanned, has provided many more facts about the solar system than could be known by peering through telescopes. Electronic microscopes

---

[1]Rodney Collin, *The Theory of Celestial Influence* (London: Vincent Stuart) p. xv.

have enabled scientists to look at the workings of the brain, blood stream, nervous system, and other organs. Medical research has provided evidence about the functions of the endocrine glands and the hormones they produce and release. Psychiatry has documented some of the effects these hormones have on human behavior. Modern psychology has devised sundry testing instruments which purport to classify different types of abilities, learning approaches, personalities, etc. in human beings.

Since what I am discussing in this book is a description of human essence types that are determined by planetary influences and governed by endocrine secretions, it seems reasonable to take at least a brief look at what has been going on in related fields of inquiry.

Space exploration has been the most dramatic and well-publicized area of fact finding. Notions about what is out there beyond the Earth's atmosphere have changed quite dramatically in the last twenty-five or thirty years. The immense spaces between planets once thought to be a complete vacuum are now filled with solar wind. The surfaces of planets concealed by cloud cover have been mapped. We have seen photographs of distant worlds, photographs which reveal such astonishing beauty that the real wonder is that we didn't fall to our knees in awe to worship whatever higher intelligence is responsible for such splendor. And we have seen photographs of our own planet, dear and beautiful beyond hope or redemption, taken from far out in space where we can see it suspended unique and alone, separate from its fellows and yet belonging more to them than to us.

There is a mountain of data about the planets available now, probably more than any one person could completely understand. In all of it there is not, to my understanding, anything that contradicts the basic premise here. If anything, that premise—that the solar system is intricately and pervasively interconnected, and that the planets affect each other and what goes on on their surfaces profoundly—has been immeasurably strengthened by myriad specific examples. Furthermore, many of the specific facts gleaned from probes that recorded images and measurements of the planets have given startling substance to the old maxim "as above, so below." Many of the facts learned about individual planets seem to be remarkable metaphors for the psychological tendencies of the human types those planets are thought to influence.

Mars, for example, although called "the angry planet" because of its red color, was thought to be like the Moon in its inert lack of any activity. In 1965 the Mariner 4 spacecraft sent back low-resolution images of Mars that recorded what seemed to be a bleak and cratered landscape like the Moon's. Other pictures from other Mariners seemed to confirm this impression. Then, in 1971, Mariner 9 orbited Mars to photographically map the entire planet. But the project couldn't even begin until a months-long global dust storm cleared. And when the pictures began to arrive back on Earth, they provided evidence of violent volcanic activity that changed the accepted notion of a static Mars to one of a dynamic world that seemed angry indeed. Huge volcanoes were caught in the act of erupting. Mars, in fact, has what is currently believed to be the largest volcano in the solar system, which is quite a distinction considering that there are lots of them. Scientists were sufficiently intrigued by this changed view of Mars that in 1976 four Viking spacecraft went to find out more. Two of them landed and sent back thousands of photographs from the surface, sampled the soil, and carried out numerous experiments. The craft which landed on the Martian surface monitored the weather for a full Martian year (about twice as long as a year on Earth). They found long periods of rather monotonous weather with little day-to-day variation, but also, toward autumn, sequences of cyclones and anticyclones that raged at the rate of about one per week.

While all this recording of information about the surface of Mars was going on, the distant Saturn was approaching a position where flyby probes might provide visual images never attainable through telescopes on Earth. And indeed they did. Voyagers 1 and 2 in 1980 and 1981 provided photographs of a ring system so amazingly complex, and satellites so different from one another, that the many factors involved in this incredibly intricate system boggled everyone's mind.

If scientific exploration has revealed a great deal about the planets recently, and it certainly has, science has also provided the same sort of information explosion about the endocrine glands and the hormones they release. Considering the planets, one august source contemptuously dismissed the claims of astrology on the subject of planetary influence by saying, "No serious explanations seem to exist regarding the alleged nature of their influences, or the manner in which they are received."[2] This of course is not so—particularly regarding the last allegation.[3] According to the Fourth Way system, the endocrine glands are the system within the human body which receives the influences of the planets and responds to them by differentiating the human types.

As recently as twenty-five years ago, approximately the time we first walked on the Moon, scientists had identified only about twenty hormones. Now the existence of more than two hundred has been documented, and the number is rising. The endocrine glands produce and release many of these hormones, as has long been known. The definition of the term "hormone" has, however, been broadened to include virtually anything produced by a cell that gets to another cell somehow or other and changes what that second cell does. Hormones are messengers that regulate the many delicate and complex functions carried on by the body.

The main thrust of research in this area has been medical science's concern with fixing things that go wrong. In the endocrine system, a messenger either wakes up or silences another, and the second messenger goes on to wake up or silence a third, and so forth. If some of the messengers are missing or on vacation, the whole system can get badly out of kilter. In pathological instances, cases in which too much or too little of a particular hormone may be causing disease or undesirable behavior, doctors have searched for ways to artificially produce, or stimulate the production of, hormones that will alleviate the symptoms.

---

[2]"Occultism," *Encyclopedia Britannica* Vol. 25, p. 85.
[3]See particularly Percy Seymour, *Astrology: The Evidence of Science* (London: Arkana, 1990) pp. 136–143.

When we examine the specific functions of the endocrine glands, as we shall be doing in some detail when we talk about the separate body types, we see many striking correspondences between the known effects of the hormones that a gland produces and the psychology and physical appearance of the human body types in which that gland predominates.

The science of endocrinology is in its infancy. There are far more questions than answers about the workings of even the most well known of the hormones. Since the motivation for studying the action of the hormones is primarily the concern with curing diseases, it is not surprising to find that the most research has been done on the hormones which are involved in the most prevalent diseases. Insulin, for instance, has long been used to treat diabetics, and diabetes is the most common endocrine disorder in the world. Most of the research related to the pancreas, the gland which governs the Lunar type, centers on the beta cells in the Islets of Langerhans, for it is by these cells that insulin is produced. Other functions of the pancreas, such as its relationship to the lymphatic system, are relatively ignored as researchers concentrate on the problems related to insulin production.

Some of the glands remain mysteries. Only one or two hormones produced or secreted by the thymus gland, for example, have been isolated and studied. This gland produces a series of compounds called thymosins. While the actions of these hormones are not completely understood, too much or too little of them is believed to either cause certain diseases or to make these diseases more easily contracted. The thymosins, or some of them, seem to be messengers which activate lymphocytes, the white blood cells which are capable of killing disease-causing microorganisms. Because of this relationship to the body's immune system, the thymus gland and its thymosins are under intense scrutiny in hopes that more knowledge about this gland will help in the battle against AIDS.

About other glands, such as the pituitaries, a great deal is already known. At the same time, for every messenger function that is at least partially understood, there seem to be more questions raised. The anterior pituitary produces hormones that are messengers sent to the other endocrine glands telling them when to secrete their particular hormones. When there is some sort of hormonal deficiency, it is difficult to tell where in the chain of interactions the problem is occurring. Did the pituitary not send the right messenger, or send too many messengers? Did the gland intended to receive the message misinterpret it, or is that gland not functioning properly? The intricacies of the endocrine system are only beginning to be understood.

As with the information learned recently about the planets, there is nothing in the new data about the way endocrine glands function that would negate the theory discussed here about the relationship of the endocrine system to human types. On the contrary, many of the new discoveries seem strong confirmations of the relationship of particular glands to the characteristics of the types they are thought to influence. These correspondences will be discussed in detail as the several types are described.

Turning from the sciences to the social sciences, most particularly psychology and all the types of therapies available, we find what could legitimately be called a craze for "enneagram personality types." The enneagram, the figure itself, seems to be as ubiquitous as Teenage Mutant Ninja Turtles although presumably appealing to a slightly older age group. In the summer of 1994 the First International Enneagram Conference was co-sponsored by the Center for Enneagram Studies and the Stanford Medical School Department of Psychiatry. Over 150 presenters from several different countries offered lectures, videos, training sessions, seminars, workshops, meditation, publications, movements, massages, classes, dance techniques, and all manner of other activities and ideas related to the enneagram either directly or tangentially. Several thousand people attended this conference which lasted for three days.

Although the many writers, lecturers, therapists, and healers who have used this device have different names for their "enneagram types," for the most part the emphasis seems to be on classifying different personalities rather than on classifying actual types of human beings. For example, the terms used by Helen Palmer, whose book *The Enneagram* is considered a basic text in enneagram circles are: 1) The Perfectionist, 2) The Giver, 3) The Performer, 4) The Tragic Romantic, 5) The Observer, 6) The Devil's Advocate, 7) The Epicure, 8) The Boss, and 9) The Mediator. Since there are nine equidistant points on the circle containing the enneagram, the nine personality types have been placed by these points. For the most part there doesn't seem to be any advantage gained by putting the names around a circle over putting them in a list—except that the enneagram is a rather pleasing design. Little is made of the figure itself.

The descriptions of these personality types in Palmer's system, and in most others, seem to be descriptions of character defects, or what in Fourth Way terminology would by called features, that people develop. Quite likely if the main concern of therapy is to assist people to be more pleasant to be around, to help them increase their social skills or ability to sell real estate or automobiles, then this attempt to study personality traits may be useful. Personality is, as the New Testament metaphor puts it, like a house built on sand. With no solid foundation the house collapses easily, so at least it is easy to get rid of. Unfortunately, the next one built on that foundation will collapse, too. There is nothing permanent in personality, so tinkering with it in this sort of superficial way at least can do no harm.

There were one or two speakers at the conference who are involved with the Gurdjieff Work and who attempted to explain the differences between different types of human essences and differences in personalities. Concern at seeing the enneagram popularized with such simplistic applications was expressed during the conference, but hardly seemed to register. There is nothing that can be done to avoid having esoteric knowledge purveyed like some new kind of potato slicer in the marketplace. Of the several ways to discourage the actual use of such knowledge, I would suspect that making it a media event with newsletters, talk shows, and international conferences is far more effective than having it suppressed by totalitarian regimes. At least in the latter instance the seriousness of such knowledge is acknowledged.

But if there is much that is slick and specious in the way the study of types is approached by psychologists, therapists, and sundry New Age healers, there are also quite serious inquiries being conducted. While Ouspensky, Gurdjieff, and others who were Fourth Way teachers were concerned with the psychology of what a human being might become, others were developing psychological theories about people as they are. One of these, C. G. Jung, wrote extensively about many of the same ideas that intrigued Ouspensky. Both were convinced that ancient systems like astrology, alchemy, and the tarot held keys to human psychology. It seems incredible that these two men did not know of each other's work. Perhaps they did. They were exact contemporaries and were deeply concerned with similar ideas. They were both widely read writers and both influenced many of the artists and intellectuals in Europe between the two world wars. If they did know of each other's work, there doesn't seem to have been any acknowledgment of the awareness. There is one rather acid passage where Ouspensky answered someone's question about the unconscious by retorting that there could be no unconscious because there is no consciousness in human beings in their ordinary state. This, however, is hardly an indication that Ouspensky was aware of Jung's work since Freud and many others also used the term "unconscious."

C. G. Jung was also concerned with the development of consciousness, a process he termed "individuation." In the course of his psychiatric practice—he had many private patients and was associated with several hospitals—Jung became aware of the differences in human types. When mentioning his work, *Psychological Types*, Jung commented, ". . . it is one's psychological type which from the outset determines and limits a person's judgment."[4] Jung's method of working and thinking was rigorously inductive. He proceeded cautiously, and always from his direct

---

[4]C. G. Jung, *Memories, Dreams, Reflections* (New York: Vintage Books, 1989), p. 207.

observations of his patients. For this reason, the classifications he has discerned are of particular interest here. Jung was not beginning with preconceived ideas about human psychology and shoehorning his patients into already defined categories. He was groping his way to an understanding of types by listening to and observing people. The major difference which he observed he describes by saying:

> I have long been struck by the fact that besides the many individual differences in human psychology there are also typical *differences.* Two types especially become clear to me; I have termed them the introverted and the extraverted types.[5]

Jung's introduction of terms like "introvert" and "extravert" have permanently changed the standard language of psychology and entered the common vocabulary.

It seems apparent that Jung also observed the four functions, although the difference in vocabulary makes it difficult to align his system with the Fourth Way description of the four types of intelligence operating in human beings.

> [B]asic psychological functions, that is, functions which are genuinely as well as essentially different from other functions, prove to be *thinking, feeling, sensation,* and *intuition.* If one of these functions habitually predominates, a corresponding type results.[6]

Jung's description of psychological types provides many insights into the essential differences in people, and the painstaking accuracy of his methods of observation make this particular body of work an important one for anyone interested in the classifica-

---

[5]C. G. Jung, *The Essential Jung* (Princeton: Princeton University Press, 1983), p. 129.
[6]Jung, *The Essential Jung*, p. 133.

tion of human types. Jung did not, however, develop a coherent typology.

The job of developing a system of types was left to Jung's followers. From the conceptual framework established by Jung, Isabel Briggs Myers spent decades developing and administering a testing instrument which is known as the Myers-Briggs Type Indicator. This psychometric questionnaire is now so well known and so widely used that it is referred to simply as the MBTI. This Type Indicator has become the most widely used personality measure for non-psychiatric populations.

The classification which results from Isabel Briggs Myers' test is sixteen different types which are arrived at from the determinations of four paired characteristics taken from Jung's observations. The first of these pairs is extraversion or introversion, designated by E or I. The next pair distinguishes between the person's preferred method of perception, sensing or intuition, designated by S or N (since "I" was already used to designate introversion). The third pair is the contrast between feeling or thinking as preferred ways of making judgments, F or T. And the last pair makes a choice between the two previous pairs, that is whether perception or judgment is the favored mode of dealing with the exterior world. The resulting types are designated by the four letters arrived at. The type ESTP would be a person who is extraverted, relies on sensory perception of facts rather than on intuition, is logical rather than emotional in making decisions but relies more on perceptions than judgments of any kind. On the other hand, the INFJ type person would be an introvert who relies more on intuition than sensory data, and makes decisions on the basis of feeling rather than thought. There's an extra intricacy in this system, because the last letter, "J," indicates that judgment (in this case arrived at by feelings) is how this type would deal with the exterior world. Since the person is an introvert, however, the interior world is more important and there the opposite mode, perception, is dominant. The INFJ type would therefore appear to function by judgments made on the basis of emotion, but the inner reality would be governed by intuitive perceptions.

If this seems complicated, it is. Nonetheless, it is widely used by colleges and universities, businesses, government agencies, and other sectors both public and private in many different countries. Many of the major Japanese corporations use the MBTI to insure that their employees are placed in jobs where they will be the most productive and efficient, receive the greatest satisfaction from their work, and thus be loyal employees.

Whatever the MBTI measures, it evidently measures something. College counselors, placement specialists, and personnel departments continue to have success in using it as a predictive test to determine academic and career aptitudes and abilities. Because this test is so widely used, there is a huge amount of data available. This data has been subjected to rigorous statistical analysis—which of course is what science does best. It is clear that certain professions attract a predominance of certain of the MBTI types. Over 60 percent of the science majors at universities were intuitive-thinking types, and nearly 40 percent were introverts as well. (If I am correct in my assumptions about how the MBTI corresponds to the Fourth Way system, this profile, the INTJ, is what would result if an intellectually-centered Lunar took this test.) Among finance and commerce students, on the other hand, about the same percentages applied to sensing-thinking types, with by far the majority of those being extraverts. The intuitive-feeling introverts show up as art majors, and so on.

It seems that the MBTI does give a rough-cut indication of tendencies in essence, or it would not have the predictive validity it has been shown to have. If it were only measuring personality—or at least personality in the sense that Gurdjieff and Ouspensky defined it—it seems unlikely that there would be the long-term career satisfaction that there seems to be. As Isabel Briggs Myers observed in *Gifts Differing*, "The best adjusted people are the 'psychologically patriotic' who are glad to be what they are."[7] Speculation about what is being measured is tempting, even though there is no way to verify if or how the Jungian

---

[7]Isabel Myers and Peter B. Myers, *Gifts Differing* (Palo Alto, CA: Consulting Psychologists Press, 1980), p. 38.

theory-based system of types relates to the Fourth Way system of essence types. Certainly the thinking or feeling contrast seems to be similar to the idea of either the intellectual or emotional function being dominant. And it may be that Jung's perceptions about introverted and extraverted types are somehow related to whether the persons were passive types or active types. But this sort of associative attempt to make correlations moves away from observation of actual behaviors.

In another area of psychological study, child development, the results of research have clearly substantiated the existence of essence types. Although again the terms used are different, in this instance there can be no doubt that what child psychologists refer to as "temperament" is the same thing that is referred to as "characteristics of essence" in the Gurdjieff Work. The distinction researchers are making between personality and what they call temperament is the same distinction that the Fourth Way system makes between personality and essence. The definition of "temperament" is "relatively consistent, basic dispositions inherent in the person that underlie and modulate the expression of activity, reactivity, emotionality, and sociability."[8] Researchers in the field of child development are finding that these aspects of temperament are apparent in the first months of life and are consistent throughout the person's life. This has caused serious questioning of the theories based on Freud's work which have assumed that every aspect of a person's psychological development is determined by the child's early environment rather than on innate characteristics. The resulting pressure on parents to be perfect, and the Mom-and-Dad bashing that has resulted when children have problems, may finally be alleviated by a more realistic approach to human types.

The best-known and most extensive study of temperament in infants and children is called the New York Longitudinal Study. It is "longitudinal" because in this study babies were studied in the first days and months of life, and follow-up studies

---

[8]Bill Cunningham, *Child Development* (New York: HarperCollins, 1993), pp. 128–129.

were carried on not only in childhood but on into adolescence and adulthood. It was determined that temperamental characteristics showed stability. The researchers considered several characteristics such as activity level, approach or withdrawal, adaptability, distractability, quality of mood, threshold of responsiveness, and intensity of reactions. Other studies have also confirmed that certain temperamental characteristics that are apparent in the first months of life remain constant as the child gets older.

One study that has dramatically confirmed that humans are born with predetermined characteristics is being carried on by the University of Minnesota's Center for Twin and Adoption Research. Pairs of identical twins who were separated at birth and adopted and raised apart have been found to have so many similarities—two of the men showed up wearing exactly the same shirt and were married to women who had the same name—that the nature vs. nurture argument seems to have been decisively won by nature. Despite the evidence that has accumulated which leads to the inescapable conclusion that there are distinct human types, there are still very strong forces that attempt to negate such evidence.

The ideological vested interests which oppose any suggestion of distinct human types are very powerful. The field of psychology was completely dominated by the Freudians up until very recently, and, as the previously mentioned emphasis on "personality types" indicates, there is still an enormous therapy industry operating which strongly resists any suggestion that people cannot and should not be "healed" of their differences. Two other very serious areas of social and economic pressures are also affecting attitudes toward the research that is confirming the existence of human types. One of these is the problems of the relationships between different races and the fear that evidence of the existence of different types will be used to promote theories of racial superiority or inferiority. That this fear is legitimate is demonstrated by Adolf Hitler's theory of a master race which was applied by Germany during World War II in its effort to eliminate supposedly inferior races. It is perfectly reasonable for any decent person to want to avoid any repetition of the horrors that occurred on an enormous scale as a result of these theories. Another problem area is the political system of democracy which is based on a valuation for human equality. Because of confusing equality with sameness, many theorists wish to ignore the evidence that demonstrates there are different types. Even though this evidence has accumulated to the point where such research has at least begun to be intellectually respectable again, there are still those who consider it a right-wing theory of predestination. One investigator has been called a "biological fascist" for his findings because his research has indicated that certain characteristics predominate in prison populations—and those populations contain a percentage of minority groups, Black and Hispanic, which greatly exceeds the percentage in the total population.[9]

Child development specialists are not, however, assuming that consistency of temperament indicates that there is nothing that can be done to alter a person's character and tendencies as he grows and learns. On the contrary, they emphasize that it is of paramount importance that the child's tendencies be observed carefully so that he can receive the guidance and nurturing that is appropriate for his type so that he will develop in ways that will ensure healthy growth and fulfillment. The prison studies mentioned above indicated that, as we might suspect, the inmates included a very high percentage of persons with temperamental tendencies toward agressiveness which were triggered by the predominance of certain hormones, such as testosterone, and the deficiency of other hormones like serotonin. In short it is being clinically confirmed that certain temperaments are associated with definite endocrine patterns, and that without proper understanding severe personal and social problems can result.

The existence of such heated controversy points up one of the central tenets of the Gurdjieff Work, which is that ideologies and belief systems form one of the most dangerous components of the human condition. Because we habitually substitute our

---

[9]Winifred Gallagher, "How We Become What We Are," *Atlantic Monthly* 274, no. 3 (September 1994): 38–55.

favorite illusions for the consciousness that we might otherwise develop through observation, we perpetuate injustice in the name of justice, inequality in the name of equality, oppression in the name of freedom, and all the myriad absurdities experienced in all aspects of our lives.

Rodney Collin defines the problem of understanding this way:

> [P]resent-day science, *without principles*, is headed toward ever more pointless specialisation and materialism; and on the other hand, religious or philosophical principles, uncoordinated with the scientific knowledge which characterises our age, can appeal only to a minority. . . . For those who are willing to accept both methods, it is hoped to present sufficient evidence to enable each reader to attempt to bridge the gap between the world of everyday fact and the world of great laws—*for himself.*[10]

Consciousness can only be developed in individual human beings. It cannot be a quality of any aggregate whether they be groups or religions or academic disciplines or political movements. The validity of any system can only be determined by you.

---

[10]Collin, *The Theory of Celestial Influence*, p. xvii.

CHAPTER 4

THE FOUR FUNCTIONS

Gurdjieff classified people according to the type of intelligence that was dominant in them, and taught that one of the main reasons for our lack of unity is that we have four different brains rather than one. These four brains compete with each other for energy, and each one claims to be the true identity of the person within whom it functions. Each mind calls itself "I" and attempts to speak for the whole person.

Gurdjieff's description combined the moving and instinctive functions and referred to those persons who habitually manifest from those functions as Man No. 1. Those who were emotionally oriented he called Man No. 2, and those who are intellectually centered, who operate with concepts and ideas, he called Man No. 3. These three types make up human beings in their natural condition.[1] All three are on the same mechanical level. They do not understand each other, they see the world very differently, and they act from entirely different motives.

These four lower functions, or types of intelligence with which humans operate, are what we have in lieu of consciousness. These functions can operate with no attention at all, and

---

[1] P. D. Ouspensky, *The Psychology of Man's Possible Evolution* (New York: Alfred A. Knopf, 1974), p. 53ff.

they usually do. Because no attention is focused on most thoughts, feelings, or actions, they leave no memory trace. At the end of any particular day, or week, or lifetime, people may be aware that certain things must have happened, but since they were not present and giving them attention when they occurred, they have no memory of them. If a man works on the sixth floor of a building, and takes the elevator to his office every working day, he will assume that he must have taken the elevator that day. But he has no memory of it—he was not present to his elevator ride because he was preoccupied with either some past event or some imagined future event.

Sometimes, when there is a particularly strong identification with some exterior or interior stimulus, there is attention, but that attention is controlled by the object—as when we are very hungry and have to wait in line before being seated at a restaurant. Our attention is held by the smell of food and the sight of it being served to others, and some dim memories of the event will be formed. And, rarely, the attention is controlled by the effort a person makes. This latter instance would be the beginning, the seed, from which consciousness might develop.

The four functions, also referred to as centers, are the instinctive, the moving, the intellectual, and the emotional. The instinctive intelligence is the one that keeps the organism alive. It controls the various systems of the body, the circulation of blood, the digestion, fighting disease or infection, breathing, the metabolism, all of the many and intricately connected processes that keep the life force flowing in a healthy body or try to establish its flow in an unhealthy one. The instinctive center also receives sensory perceptions—not only sight, hearing, taste, smell, and touch, but also sensations of warmth or coolness, wetness, weight, and so forth. This center monitors the energies of the body. The instinctive mind can provide tremendous amounts of energy in times of danger, and it can allow the body to go into the first, or lowest state of consciousness (see p. 11) when it needs to replenish its energy supply.

The moving brain controls learned movements. This intelligence works closely with the instinctive mind but is separate from it. If there is any doubt about whether a particular action or activity is controlled by the instinctive or the moving brain, consider whether a newborn baby could do whatever it is. If the answer is yes, the activity is instinctive. If it is something the infant must learn, then the moving brain is responsible. The instinctive brain, for instance, knows how to suck, but the moving brain has to learn how to hold a bottle and later a cup and a spoon. After the moving brain has learned how to perform certain movements, even very complicated movements such as are required for driving a car or landing a jet aircraft, it is possible for the person to perform the actions without attention. It is very difficult, for instance, for a small child to learn how to tie her shoes, but once she has learned, and has done this action hundreds of times, she does it without noticing.

The intellectual brain is the one generally considered to be *the* brain. Although it is only one type of intelligence that humans have, and is the latest to develop, the most fragile, and the most unreliable, it is still the one generally indicated by the term "intelligence." This is the brain that differentiates humans from the other animals in their ability to manipulate symbols.

The emotional function is the one with which we relate to other people and make aesthetic discriminations. Where the intellectual function produces words, the emotional function produces images. These two brains use different types of symbols and have difficulty transferring their ways of knowing to each other.

Each of these four types of intelligence has a positive and a negative part, although this division is quite different in the separate functions. For the instinctive center the contrast is between comfort and discomfort, pleasure and pain. For the moving center the contrast is between movement and rest. For the intellectual center the paired opposites are yes or no, true or false. And for the emotional center the contrast is between like and dislike.

Each of the centers can, and usually does, work alone without connection with the others, even though they are operating simultaneously. Consider, for example, a young woman walking down the street. Her blood is circulating, she is breathing, her hair and fingernails are growing, in short, all the processes of her body are operating as they usually operate. She is walking. Her left leg swings in rhythm with her right arm. Then as her weight shifts to her left foot and her body moves forward, her right leg swings out as her right arm goes back and her left arm moves forward. She has no sense of where her legs and arms are or how they move in relation to each other, any more than she is aware of the digestion of her lunch. She probably does not know what the name of the street is, nor does she look at the other people walking on the same street except with the minimum amount of attention needed to avoid walking directly into one of them. She is unhappy. She has just left her boyfriend at the bookstore where they had an argument. In order to avoid the feelings of unhappiness, the fear of being alone if he leaves her, she is thinking about how much money she will get in her paycheck this week. She thinks that she will have enough to buy the sweater she saw in a shop yesterday. Her mind is calculating how much she will need to pay for food for the week and how much she will need to spend on the medicine her mother needs.

If you stopped this young woman and asked her if she were conscious, she would say that she was, since her idea of consciouness, like most people's, is that if she's not in the first state, she's conscious. And for that moment, surprised by your question, she would certainly be more conscious than she was before you stopped her. But before that, what was she conscious of? The associative mind activity about how much money she will get and how much she needs to spend for this and that can hardly be categorized as consciousness. She neither has the money in the present moment nor is in the vicinity of any of the items she may or may not spend it on if she gets it. She is actually just four functions operating independently of each other, with nothing watching them or aware of them.

The four lower functions are like machines within a machine, each operating with its own fuel and at its own speed. Frequently they operate inefficiently, getting in each other's way, interfering with each other's work or trying to do things they weren't designed to do. The young woman we observed, for instance, uses her calculations about whether she has enough money to buy a pretty sweater to avoid feeling the fear and unhappiness her emotional center is experiencing. She avoids her feelings of insecurity about whether her boyfriend really cares for her. In other words, she uses one center to avoid awareness of another center. And since she is paying no attention to her surroundings, she is about to stumble when she comes to a curb that is higher than usual.

Each person has one function which predominates. This is called the person's center of gravity, and is the way that person habitually perceives and deals with the world. None of the functions has any advantage over the others, either as a mode of perception or in terms of the person's chances of developing consciousness. Each has its own correct work. Each does, when it is the dominant function, modify and affect the person's physical and psychological essence type. The body type of any human is quite distinct from the functions operating in that person. All of the types have each of the four lower functions, and all people have one function that is the one from which they are most likely to operate, or of which they are most aware. It is important to keep this in mind when trying to determine what type a person is.

People who are instinctively centered tend to be more solidly built, regardless of their body type. Those whose center of gravity is in the moving center are more slender and at the same time muscular, while intellectually centered persons are frequently thin without being particularly strong. Emotionally centered people tend to be plump and rounded. These differences will alter, to some degree at least, the typical appearance of an essence type. And of course the center of gravity is an integral part of the essence.

Not only are there four separate types of mind in each person, but each of these minds has three distinct divisions. These divisions are made according to the attention required for the part to operate. At the lowest level of awareness—which is no awareness—are the moving and instinctive parts of each center. Since these two parts work with the same lack of attention and the same speed, the distinction is not important for beginning work.

The two will therefore be treated as one, which is called the mechanical part. Each of the four centers has a mechanical part, and this mechanical part may be primarily moving or primarily instinctive, but operates without attention in either case.

The next level in each center is the emotional part. This part of the center operates with attention, but it is attention which is held by an object and identified with the object. There is no, or very little, attention given to anything else. The emotional part of each center is functioning when that center has taken control and is fixed on a particular manifestation. A person on a roller coaster, for example, would have all attention held by the sensation of movement, and very little awareness of anything else. This would be the emotional part of the moving center manifesting. A very hungry person who has just been offered a hot pizza would have all attention focused on the food. This would be the emotional part of the instinctive center, because the attention is held by an object, in this case a fresh pizza.

The highest level in each center is the intellectual part, the part that performs the type of cognition that is the center's specialty. In the intellectual part of each center the attention is held by effort. The attention is controlled and directed by the person. This ability to control attention is the starting point in any effort to become more conscious. When functioning from the intellectual part of centers we are much more aware not only of what we are holding our attention on, but of our surroundings, and particularly of the effort and energy it takes to control the attention. Anyone who has ever studied for a test when he or she would rather be at the beach surfing, or who has changed a lock on the front door when really wanting to watch football on television, has experienced the intellectual part of the intellectual and moving centers. By holding the attention on the necessary activity, the intellectual part of the center is evoked.

There is an even finer division within each part of each center. Each of the three levels of each center is in turn divided into a mechanical, an emotional, and an intellectual part. This can be verified, but takes many observations over long periods of time.

For our purposes here it is sufficient to be able to observe the three main divisions of each center.

The tarot deck may have been one way of communicating this information about the four functions and parts of functions. Esoteric ideas have frequently had to be passed on through symbols during periods when the dominant religion or government opposed them. Ouspensky has suggested that the tarot cards were a way of preserving this knowledge during the Middle Ages when the church would have persecuted anyone speaking of these things as a heretic.

Whether or not this connection of the Tarot with a Fourth Way system is valid, an ordinary deck of modern playing cards can be used as a shorthand system for designating the different functions and their parts. (See figure 1, between pages 60–61) This makes discussing and classifying one's observations easier, since it is far easier to refer, for instance, to "the five of diamonds," than to say, "the mechanical part of the emotional part of the intellectual center." The playing cards have many ideas about the centers represented in their imagery. Each face card has two halves, which can be used to indicate that each part of each center has two halves, one positive and one negative. (These will be discussed in considerable detail when the individual centers and parts of centers are described.)

In each suit, the ace is understood to represent the center as a whole. The ace of clubs stands for the instinctive center, the ace of spades for the moving center, the ace of diamonds for the intellectual center, and the ace of hearts for the emotional center. The three face cards of each suit represent the three division of each center. Taking clubs as an example, the jack of clubs represents the mechanical part of the instinctive center, the queen of clubs the emotional part, and the king of clubs the intellectual part. In each center this is the case: jacks stand for mechanical parts, queens for emotional parts, and kings for intellectual parts.

The numbered cards in each suit are used to represent the finer division of parts of centers mentioned above. The two, three, and four are the mechanical, emotional, and intellectual divisions of the jacks, or mechanical parts of centers. The five, six, and seven are the mechanical, emotional, and intellectual divisions of the queens, or emotional parts of centers. The eight, nine, and ten are the mechanical, emotional, and intellectual divisions of the kings, or intellectual parts of each center.

Each of the four functions has its own way of seeing the world and of reacting to the world, and each person has one center which is the one from which he or she most frequently manifests. This dominant mind, called the person's "center of gravity," is like a window from which that person views the world. Looking out at exactly the same scene and having exactly the same opportunities for observation, people with different centers of gravity are likely to have entirely different experiences. One of the world's most familiar esoteric teaching tales, "The Story of the Blind Man and the Elephant," illustrates this truth. Let us imagine four people, each with a different center of gravity, seated at a table in a crowded restaurant. The instinctively-centered person is likely to be aware primarily of the food, its quality, whether it was served hot enough, whether the quantity was sufficient. He will notice whether the room is too hot or too noisy, whether the chairs are comfortable.

Meanwhile the moving-centered person notices entirely different things. She sees the locations of the tables, how far apart they are and how easy or difficult it is for the waiters to maneuver between the tables with their trays. She is aware that a busboy is having difficulty stacking plates on a tray because he is putting large ones on top of small ones, and sees a near collision which occurs when the busboy enters the swinging door by which waiters leave the kitchen.

The emotionally-centered person at the table focuses on the people in the room. He overhears part of a conversation at the next table and is aware that the man and woman at that table are having an argument, even though they are speaking in low and carefully controlled voices. He notices that their young son, seated between them, looks acutely miserable. At the same time this emotionally-centered man is trying to respond to the conversation his intellectually-centered wife is initiating at his own table, although he does not find the topic particularly interesting.

This intellectually-centered woman is discussing an article she read about the correlation between currency exchange rates and political unrest in emerging nations. Her moving-centered companion is nodding automatically, and her emotionally-centered husband is looking at her attentively even though his attention is actually on the conversation at the next table. Her instinctively-centered friend looks up dutifully now and again, so she has no awareness that no one is listening to her. She probably is not even listening to herself.

Since our center of gravity is reality for us, the way the world looks to us and the way we feel it is most reasonable to respond to our experiences, it is difficult to see what that center of gravity is without assistance. This is why our efforts at self-observation can be greatly assisted by working with others who have the same aim of developing more understanding and a higher level of consciousness. And this is why it is crucial to work under the direction of a teacher who has achieved this understanding and higher level, and is experienced in assisting students as they go through the same process. Since others see the world differently, we can, by comparing observations, make more rapid progress in understanding our own subjectivity by working with them than by working alone. The more we are able to disabuse ourselves of the notion that our way of experiencing the world is the only way, or at any rate the only correct way, the more progress we will make. This, however, is a very difficult process, since we have a huge psychological investment in our own version of reality, and we defend it by automatically believing that anyone who does not see things the way we do is wrong.

In order to get a glimpse of what another's center of gravity might be, I have found it useful, when time and circumstances permit, to ask that person to tell me about his or her life. Since our attention is usually focused on those aspects of our experiences that relate to our center of gravity, and since it is attention which creates memory traces, most people will reveal their center of gravity as they tell about their lives. Imagining exactly the same history for three different people, here is what you might hear as they tell about their lives:

"I was born on an Air Force base where my father was stationed in Germany, but we moved to the Philippines when I was 3 years old. When I was 5 we moved to California so I started school there. I remember the big yellow school bus that picked me up on the corner by my house and took me to school." One minute of listening to her narrative, and you will have a strong hunch that this person has her center of gravity in the moving function.

"My parents were both past middle age when I was born, so I was an only child. I was lonely and always wished I had brothers and sisters. I was embarrassed because people would assume that my mother was my grandmother—I wished that she were young and pretty like my friends' mothers. She was German, and her accent bothered me, too. One of the biggest regrets I have is that I didn't understand how difficult it must have been for my mother to cope with all of the problems of living in a new country with a daughter who was ashamed of her." Again, you hardly have to hear more than the first few sentences to form the hypothesis that you are listening to an emotionally centered person.

"I was a military brat, so I got a good dose of authoritarian doctrines at home. Then when I started school I encountered an environment predicated on the ideas of Dewey and Piaget, sort of permissive child-directed theories, and I was completely confused. I guess having this chance to see the practical applications made me curious to learn about different psychological theories." Here, of course, you are listening to the intellectually centered version of the same experiences.

I have used extreme examples as illustrations, but it is frequently just this clear which of the functions in a given person records the lion's share of the surrounding impressions during the process of growing up. I have given no illustration of the life story of an instinctively centered person having the same experiences because this function does not usually reveal itself with the same clarity. Perhaps instinctively centered people do have more memories in the form of sensory images, but they don't seem to be communicated as often as do the preoccupations of the other centers. The instinctive center might be tentatively considered as a center of gravity if the life narrative does not clearly point to one of the other functions.

Systematic efforts to tell yourself your own life story—not the mechanical maunderings about the past induced by identification, but the use of directed and controlled attention to the reconstruction of your memories—can be useful in the attempt to determine your own center of gravity. Trying to see yourself objectively, as a character in your own movie, resisting the mechanical impulse toward judgment or regret, praise or blame, you may come upon many useful observations that will indicate the function from which you spend the most time operating. The more detailed discussions of each of the four lower functions presented in the following chapters may help you to see which ways of experiencing the world are most familiar to you.

CHAPTER 5

THE INSTINCTIVE MIND

The instinctive function, or intelligence, is the animal mind, the mind that humans share with other members of the animal kingdom. It is an extremely powerful mind, and one that can override the other types of human intelligence whenever situations occur which threaten the survival of the organism. Maintaining life is the primary business of this intelligence, and it is both relentless in its performance of duty and oblivious of the fact that it will ultimately fail.

The instinctive center does not like to be observed and will employ various stratagems to avoid attention, either from other people or from the other centers functioning in the same body. Like any animal, this center feels safer when concealed and anxious when it knows it is being observed. We are taught as young children that it is not polite to stare, and we are aware as adults that prolonged looking is taken as an act of hostility. Yet we are also aware that we want to look at others, to know what they are doing, what they look like—particularly if there is anything strange about them. We want, with an almost obsessive curiosity, to look at accidents because the instinctive center realizes that another member of our species has been injured and wants to know about it. We want to look at people who are disabled or deformed, and even if we don't actually buy the sensationalist newspapers devoted to freaks of nature and horrible perversions, we nonetheless read the headlines while standing in the supermarket checkout line. We are struck almost dumb when faced with the prospect of relating socially to the severely disabled because our own instinctive center is so preoccupied with the nature of the affliction and concerned to know whether it might happen to us.

Gurdjieff referred to the instinctive center as "the wolf" and cautioned that the wolf must be fed. The instinctive needs can be ignored only so long before this center will take control and destroy the efforts of the other centers. It is important to observe and begin to understand the instinctive function or we will not have accurate information about our limitations. The other centers tend not to take the instinctive center into account and therefore imagine that we are capable of doing far more than we actually are able to. We have a finite amount of energy available, and the energy must constantly be replenished by food and rest. The other centers usually underestimate the amount of attention which the instinctive center will demand.

The moving center, for example, loves to travel, to experience new places. Backpacking through the Yucatan is a prospect the moving mind would contemplate with delight. Once in the Yucatan, however, it is the instinctive center which actually experiences the drenching of sudden tropical downpours, the buzzing and biting of swarms of mosquitoes, the diarrhea caused by unfamiliar food or impure water, the aching muscles and sore feet after days of hiking along isolated roads through the jungle. After about four or five days of actually experiencing this tropical idyll, check out which of the four functions is taking the most attention and energy.

Or, again, the emotional center may feel confident that it is so devoted to a loved one that there is nothing that it wouldn't do to care for that person in time of need. Check that out after two or three days of caring for a sick friend day and night, having not a minute to yourself, no time for a hot meal, no more than a half hour's sleep now and again. For another example, the intellectual center may be convinced that nothing would cause us to betray our beliefs, our principles, our convictions. But chances are we know enough of pain not to think ourselves any stronger than those who have broken under the pressure of torture or deprivation.

The instinctive mind is similar to the other kinds of intelligence in many ways, yet it is also different in many ways. Like the other brains, or centers, it has a positive and a negative half. The positive half of the center registers impressions of proper functioning, of health, of pleasure, of things that are wholesome and useful for the well-being of the organism. The negative half of this center detects what is dangerous, unhealthy, painful, or diseased. Like the other centers, the instinctive center is aware of how that center is functioning in others, and, in the case of those who are natural healers, may even be more aware of another's instinctive center than that person is. Also like the other centers, the instinctive center is divided into three main sections depending on the attention required for the functions of the center and how the attention is directed.

The instinctive center differs from the other centers in that it not only requires energy for its functioning but, to a certain extent, controls the energy that is allotted to the other centers. When we are ill, for instance with a bad cold or a case of flu, the instinctive center will cut off most of the energy to the other functions. Until the illness has been defeated, the immune system will command all of the energy at the organism's disposal. The person will have no interest in movement, in talking with friends, in reading or thinking about ideas. The normal activities of the other minds will be shut down until health has been restored. For this reason, chronically ill people are seldom pleasant or interesting for others to be around because they have been reduced to the animal mind's struggle for survival.

The instinctive center is also more difficult to observe than the other centers because, as mentioned before, it does not want to be observed. We all tend to be much more aware of other people's instinctive habits than we are of our own. We notice when others have poor eating habits, bad table manners, unpleasant habits of belching or coughing or sighing, spend inordinate amounts of time in the bathroom, and so forth. The closer our contacts with others, particularly others who share the same

living or working space, the more intensely we are aware of instinctive manifestations of which they may be entirely unaware. It
takes quite long and determined self-observation before we are as
aware of our own instinctive habits as the person who works at
the desk across from us in an office probably is.

The mechanical part of the instinctive center differs from
the mechanical parts of the other centers in that it is fully programmed at the time of a person's birth. The medical profession
has a very limited ability to intervene in cases where an infant's
instinctive function is defective in some way. Unlike the other
types of intelligence in humans, the instinctive mind does not
learn and then store what it has learned in the mechanical part of
the center. Instead, the mechanical part of the instinctive center is
the foundation for all of the centers. Its capacities and limitations
will determine the effectiveness of the other minds. Because the
workings of the instinctive center are so complex and so little understood, it is extremely unwise to tamper with the functioning
of the mechanical part. Experiments with breathing techniques,
extreme diets which affect the metabolism, long fasts, and other
disruptions of the normal working of this center should be undertaken only with great caution and under the supervision of
competent experts.

Although it differs from the mechanical parts of other centers in many ways, the mechanical part of the instinctive center
does provide an excellent illustration of the way the mechanical
parts of all centers operate. It is very clear that all of the myriad,
intricate, amazingly complex functions that this part of the instinctive center performs occur without attention. Unless something goes wrong, most of us, most of the time, are completely
unaware of the beating of our hearts, our breathing, the rate of
growth of our hair and toenails, the digestion of our breakfast, or
the healing of the small cut we got nicking our thumb with the
bread knife. We may sometimes be aware of marked fluctuations
in the amount of certain hormones in our blood, such as the
adrenaline rush that comes in moments of danger. Usually, however, we find our attention riveted on the stimulus which caused
this response in the instinctive center—the driver who cut ahead

of us on the freeway, the strange sound downstairs that may indicate a prowler is in the house—rather than being aware of the functioning of our endocrine glands.

Despite all the many things that medical science has learned about the functioning of the mechanical part of the instinctive center, not very much is known in comparison to what is unknown. In our ignorance we have concocted an odd mythology which invests doctors with great status, and we pay them far more for their labors than we pay almost any other workers. In this way we buffer our terror at being almost entirely helpless in the face of failure of the instinctive center to function correctly or indefinitely.

The mechanical part of the instinctive center is designated as the jack of clubs in the shorthand system which uses the face cards of an ordinary deck of playing cards to represent the parts of centers. People who habitually function from this part of themselves, who most frequently place their valuation on the operation of the bodily functions, are said to have their "center of gravity" in this part of this center. This does not necessarily mean that the person centered in the jack of clubs will be a hypochondriac, although it may turn out that way. It simply means that a lot of energy will be devoted to this aspect of life. This person automatically eats a balanced diet, and gets enough exercise, without giving these matters much attention. His notion of an act of friendship will be to share with you a new lemon juice and water and blackstrap molasses regimen that will flush your liver. All other functions often seem placed in the service of the basic maintenance of the organism.

Because of this care for the functioning of the body, people centered in the jack of clubs are usually in good health, and frequently make suggestions that can be of real practical value to friends and family members. Since it is this basic level of the body's functions with which they are most concerned, people with this center of gravity are usually even tempered and congenial, although perhaps not the most stimulating companions one could wish for. Travel, adventure, experiencing different cultures, experimenting with exotic cuisines, exploring new ideas, meeting new people are all activities which this type views with mild alarm and certainly would not seek out. Jack of clubs people are just common ordinary people who go about living their lives without much fuss or bother.

This center of gravity may be hard to recognize, since the preoccupation with bodily functions is quiet and unobtrusive. We are unaware, nearly all of the time, of what is occupying the attention of even our closest and most intimate family members. Indeed, we are usually unaware of our own mechanicality most of the time. People centered in the jack of clubs may seem enigmatic, hard to get to know, even standoffish because they are not really all that interested in sports, in new ideas, in people. They may be very good at their professions without seeming really involved beyond the level of disinterested competence. If they do travel, they are likely to be extremely fussy about packing since it is essential that they have everything with them that they could conceivably need for physical necessities. Even when traveling to a nearby city they don't feel confident that exactly the right brand of vitamin supplement is going to be available, or the right antacid in the event that unfamiliar food might cause some gastrointestinal distress. In short, for the jack of clubs, what is familiar and wholesome is good, and all else is vaguely suspect or outright threatening.

While the mechanical part of the instinctive center is placid and usually quite passive, to the extent that it will temper the activity of a basically active person, the emotional part of the instinctive center is very different. In the instinctive center, as in all of the centers, the emotional part is the most obvious, the most visible in its manifestations, by far the easiest part of the center to identify. When emotional energy activates a center, it is vivid and active. The emotional parts of centers are emotional about that function, whatever it is. When we say that someone is enthusiastic about something, we are observing that the emotional part of a center has been activated.

The emotional part of the instinctive center is emotional about sensations. It is the location of the five senses and the part of the organism which receives impressions from the environment and determines whether those impressions are good or bad—that is, pleasurable or unpleasant. The emotional part of the instinctive center may not, however, actually be a very good judge of what is conducive to health and well-being. It only evaluates the nature of the stimulus, whether it feels, smells, tastes, sounds, or looks nice or nasty—not whether it actually is good or bad for the health of the person. Food that tastes good, as fats and sugars almost always do, is preferred to food that may be more nutritious but not as tasty. When cravings and bad habits are indulged, the emotional part of the instinctive center can operate to the detriment of the body. This is what occurs in the case of addictions to harmful substances. Initially the stimulus is experienced as pleasurable, so the queen of clubs wants to experience it again, and then again. Eventually, in the case of substances such as heroin, freebase cocaine, alcohol, or nicotine, the amount of pleasure diminishes, but the absence of the substance causes severe discomfort, so the instinctive center is driven to use the substance to avoid pain rather than to experience pleasure. Because the instinctive mind is so powerful in human beings, as in all animals, addictions are very hard to overcome.

The instance of chemical addiction illustrates an important fact about the emotional parts of centers, in this case of the instinctive center. In the emotional parts, the attention is held by the object. In instances of drug addiction, it is apparent that most of the person's energy is absorbed by the attention held by the substance. Getting the drug, using the drug, insuring that there will be a continuing supply, associating with others who are similarly addicted, and being involved in activities centering around the substance, even when those activities are clearly criminal and place the person in danger, all of these behaviors result from having the attention held by the object, of being identified with it.

Because this most powerful of the human minds has become enslaved, as it were, the actions of addicts seem incomprehensible to those who do not understand the instinctive center. Until legislation and education that purport to control drug use are based on an accurate understanding of "the wolf," as Gurdjieff called it, it is unlikely that we will see much change—and the wolf will continue to eat our children. Most of the educational materials that are given to children to teach them about drug use ignore or actively misrepresent the fact that the initial experiences with addictive drugs can provide intensely pleasurable sensations—in fact these materials make it seem as though drugs provide unpleasant experiences right from the start. When the young instinctive center learns that it has been lied to, that the experience can feel very good indeed, all of the warnings are likely to be dismissed as lies. The other centers cannot convince the queen of clubs of anything that is contrary to her experience. The emotional part of the instinctive center knows what it knows, and what it knows is whether something provides pleasure or not. I was a cigarette smoker—consuming several packs a day—for over thirty years before I finally overcame my addiction to nicotine, so I can speak from experience of the power of addictions to control the instinctive center. I also come from a family which has had a marked tendency to alcoholism for all recorded generations, so I have watched many people who are close to me struggle with their compulsion to drink. These experiences and observations have convinced me never to discount the power of the instinctive center, and particularly of the emotional part of that center.

The queen of clubs is also easily observable in less harmful situations than drug use. Consider how much, when we are really hungry, we are interested in food. Consider how much, when we are cold and wet and chilled to the bone, we are interested in a hot bath and a warm bed piled high with blankets. Consider how much, when we are exhausted after a long day of physical activity and still have 100 miles to drive before we get home, we want to go to sleep. If we remember such moments, or observe ourselves in the middle of such experiences, we will have an understanding of what it means to have the attention held by an object.

It is, of course, through the senses, through the instinctive center, that all impressions are received by any of the centers. But those persons who have their center of gravity in the emotional part of the instinctive center are much more aware of these impressions than most other people. This type luxuriates in impressions that are sensuous and pleasurable and suffers acutely from impressions that are unpleasant or disgusting. The queen of clubs is greatly interested in creating comfortable environments, and will have her attention attracted by rich fabrics, polished wood, and all manner of textures and materials. A person with this center of gravity might be attracted to a career in interior decorating, clothing design and construction, weaving or ceramics, or any activities in which tactile and visual stimulation are constantly present. This center of gravity might also be attracted to gourmet cooking and wine tasting, would enjoy perfumes and incense, and could become fanatic about exactly the right stereo components to produce the best sound quality possible.

People centered in the queen of clubs are usually very attractive to others, whether or not they are actually physically good looking. The sensuality of this type evokes sensuality in others with its animal magnetism. People of this type have such an interest in comfort and pleasure that they create environments which others can enjoy as well. They genuinely want their friends to be comfortable, well fed, wearing snuggly clothing, and sitting in front of a fire drinking hot cocoa. Much of their energy is spent providing creature comforts for themselves and others. Their interest in sensuality definitely includes sexual pleasure. The queen of clubs considers the idea of celibacy to border on madness and frequently has a completely amoral attitude toward sexual activity: if something feels good, it is good, and that's the end of that discussion. People centered in the queen of clubs can have a sexual magnetism that can be overwhelming—and they frequently seem not to be aware of it. They are only aware when their own attention is held by some object, in this case someone they are sexually attracted to, not of the emotional and instinctive havoc they may be causing in others.

The queen of clubs is also the location of maternal feeling and other instinctive emotions. The bond between mother and child has its origins on the cellular level—bone of my bone and flesh of my flesh—since the child was formed within the mother's body. When this bond is formed properly, the mother is able to sacrifice her own instinctive needs and safety for her child if a situation requires this. This function is necessary for a species which has young which are dependent for many years. And when the bond does not form for some reason, such as the separation of mother and child in the period following birth, the young are in a perilous situation. At any rate, women centered in the queen of clubs usually make very attentive mothers, at least as far as the instinctive well being of their children is concerned.

Another attribute of the queen of clubs—one which is shared with the emotional parts of all the centers—is the tendency to flip from the positive half of the center to the negative half, and back again. This instability of emotional parts makes people who have their center of gravity in one of the queens unpredictable and subject to revulsions that are as strong as their enthusiasms—and these revulsions and enthusiasms can be evoked by exactly the same object. To take an example from the queen of clubs, you may have a friend of this type who has a passion for Baskin and Robbins Pralines 'n' Cream ice cream. Every day during lunch she stops for this kind of ice cream. So, on her birthday, you buy her a half gallon of Pralines 'n' Cream. When you give her the ice cream, her response is definitely not enthusiastic. "Oh, I really don't care for that kind," she says, "I'm sick of it."

The queens of centers tend to extremes, and the further they veer in one direction, the further they will react in the opposite direction—the pendulum effect. This is an important thing to understand about people whose center of gravity is in the emotional part of a center. Many times others think they can experience the positive energy, the enthusiasm, the vivacity of a friend who is centered in a queen without also experiencing the negativity and revulsion that these types express. This is not possible; the extremes of either side are a package deal.

Advertising takes full advantage of the impulsiveness and lack of self-discipline of the queen of clubs. In fact, a consumer economy could not function without this part of human machinery. The desire of the emotional part of the instinctive center to have more, to have better, to have different is insatiable, and as long as advertising campaigns can convince the queen of clubs that there exists a glossier lipstick, a more exotic fragrance, more elegant jewelry, more luxurious automobiles, then the attention of this part of the person will be held by those objects until they are possessed.

Unlike the emotional part of the instinctive center, which is profligate with energies spent in the pursuit of pleasure and comfort, the intellectual part of the center is extremely cautious in using the energy that might be needed to sustain the life and health of the organism. This part of the instinctive center, the king of clubs, is extremely hard to observe: it is concerned with seeing without being seen. For this reason, the intellectual part of the instinctive center remains mysterious, and even a bit sinister in its workings. This is the animal mind at its most perceptive and cunning: it is aware of much and has many powers that we neither use nor recognize in the humdrum sameness of our daily lives. The king of clubs, unlike the intellectual parts of the other centers, does not have its attention directed by the person. It is said to be conscious for itself; that is, when the heightened awareness of this part of the organism is needed in situations requiring unusual caution or the efficient functioning of other centers, the king of clubs kicks in without any intentional decision.

Imagine a person walking down a dark street in the very early hours of the morning—a young man who has just spent a long evening with friends at a party, and had good food and quite a bit more to drink than usual. He's a little drunk, thinking romantic thoughts about a girl he met at the party who agreed to go out with him next Saturday, and is humming one of his favorite show tunes. Suddenly he hears rapid footsteps behind him and he becomes, instantaneously, a different person. The effects of the alcohol that had blunted his perceptions just a moment before are entirely gone, as is the inner haze of scraps of memory suffused with warm fuzzy emotions mixed with pleasant imaginings about the date next week. Instead, he is intensely aware of his surroundings, how far it is to the corner, what doorways are open onto the street, how far from the ground the windows are and whether they are barred, anything that may be useful if he needs to escape. His mind is rapidly reviewing all he knows about self-defense, his fingers are quickly unbuttoning his overcoat which would slow him down if he has to run; his blood is flooded with adrenal hormones preparing for fight or flight. Then he hears the footsteps cross to the other side of the street, turns and sees a middle-aged man wearing workman's overalls who soon turns into one of the doorways and goes inside. For the rest of the walk home, the young party-goer remains intensely aware of his surroundings and uncomfortably stimulated, to the extent of feeling a bit queasy, with his own adrenalin.

In other situations the intellectual part of the instinctive center has the ability to shut down awareness. A very severe injury, for example, may not cause any pain at all. I once twisted my leg badly, dislocating the knee, flipping the knee cap over so that it looked like a cup under the skin, and bending the lower half of my leg sideways. I remember looking at this strange configuration curiously and wondering why there was no physical sensation. There was no pain while waiting for the ambulance, nor on the way to the hospital, nor while waiting for the doctor and the preparation for the operating room. Later, when I came out of the anesthetic in a comfortable hospital bed with a large cast on my leg, the pain was so great I thought I would be unable to bear it. The king of clubs seems to make decisions about how much pain is felt on the basis of its usefulness for survival. If I had been a wounded animal trying to escape from a predator (instead of a rather clumsy teenager practicing cheerleading jumps), I would have needed to escape without being hampered by pain.

The intellectual part is the part of the instinctive center which controls the energy of the whole person, the part which cuts off energy to the other centers when the person is ill, the part that can release incredible energy for strength in situations of danger, as in a case where a small woman is able to lift a heavy beam weighing hundreds of pounds to release her trapped child. Such virtually miraculous feats of strength sometimes occur in crisis situations. The king of clubs can also change the perception of time, as in those experiences of danger where everything seems to be happening in very slow motion so there is plenty of time to consider what action to take and to take it very slowly and deliberately. Again, I have had personal experience of this, as most people probably have. I was driving rather too fast at night on a country road when a cow started out into the road just a few yards ahead of me. Immediately the action went into a very slow dream sequence of almost suspended animation. I remember that the cow seemed to be floating in a light mist, and that I thought for what seemed like a long time about whether the cow would be startled by the headlights and freeze, or keep moving. Since the cow did not seem interested in the car, I decided she would probably continue her amble across the road. I then turned my attention to the amount of road and gravel shoulder behind the cow and calculated how far I should turn to go around the cow. Having carefully made these calculations, I adjusted the steering wheel with great precision, made a neat little arc around the cow's tail, and with equal precision adjusted the trajectory of the car to coincide with the direction the road was taking. All of this seemed to take several minutes but probably did not occupy more than half a second of measurable time. Again, such instances of people performing maneuvers with considerable skill which they might not otherwise possess (I have trouble getting out of the driveway without knocking over two bicycles and the trash can) are not at all unusual, and most of us probably have such tales to tell.

The abilities and powers of the king of clubs are probably what produce many experiences which are considered paranormal or extrasensory. Telepathy, clairvoyance, and such phenomena may be functions of the king of clubs, or of the king of clubs in some people. People who have their center of gravity in the intellectual part of the instinctive center are likely to seem formidable to others. They are not approachable, or comfortable to be around, until one has come to know them quite well—and this will occur only when and if they wish someone to know them. The king of clubs has the ability to put an invisible wall, almost a force field, around itself to repel unwanted advances from others. People centered in the king of clubs can seem brutal, and can verge on paranoia in their concern for safety. This part operates all the time, but people with this center of gravity seem more aware of its functioning. The omnidirectional awareness that lets us know when someone behind us is looking at us is more developed in this type, and they will seldom sit with their backs to an open door, or to any part of a room where someone could enter without being seen. People centered in the king of clubs can be described as calculating—about diet, about circumstances, about life in general.

People with this center of gravity may be healers with amazing sensitivity not only to their own instinctive needs, but to the instinctive centers of others. Sometimes this type is able to see the auras of others, and is able to determine where others are having problems with the circulation of energy. It seems that many of the Eastern forms of healing require an intentional development of the king of clubs, which is probably much more sensible than the Western tradition of relegating the practice of medicine to the intellectual center. Ideally, a doctor, nurse, or paramedic should have both a highly developed instinctive awareness and a knowledge of scientific data, but if I had to choose one or the other, I would definitely opt for a physician with instinctive sensitivity.

People centered in the king of clubs can have great charisma. Mystics like Rasputin, who have exerted great psychic or hypnotic influence over their followers, are probably of this type, and it is this type which is depicted as the villain in many a cinematic thriller. The gunslinger with the black hat, steely gaze, and preternaturally fast and accurate draw is the archetypal portrait of the king of clubs. It is not surprising that this most highly developed part of our animal nature has been selected to represent the forces of evil. The king of clubs will attempt to undermine any activities which require sustained efforts from the other centers, and thus can be a constant energy drain. The king of clubs is a liar and will claim to be too exhausted to go to a concert, too hungry to study right now, too tired to go visit friends, too sick to go skiing.

The king of clubs' reluctance to release energy for the interests of the other centers becomes more and more pronounced as a person ages. If this progression is not intentionally resisted, the older person is reduced to a very limited sphere of activity, even though in fact there is ample energy available if only it is used. Of course the less one does, the more easily one becomes tired from any activity, and the more the king of clubs attempts to shut down the other centers.

The king of clubs is one of the most determined opponents of the efforts to work on oneself. It will undermine efforts at self-remembering any way it can, and will resist the attempt a person makes to be in the intellectual part of other centers because of the energy and attention required.

CHAPTER 6

THE MOVING MIND

The moving center, or type of intelligence, has the functions that are the easiest to observe. The results of its functioning are right out in the open for everyone to see: either a person is moving or he is not moving. Paradoxically, it is this type of intelligence that has been consistently overlooked in systems of human types and in studies of different forms of intelligence. We have what amounts to a genius for not noticing the obvious.

It is true that some observers have come close. Piaget, the central authority in child-development theory, was observing the moving center in infants when he termed his first stage of development the "sensory-motor" stage and hypothesized that all learning must begin with learned movements and the manipulation of objects in the child's environment.[1] Howard Gardner, in his discussion of different types of human intelligence in *Frames of Mind*,[2] has included two categories that are the province of the moving center, his "Spatial Intelligence," and "Bodily-Kinesthetic

---

[1]Jean Piaget, *The Child and Reality*, Arnold Rosin, trans. (New York: Grossman, 1973), pp. 54–57.
[2]Howard Gardner, *Frames of Mind: The Theory of Multiple Intelligences* (New York: Basic Books/HarperCollins, 1985), pp. 170–236.

Intelligence." Nonetheless, there have been very few serious examinations of the moving mind, even though we reward those who excel in this type of intelligence—professional athletes, inventors, computer software designers—very well indeed, with high salaries and, in the case of athletes, with public adulation.

The moving intelligence is, like the instinctive intelligence, a mind that is shared with other higher animals. It is so much more highly developed in humans, however, as to be almost different in kind. It is true that other animals may surpass us in specific kinds of moving performance, but those kinds are relatively unsophisticated. No human can run as fast as a champion race horse, for example, but you will never find a horse that can dance like Fred Astaire (or at all beyond the most crudely executed circus tricks).

In other animals there seems to be a much closer relationship between the instinctive and moving centers than there is in humans. This is an area of considerable conjecture for those who study animal behavior. On the one hand, many animals perform very intricate moving patterns that seem entirely instinctive (the criteria here is whether the organism is born with the movement already programmed into it or whether it has to learn the movement). Elaborate mating rituals of some species seem to be automatic rather than learned responses, as do such actions as the feigning of a broken wing by a mother bird trying to decoy a predator away from her nest and helpless young. On the other hand, there are also instances when animals clearly teach their young useful movements, as wolf packs educate their young in the art of hunting.

But whatever the nature of the moving function in other animals, in humans this function can be distinguished from an instinctive function by asking, "Can a newborn baby do it?" If the answer is yes, the manifestation belongs to the instinctive center. If the answer is no, if it is something that has to be intentionally learned, then it is the moving center which is functioning. We are usually imprecise in making this distinction. Take, for example, the familiar experience of catching a falling object before the other centers are even aware the object is falling. It may well be the king of clubs which initiates the action, but it is the moving center which performs the action. A 2- or 3-year-old child has not yet learned the movements which make such a reaction possible, and some people whose moving memory has not recorded the history of many games that require catching balls, or who are not well-coordinated, never develop this ability. Although we may say that such a feat as the quick catch is "instinctive," it is really a learned movement operating automatically.

The moving center, then, is the intelligence that controls the movements and spatial relationships we have to learn. Like the other centers, this center has a positive and a negative half, which, in the case of the moving center, is the contrast between movement and rest. Also, like the other centers, it has three divisions: the mechanical, emotional, and intellectual parts. These are represented by the face cards of the spade suit, the jack of spades standing for the mechanical part of the moving center, the queen of spades for the emotional part, and the king of spades for the intellectual part.

The mechanical part of the moving center is where the memory of learned movements is stored. Most adults have quite an amazing accumulation of moving abilities available in their jack of spades which, like all of the mechanical parts of the four centers, functions without attention. The ability to walk up and down stairs, tie shoes, ride a bicycle, drive a car, swim, use an automatic teller machine, operate a keyboard, and many other quite complex movements are so firmly programmed into most people's moving memory that they can perform these actions without even being aware of them. As I sit and type, for example, I am aware of words and ideas, but have no awareness of which finger moves to which key of the keyboard in order to form the words from the letters. Yet, at one time, it required great concentration and repeated practice in order to learn these movements and have them become automatic.

Because the moving center is the easiest of the functions to observe, it can be studied not only for its own quite fascinating sake, but also to understand how the three divisions of any of the centers work. The mechanical part of the moving center, for example, demonstrates what it means for a part of a center to operate without attention. There simply is no awareness invested in the performance of many learned movements. All the complex movements that go into walking, talking, writing, reading, watching images on film or video, eating, etc., go on without our being aware of them. We even carry them out when we don't intend to. For example, we may start out to go to the hardware store on a Saturday morning and suddenly find ourselves in the parking lot of the building where we work. The mechanical part of the moving center is so used to driving to the office every day that it has driven there when we didn't intend to go there. Or perhaps we intended to stop to visit a friend on the way home from work, but instead drive right by that freeway exit and turn off on the exit ramp closest to home. We may tell ourselves we decided not to see the friend after all, but the truth is there was no decision, and no awareness involved. The jack of spades just took us home.

Gurdjieff called humans "sleeping machines" exactly because we can function without being aware that we are functioning, and do most of the time. To a certain extent, the mechanical parts of centers have their appropriate use, and are usually considerably more efficient than the higher parts of centers which do require awareness. The jack of spades should certainly not be interfered with, any more than the jack of clubs should be interfered with, when its most effective actions are needed. It is fine to try to observe the movements you make while driving, as long as you are in a deserted parking lot late at night, but a freeway during rush hour when the traffic is moving at 70 miles an hour is no place for exercises in self-awareness directed at the moving center. And when you have a writing deadline coming up, it is no time to try to observe which finger hits which letter on the keyboard. Just leave the jack of spades alone and it will do its job much better than it will when you try to be aware of it.

People who have their center of gravity in the jack of spades are probably those described by the phrase "the salt of the earth." This center of gravity is remarkably steady, enjoys routine, has a great tolerance for repetitive tasks that would bore others beyond endurance, is efficient and consistent in performance, capable of working long hours without tiring, and usually quite even in disposition. In brief, the person centered in the jack of spades is just about the perfect employee for many jobs. Any employer who needs workers for assembly, data entry, keyboarding, routine repairs, agricultural work, food service, or warehouse stock control can only hope that the people applying for positions are centered in the jack of spades. In fact, this center of gravity does seem to be prevalent. Humanity is well designed for the things that need doing. We might even conjecture that the species would be better off if these people, who are quite content with the simple repetitive tasks of sowing and reaping, cooking, and building, were all there were.

It may be difficult to determine whether this is a person's center of gravity until you know the person quite well. After all, most people, whatever their center of gravity, spend most of their days going through familiar automatic movements to which they give little or no attention. One way of observing whether or not this functioning of the mechanical part of the moving center is actually preferred is to watch whether it is resorted to in times of stress or confusion. In times of emotional conflict, for example, we might observe that a person with this center of gravity would turn to some repetitive action for solace. During a domestic argument a man centered in the jack of spades might abruptly go outside and start digging up the garden, while a woman with this center of gravity might start chopping up vegetables to make soup. The frustrated spouse may wonder how, in the midst of important emotional issues, the person centered in the jack of spades could be involved in these mundane activities. (This may actually become an emotional issue in some marriages.) But if we understand that people are much more likely to manifest from their center of gravity when experiencing stress, we can understand that they are not being insensitive, but are dealing with their emotional pain as best they can, and we also have a good indication of what their center of gravity is.

On the other hand, because of the steadiness of the jack of spades, it may be necessary to work by the process of elimination, as is frequently the case with instinctively-centered people. It will be clear that the person centered in the mechanical part of the moving center is not emotionally centered, or centered in the emotional part of a center, because of his steadiness and the absence of erratic shifts from the negative to positive halves of centers. The probable lack of concern with ideas and theories will suggest a person not intellectually centered. Gradually, through observing the prevalence of movement, you will be able to narrow the possibilities down to either the intellectual or the mechanical part of the moving center. Keeping in mind that the intellectual part tends to lose interest in processes once the movements are understood or mastered, the key to identifying the jack of spades as a center of gravity will be the tolerance for, indeed enjoyment of, repeating movements, performing the same tasks over and over, and living in the same neighborhood or working at the same job year after year without experiencing frustration.

While the mechanical part of the moving center can be recognized by its steadiness, the emotional part of this center is characterized by the lack of stability. As in the other centers, the emotional part is emotional about that particular function and has its attention held by a particular kind of object, in this case a movement or spatial problem of some sort. The emotional part of the moving center, the queen of spades, has great enthusiasm for sports, although this enthusiasm does not necessarily mean that the person will excel in a given sport. The practice required for excellence is not really to the queen of spades' taste. This part of the moving center may love skiing, and even be quite good at it, but probably will not have a tolerance for the amount of disciplined practice required to be exceptionally good. In fact, this part of the moving center, with its penchant for risks, may cause people to be carried off the slopes with broken legs.

If the emotional part of the moving center cannot be experiencing movement directly, it will be watching movement. The queen of spades has its attention held by movement wherever it occurs. Sports in stadiums or on television, video games, pinball machines, roller coasters and other amusement park rides, fast cars, all appeal to this part of the human makeup. When we consider the amounts of time, energy, and money devoted to such activities, we can suspect that this part of the moving mind is quite powerful, particularly in the younger members of the species.

People centered in the queen of spades are relatively easy to identify. Their preoccupation with movement is readily observable, and they tend to move more than is necessary or efficient in the performance of any activity. These people may have an extravagantly gliding, springy, or swaggering walk, may gesture dramatically when speaking, may emphasize the pronunciation of words with more stylization or drama than is strictly necessary.

The queen of spades also demonstrates the tendency to flip from intense involvement to complete lack of interest in an activity. A person centered in the emotional part of the moving center may pursue an activity with almost obsessive interest, may learn square dancing, for instance, and go to square dances three or four nights a week. And then suddenly the same person is completely involved in rock climbing and never goes square dancing again. The queen of spades will participate in a strenuous sport like beach volleyball for three or four hours without taking a break, and then suddenly flop down on the sand and declare that she will never move again, much less play volleyball.

The emotional part of the moving center likes to travel, and people in whom this part is active usually have seen quite a bit of the world. The person centered in the queen of spades is frequently not content with the travel opportunities afforded by a two-week vacation, but is likely to actually move to another country for a while, explore that piece of the planet while there, and then move on to somewhere else. There is a whole fraternity of international travelers who probably have this center of gravity. Far from being wealthy, this group of contemporary nomads has learned to live on practically nothing in order to avoid the ghastly fate of working at a boring and repetitive job (the kind the jack of spades would genuinely enjoy) and staying in one place for any amount of time. They are not to be found at the big flossy resort communities, but on the obscure little island next door—not Cancun, but the beaches of Isla Mujeres, not Mykonos or Santorini, but Milos. For the most part these adventurers stick to the poorer countries where strong currencies go a long way, where public markets sell food cheap near closing time, where warm climates make living on the beaches reasonably comfortable. They frequently congregate in the same camping area, sharing the bounty the day has brought—a good catch fishing, day old bread from the bakery, a bottle of local wine—with other travelers around the campfire and exchanging tips about how to make some money on the black market in the next country, or how to cross the next border without a passport, or how to get through expensive countries like the U.S.A. or Germany as quickly and cheaply as possible and so get on to Mexico, or the Eastern Bloc, where the economies are not so demanding. Sometimes the members of this traveling fraternity have been on the move for three or four years without stopping at even a semi-permanent place of residence. At this point most people would consider such a life to be hard work, but for those who are strongly emotional about moving, who just have to see what's at the end of the road or across the next border or on the other side of that mountain range, the experiences are worth the discomfort.

While the emotional part of the moving center has its attention held by a particular object—hang gliding, climbing Mt. McKinley, taking karate lessons, white water rafting—the intellectual part of the center requires directed attention to function. The king of spades is much slower than the other divisions of the moving center, operating carefully and being intentional with its movements. Heavy equipment operators need to function from this highest part of the moving center much of the time because their work requires them to be alert and aware of what these large machines are doing. If their attention fails and they are operating from the mechanical part of the moving center, they may find they have broken a water main or cut through a power cable rather than excavating the area intended.

The king of spades is the primary creator of technology. It is the part of humans that invents better, easier, more efficient ways of doing things. Human beings are sometimes defined as the tool-using animals, indicating that this part of the moving center provides one of the definitive differences between humans and other large anthropoids. While there are some apes, chimpanzees for example, who seem to have very rudimentary tool use, it is our species who is distinguished by the proliferation of devices to do our work. Indeed, this seems a sort of compulsion for our species to the extent that most of our work consists of tending the machines and gadgets we have devised to do our work.

At any rate, once the king of spades realized the basic principle of the lever, this part of human functioning never slowed down. From there to the components of the information superhighway has been one long ever-increasing avalanche that shows no sign of diminishing.

In any person, it is the intellectual part of the moving center that figures out how things work. Anyone who has ever put together a tricycle on Christmas Eve has functioned from the king of spades. When the king of spades falters, we resort to the written directions, which means that the moving center needs to be assisted by the intellectual center rather than being able to solve the problem entirely with its own kind of intelligence.

Persons who are centered in the king of spades are greatly in demand in our technologically based economy. Not only are they highly rewarded for their inventions, and for improvements and refinements of these devices, but they are then needed to repair these things when they break down or are hopelessly snarled up by people who are not moving centered and who don't have the foggiest notion of how they work.

Those who have the king of spades as their center of gravity are capable of great efforts of sustained attention when they are trying to solve a particular problem. The athlete developing a slightly different twist to his body that will enable him to break the world's pole-vaulting record, the animator envisioning a new method of clay animation, the video game designer creating a more perilous environment over which Mario can triumph, the race car engineer figuring out a more powerful thrust for an engine's pistons all control and direct their attention until the problem they are working on is solved, whether it takes days, months, or even years. This part of the moving center receives considerable satisfaction from the process of problem solving.

After the problem is solved, however, the intellectual part of the moving center has little further interest in it. The king of spades has very little tolerance for repetition of the same movements. The pole-vaulter's record will soon be broken by other athletes who have the patience and endurance to practice his new method over and over. The animator's film sequence will remain unfinished once the technique is perfected—unless studio animators complete it. This part of the moving center is very good at creating new ways of doing things, not so good at actually doing them. Leonardo da Vinci's career was strewn with incomplete projects and irate patrons who wanted a finished product delivered. Many other brilliant inventors have failed to actually produce a product after the basic problems they were working on had been solved.

The king of spades works not only with movement but with spatial relationships as well. This is the part of the moving center that can look at a sofa and tell whether it will fit through a particular doorway and how it will need to be turned to do so. Visual composition is the province of this center division, whether it is a repeat pattern for wrapping paper or a new glass-skinned skyscraper. Not only understanding spatial relationships, but handling them in harmonious and aesthetically satisfying compositions, is one of the functions of the king of spades. Architects and engineers need a strong intellectual element in their moving center, and surgeons should certainly excel in this type of intelligence.

The three divisions of the moving center, the intellectual, emotional, and mechanical parts, provide a good illustration of how attention differs in the functioning of parts of centers. This center also demonstrates how the divisions function in relation to each other. It is the emotional part of the center which first becomes aware of a particular moving activity and has its attention drawn to that activity. But it is the intellectual part of the center which must actually learn to perform the movements by controlling and directing the attention. If these movements are learned thoroughly through frequent repetition, the memory of how the movements are performed is stored in the mechanical part of the moving center, which means that the person can now perform the actions without awareness of how the movements are being executed. We often hear people marvel that they can still do things they haven't done for twenty or thirty years, such as riding a bicycle. This indicates that once a movement has been firmly recorded in the jack of spades, it stays there.

In the above example, riding a bicycle, we can trace the movement to the different divisions of the moving center. When the infant or toddler first sees other children riding bicycles, it probably seems like an impossible miracle, that fast swooping movement almost like birds flying. Gradually, the young child realizes that these movements are being experienced by children like her, only a little older. From that moment her queen of spades yearns to experience that amazing movement that seems so effortless. The child pesters her parents for a bicycle until finally they relent and there it is, on a birthday or on Christmas morning under the tree: her very own bright red bicycle.

The emotional energy of the queen of spades is the motivation, but for a long painful time it is the king of spades that has to do the work. The child has to concentrate on many movements at the same time—feet turning the pedals, hands adjusting the handlebar direction, whole body trying to maintain balance, legs pumping fast enough to get some momentum to aid the balance, but not so much that it will be a disaster if she falls. Time after time she does fall, and then gets up, climbs back on the bicycle, and starts again. There may be an adult who helps, running behind the bike to keep the momentum up and to steady her when she wobbles, but for the most part it is the king of spades that learns the necessary movements through directed attention. Finally, after more than a week of skinned knees and bruised bottom and scraped elbows, the child performs well enough that she experiences the swooping speed the queen of spades was seeking. There will be some more falls, of course, until all of the maneuvers have been mastered. Two weeks later, however, the child will be seen riding her bike next to a friend, deep in conversation about how unfair their teacher is to assign so much homework, both girls negligently guiding their bikes with a casual touch of one hand on the handlebars, and no attention whatever allotted to the complex movements required by bike-riding. At this point the jack of spades has taken over, knows the movements, and will be able to do them as long as the little girl lives, and without awareness of how they are done.

It is possible, of course, that movements and other skills may be learned because of motivation originating in other centers and parts of centers. The emotional center might prompt one to learn to perform a particular action because someone loved or admired does it—a big brother who is a diving champ, or a father who loves to ski. The instinctive center might motivate learning some process because of fear of punishment or harm, as fear of drowning might motivate someone to learn to swim.

But wherever the energy that we call "motivation" comes from, it is the concentrated and sustained attention of the intellectual part of the moving center that is required for us to learn a certain set of movements. The pleasure we experience from the movement once it has been learned sufficiently well that the movement itself commands the attention rather than having the attention controlled by effort is the province of the emotional part of the moving center. And after the movement sequence has been mastered, the memory of how it is performed is stored in the mechanical part of the moving center from where it can be evoked by an associative stimulus and performed without attention.

Because this pattern of learning is so important to understand, and because it is so much more available for observation in the moving center than in other centers, another brief example is in order. Rather early in the child's development he will become interested in the process of making a bow knot. Again, the motivation might come from a number of different divisions of the centers. The queen of spades might become fascinated with watching his mother's nimble fingers tie his shoes and want his own fingers to be able to do the same thing. Or he might become aware, when he goes to kindergarten, that the other children can tie their own shoes and his emotional center will feel ashamed that he cannot. But whatever the motivation, he invests long hours of frustrating effort as his pudgy fingers attempt to make those recalcitrant floppy shoestrings go where they are supposed to. Finally, almost by accident it seems, he gets it right one time. And then for several more mornings he can't get it right, and his mother has to intervene when he is red-faced and furious, tying his shoes for him so he won't be late for school. Gradually he can tie his shoes more often than not, and for two weeks he demonstrates his ability proudly—his mother has to inspect the successful bows and lavish praise for his performance. Before very long, the thrill is gone, the attention is gone, too, and only the learned movement remains, an odd little dance the fingers do in response to the stimulus of the foot sliding into the shoe.

These steps in the learning process occur not only on the scale of the individual, but to a certain extent on the scale of the whole human species. For centuries, for millennia actually, the emotional part of the moving center in millions and millions of human beings was fascinated with flight. Watching seagulls soar, watching hawks circle, we have wanted to fly. At last it began to happen. First just hot air, then the little hop at Kitty Hawk where Orville and Wilbur's contraption actually went airborn, and on and on in a soaring rush until humans walked on the moon. In brief, the queen of spades nagged and nagged until finally the king of spades learned how to fly.

Imagine what they would have given, those towering geniuses of the past—Leonardo da Vinci, Sir Isaac Newton, Wilbur and Orville Wright themselves—to have the experiences most of us take for granted. Imagine them looking down at the cloud formations from thirty-five thousand feet in the air, seeing the patterns of cultivated fields and wilderness, passing over enormous mountain ranges, circling the planet, seeing the entire planet suspended in space, and try to feel the awe and wonder they would feel. Then, next time you walk through a large international airport, listen to what people are talking about: their luggage was put on another plane and won't arrive for six hours; their flight was canceled and they'll have to wait an hour for the next one; their plane was late and the gate for the connecting flight is at the far end of the terminal so they have to run all the way. Aunt Louisa's flight was grounded in Seattle because of fog, they've been waiting for two hours and just know as soon as they go home they'll have to turn around and come back again to meet her. And so it goes. So much for the miracle of flight. The queen is bored now. Ho-hum.

It is useful to remember this basic pattern of the learning process as it can be readily observed in the moving center because this is also the pattern of learning as it occurs in the intellectual center, which we will consider next.

CHAPTER 7

THE INTELLECTUAL MIND

The intellectual mind, the type of intelligence we are most likely to call "intelligence" even though it is not the only one, has functions that are difficult to observe. In fact, the functions of this center usually take the place of observation and actually prevent it. As one quip has it, "It isn't what you don't know that hurts you, it's what you know that isn't so."

The intellectual center works with words, numbers, ideas, concepts, theories, and abstractions. For this center experience exists in terms of terms. A process is the description of the process. An object is the name of the object. Tell the intellectual center that a rose by any other name would smell as sweet and it looks blank and walks off muttering, "A rose is a rose is a rose." The basic inability of the centers, particularly the lower parts of centers, to understand each other is partly the result of the intellectual mind's insistence that it alone has the province of intelligence and its habit of relegating other ways of knowing to inferior status.

The intellectual mind was the most recent to develop, and is the one used to differentiate ourselves from the other animals (which we call the "lower animals" although many of them are taller than we are and nearly all of them behave better). By calling ourselves *homo sapiens*, thinking man, we seem to be making a value judgment among the lower centers. Experiments being conducted with some of our supposed relatives, chimpanzees for example, are coming up with some ambiguous answers to the question of whether any other species can learn language. But whether they can or not, it seems very clear that no other animal uses language to the extent that the human animal does. The definition of humans as "the talking animal" holds up rather well.

It is the intellectual center which makes language possible, although all four of the centers must work together to produce and receive it. This capacity to use symbols has been termed "algebraic intelligence" which means that we have the capacity to let anything stand for anything else. In fact, this is not only a capacity, but seems almost a disease in its proliferation. We not only can let one thing represent another thing, but very rapidly become confused about which is which. We start out letting one thing represent another and soon think it actually is the other. It is true that Pavlov's dogs took the first step down this path when they began salivating at the sound of a bell which always accompanied the food they were given, even when the food was no longer given. There is no evidence, however, to show that these dogs would ever prefer the bell to the food if given a choice between the two. Human beings, on the other hand, can frequently be seen preferring their symbols for things to the things those symbols represent.

To take a familiar example, consider something that is seen as a symbol of wealth, an expensive automobile. Since wealth—the tangible form of energy—is something which the instinctive center wants to have, automobiles are greatly coveted. In fact, these symbols are so intensely desired that people will sacrifice what the automobiles symbolize in order to possess them. In order to have an expensive car to display, people will do without adequate housing, nutritious food, or other necessities. They will expend great amounts of energy in the form of money—not only the high price of the automobile, itself, but the finance charges over long periods of time and the maintenance costs—in order to have the symbol that stands for wealth. In the process they are ruining their chances for the practical acquisition of wealth. So much for the algebraic intelligence.

This is definitely not to say that this type of intelligence is a negligible thing. Obviously it is not. This most recent type of mind to develop is an amazing thing indeed. But we are rather too enamored of it. Truly, it is what makes us unique—our peacock's tail, our giraffe's neck—but we have every reason to take a dispassionate look at its limitations and ask ourselves what its survival value actually is. The peacock's tail, of which he seems so proud, certainly has its value in attracting lady peacocks and for finding him safe homes in ornamental estate gardens as long as people can stand his awful screeching, but how much good will it be in the wilderness if the fox population rises? If we examine the uses and limitations of the intellectual center, we will certainly find that it has value. We will also find that there are very important matters with which it is in no way qualified to deal—and in fact the intellectual function can provide a major obstacle to understanding in areas of transcendent importance.

Like the other centers, the intellectual center has a positive and a negative half. In this case the positive response is affirmation, the belief that a statement is true, agreement, saying yes. The negative response is negation, the belief that a statement is false, disagreement, saying no. Looking at the history of human knowledge, we can see that the positive or negative responses of the human intellectual center, whether in one person or in the combined minds of the many persons who make up an entire culture, have little to do with what the reality of a situation might actually be. Within the very short period of recorded history we humans have lived on a flat Earth and a round one. We've had a planet that was the center of the universe, then a sun that was the center of the universe, and now we can't even find the center of the universe. But in spite of the way the things we say yes or no to keep changing, we still keep saying "yes" to the unconfirmed assumption that the intellectual center has this right to decide about what is true or what is false.

Well over two thousand years ago, one of the most intelligent human beings who ever lived, Socrates, said that he knew more than others because he knew that he didn't know anything. We have accumulated a lot of information since his time, but

2,400 years later he could still make the same claim if he were around to make it. The intellectual center just isn't very intelligent, even at its best, and its virtual deification in the educational systems humans have devised has been and continues to be an error.

With these cautionary observations made, we can look at the intellectual mind, beginning with the mechanical division. The mechanical part of the intellectual center is where information is stored, the memory of this center. This part of the intellectual center, the jack of diamonds, is very, very good at what it does. Even humans who are considered to be very limited in intellectual attainment know an incredible amount of information.

An illiterate farm laborer has a vocabulary of hundreds, probably thousands, of words in his native language and, if he lives in a part of the world where the land owners speak a different language, hundreds of words in another language or a pidgin dialect. In addition to the language stored in his jack of diamonds, he has enough information about numbers to purchase the items he and his family need and get the right change—and he probably can draw on his memory of relative prices in order to get a good bargain. He knows the names and histories of saints or demons or deities, whatever beings populate the world of his belief system. He knows a complex set of rules governing his interactions with other human beings in his family, his social group, and the larger community. He has a lot of information about whatever job he does to earn his bread, and probably about a few related activities as well. He probably has memorized statistics about the accomplishments of some athlete who participates in the sport he prefers, as well as the rules by which that sport is played. And of course he has a wealth of political opinions which he is so convinced are correct that he will grab a gun and go out and either shoot someone or get shot, or both, if the situation arises.

It is here that we see how the mechanical part of the intellectual center causes difficulties. It is admirably designed to store information. But it cannot think, and it does not think, although it uses that particular word to designate information retrieval. "I just can't think of her name," we say when a particular piece of information has gotten misfiled or lost. The jack of diamonds also considers "thinking" to be the repetition of the yes-or-no tag that the piece of information is filed with. "I think a mile is 5,280 feet," means that this is the information I retrieved and I believe it to be correct. Correct is good. Incorrect is bad. This is what passes for thinking with the jack of diamonds.

Gurdjieff gave this particular part of us, the mechanical part of the intellectual center, its own name: he called it the "formatory center"[1] because of the preformed pieces of information, opinion, and belief stored there, frequently in the form of yes-no, black-white dichotomies, such as, "If you aren't part of the solution, you're part of the problem," or, "When guns are outlawed, only outlaws will have guns." The proper function of this part of the intellectual center is to act as a file clerk, or, in our time, a computer database. The formatory center stores information and has a system for retrieving it. Beyond that it cannot go. Decision-making is definitely not the formatory center's correct function. Indeed, it no doubt has stored maxims that will come up with opposite decisions. "Look before you leap," but "He who hesitates is lost." "Many hands make light work," but "Too many cooks spoil the broth." "A penny saved is a penny earned," but "It takes money to make money." If you've ever heard or participated in debates in which the speakers exchange this sort of conventional wisdom until they are quite red in the face and upset with each other, you have experienced what passes for thinking with the jack of diamonds.

The mechanical part of the intellectual function operates by association, which is the way most mental functioning proceeds. Casual conversations demonstrate the stimulus response activity of the jack of diamonds. You observe that a friend looks tired. He says that he is tired because he was up late taking his Aunt Louisa

---

[1] P. D. Ouspensky, *In Search of the Miraculous* (New York: Harcourt Brace, 1949), p. 235.

to the airport for her trip back to Seattle. You say that you were in Seattle for the World's Fair and had dinner in the Space Needle. He says that he had dinner in the Space Needle the last time he visited his aunt, but the food was overpriced and not too good. You say you had one of the worst meals you've ever had at the expensive new restaurant on Wilshire and he says. . . . In each statement made in these unstructured conversations, a word or phrase triggers a response from the jack of diamonds, which will produce a statement containing more words and phrases, one of which will trigger a response from another person's jack of diamonds. Occasionally conversations go so far afield and end up producing such strange material that the participants will stop to wonder, "How did we ever start talking about cannibalism among the Trobriand Islanders?" The people involved may be able to trace the associations back through the triggering terms: cannibalism, survival in snowbound disasters, the rugby team in the book *Alive!*, whether rugby is a more strenuous game than American football, who won the Monday night football game. . . .[2]

We can see from these examples that the mechanical part of the intellectual center functions without attention, just as the mechanical parts of the other centers do. Whatever is stored there will pop up when the triggering stimulus is present, just as the dance of the fingers that ties the shoes occurs when the foot slides into the shoe.

Educational systems devote most of their time and effort to programming the mechanical parts of the intellectual centers of young humans with the information, opinions, facts, and moral precepts that the mechanical parts of the intellectual centers of older humans contain and that these older humans believe are true, correct, accurate, good, and so forth. This is not easy, since many of the young would make direct observations about their experiences if they were allowed to, and might arrive at material to be stored in their memories which was different from what the

---

[2]Piers Paul Read, *Alive! The Story of the Andes Survivors* (New York: J. B. Lippincott, 1974).

older humans had. There could therefore be a conflict of opinions between generations, which happens to a certain extent under the most stable conditions, but happens to a very great degree when educational systems are not efficient or well-regulated or functioning in stable societies. We call the resulting changes in the programming of the jack of diamonds "progress."

Another characteristic activity of the jack of diamonds is to respond to someone else's "yes" with a "no." The system calls this producing "opposite 'I's." When a particular statement is made, such as, "The Moon is the Earth's satellite," the formatory mind will attempt to show that the statement is not true. "Actually," the response might be, "the Earth and the Moon form a double planet system with the two planets revolving around a common center of gravity." There are very few statements for which the formatory mind cannot find an opposite statement. A friend of mine who has this center of gravity told me that the first time he heard the idea, "The formatory center has an opposite 'I' for everything it hears," he thought to himself, "I don't believe that." And it took him fifteen years of self-observation and work on himself to see what had occurred.

People who have this part of their functions as a center of gravity are likely to have the reputation of being very intelligent because they have stored a lot of facts and are efficient at retrieving them. These people seem almost constantly in the process of assimilating more information. They read the ingredients on packages in the supermarket, the dates of birth and death of artists on the cards beside the paintings in art museums, the program notes about the baroque period at a Bach concert, the entire newspaper every morning, and any other printed material that shows up in their environment. They are not necessarily interested in or enthusiastic about information, but they keep taking it in whenever it is available. Considering how much these people know, it sometimes surprises us that they, like others centered in the mechanical parts, are not necessarily very interesting. They may not be intelligent, just very well informed.

The accumulation of information is so frequently mistaken for understanding that persons centered in the jack of diamonds can do very well in academic work in areas where a piling up of data results in publishable work. Nearly all academic disciplines have respectable specializations that consist of little more than feeding facts into computers and doing statistical analyses. Enormous research projects, such as trying to determine whether the *Iliad* and the *Odyssey* were written by the same poet by counting the uses in these works of the most frequently used conjunction in Homeric Greek, seem almost as common in the humanities as they are in the sciences, where such massive aggregates of data are to be expected. Increasingly, the activities of the mechanical part of the intellectual center are accepted as being academically valid. At the same time, the almost universal use of scantron testing (where the one right answer to a question is filled in on a bubbled computer card that will be graded electronically) is reducing the realm of learning to the retrieval capabilities of the jack of diamonds. In almost all college and university courses, as well as in the tests that screen those students selected to attend these institutions in the first place, the kind of testing done measures the programming and retrieval efficiency of the mechanical part of the intellectual center, not thinking ability. The answers which must be selected are either true/false or multiple choice (which are just a series of true/false answers to a single question). Comparing, evaluating, seeing causal relationships, tracing the connections between events, all of the processes involved in what we term "thinking" are removed from these tests except for occasional vestigial remains which might have been left embedded in a true/false response.

The contrast between the mechanical part of the intellectual center and the emotional part is as marked as it is in the other centers. The animation and enthusiasm of the queen of diamonds is very different from the dry-as-dust accumulation of facts carried on by the jack. The emotional part of the intellectual center is emotional about information, ideas, theories, ways of thinking, and ways of thinking about thinking—but not indiscriminately and not all at once. As is true of the emotional parts of all the centers, the queen of diamonds has the attention held by an object. For a while. Then the emotional part of the intellectual center flies from intense interest to total boredom.

The key to recognizing this type centered in the queen of diamonds is by his books. Usually at least one wall of his home, and sometimes several, will be floor to ceiling bookcases overflowing with books. Few of the books will have been read all the way through; the queen of diamonds frequently loses interest before a book has been completed, and the accumulation of details for their own sake holds no attraction. Since most books state their major premises in the opening chapters, the queen is likely to become bored once the basic concepts have been grasped. Also, with the attention held by some object—raising tropical fish, the culture of the Trobrian Islands, Japanese ceramics, existential philosophy, baroque music, differential calculus—the emotional part of the intellectual center may buy four or five books on the current subject of interest and then read the opening chapters of only three of them.

Like the other queens, the queen of diamonds' center of gravity usually causes these people to be sought after as friends and companions. The emotional energy feels good to be around and generates the same response in others. Having the intellectual function stimulated attracts many people, distracting them from the instinctive and emotional quagmires into which they are prone to wander. The late-night bull sessions in campus dormitory rooms, political discussions in taverns, community service extension courses for bored housewives all allow people to experience their queen of diamonds as a kind of vacation from tedium. Persons who have their center of gravity in the emotional part of the intellectual center are therefore much in demand, not only as friends but as teachers. Since they are excited about ideas, and since this excitement can be communicated to others, this type of person can make a very effective classroom teacher, particularly at the secondary and undergraduate levels.

The queen of diamonds type is usually too eclectic for the in-depth research required of scholars, but they can be effective generalists and can help young people experience excitement about ideas. The problems that such teachers may have occur when the queen of diamonds flips and is not interested in a particular area of the curriculum any more. These teachers may lack consistency in their courses, and may have difficulty covering the basic areas once those areas are no longer interesting to them.

As in the other centers, the intellectual part of the intellectual center is much more steady than the emotional part. The king of diamonds is the only part of the intellectual center that can legitimately be said to think, and is a part of the human psychological makeup that few people use any more than is strictly necessary. The effort of sustaining attention to intellectual matters is usually experienced as drudgery and boredom—or such is the conclusion arrived at from the testimony of students in secondary schools and colleges. Very seldom do we find people who derive pleasure from such activity.

Everyone who has completed any course of academic work has, of necessity, experienced the functioning of the intellectual part of the intellectual center. Even in subjects about which the emotional part of the center is enthusiastic enough that the attention is held by the subject, there come days when studying must be done even though the energy is low because of an instinctive problem such as a bad cold, or because the emotional center wants to socialize instead of studying, or the moving center wants to go skiing. On these occasions it is necessary to control and direct the attention to the material that needs to be studied, and that is the function of the king of diamonds.

The king of diamonds is the slowest part of all the functions. The intellectual mind is the slowest of the four types of human intelligence, and the intellectual division of that mind is the slowest of the three parts. It is obviously much easier to settle for the quick associative responses of the mechanical part of the center than it is to go through the laborious processes of the intellectual part. While the jack of diamonds specializes in quick and easy answers, the king of diamonds realizes that there are no answers because it is never possible to know all there is to know about anything. The jack of diamonds quickly decides whether something is true or false, right or wrong, but the king applies relativity and understands that a precept may be reasonable in one situation but inappropriate or even criminal in another.

People who have their center of gravity in the intellectual part of the intellectual center tend to be quiet and to wait a long time before speaking. Ironically, the only part of the intellectual center which actually thinks gives the impression of dullness or outright stupidity much of the time. It is the part that knows that it doesn't know. I have known only a few people who have this center of gravity, since this type is relatively rare. Also, this type is particularly hard to recognize because they are so tentative about ideas that it is difficult to see that they are, in fact, quite absorbed in ideas. It is paradoxical that those centered in the mechanical part of the intellectual center usually have the reputation of being intelligent, while those centered in the intellectual part frequently appear slow and unintelligent because they are unwilling to make assertions until they are certain of their correctness—and they are almost never certain. The person centered in the king of diamonds, when asked what center of gravity he thinks he has, almost inevitably says that he doesn't know. The one part of the human psychology that actually is intelligent appears dull-witted.

I once asked an acquaintance who has this center of gravity what it was like to observe this part of the intellectual center functioning. He said it was like building a house out of playing cards, trying to balance one more card on the fragile structure, and then another, and then one more. The king of diamonds tries to understand everything about a particular subject in relationship to everything else, to see the connections between ideas as well as the ideas themselves. This, of course, is the method of real scholarship, not simply the accumulation of great lumps of data.

In the intellectual center the correct relationship of the three divisions is extremely important. With this mind, the enthusiasms of the queen may program the contents of the jack without the attention of the king ever being involved, and the jack may feed the information back and pass this retrieval off as thought. But the correct functioning of the jack of diamonds would be in service to the king in matters where thinking is appropriate. There are, of course, many situations in which the mechanical response, occurring without attention, is all that is required: What street does George live on? What is the capital of Latvia? Matters that exist by definition and labels can be dealt with by definitions and labels. But matters of real importance cannot be dealt with this way. "Religion is the opiate of the people" is not an appropriate response to the eternal questions about whether there are higher beings, and if so, what relationship human beings have to them, and neither is any other automatic response. In other words, as soon as the questions being dealt with are of any importance, the correct use of the jack is in service to the king. The information stored in the mechanical part of the intellectual center is valuable only as it is evaluated and understood by the intellectual part of the center, which is able to compare, contrast, see causal relationships, structure logical sequences, and carry on the other processes of thought. But all too often the ready-made slogans and maxims served up by the jack of diamonds are what pass for thought, and instead of intelligence we settle for belief.

The jack of diamonds, with its labels and definitions that are applied to experiences and impressions, not only stops the thinking process but it can also stop observation. As long as the intellectual center operates without attention, or operates with its attention held by objects that appear accidentally in the environment, this is what occurs. In attempting to observe ourselves and to be aware of what is occurring around us, which is the central endeavor in spiritual evolution, we must always be trying to change our relationship to ideas. Ouspensky, who was intellectually centered, said that he "abandoned the system." Students of Fourth Way ideas have been puzzling over what he meant by that ever since. Perhaps it was his warning of the danger of letting words get in the way of the reality to which they point. When we settle for a definition of something we observe, we stop observing. For this reason the mechanical part of the intellectual center is an enemy of the aim to develop our understanding.

The intellectual part of the center, however, is one of the strongest allies of this work. Through directing the attention to new ways of connecting ideas, different angles of thought, we may find an approach and an understanding that would otherwise be overlooked.

CHAPTER 8

THE EMOTIONAL MIND

The emotional mind is the intelligence that relates to other people, that establishes valuation for things and experiences, and is the part of us that develops a sense of aesthetics, ethics, and morality. The positive half of the emotional center likes, approves, appreciates while the negative half dislikes, disapproves, condemns. The affinities and aversions of the emotional center can command the most powerful energies of the human organism, overriding even the instinctive mind's concern with the safety and survival of the body.

The emotional mind is the most difficult of the four lower functions to observe for several reasons. It is much more rapid in its operation than the other centers so that until the higher centers are developed to the point where they can observe the lower centers, only traces of the emotional function can be observed by the other three centers. It has no visible manifestations that are as easily interpreted as those of the moving and instinctive centers. It has no words or negotiable symbols with which to communicate its impressions and responses.

By far the greatest obstacle to the observation of the emotional center is the prevalence of negative emotions. It is impossible to understand the emotional center without understanding that negative emotions are wrong work of our functions and that they have no rightful place in our psychology. Negative emotions are a part, a very large part, of our false personality. We learn them largely through imitation—small children mimic the negativity of adults—and then assume they are a legitimate part of us. They are not. But because of the interference of this artificial encumbrance, which draws energy from all of the centers, it is difficult, when beginning self-observation, to see that the emotional center is primarily an organ of perception rather than one of reaction.

For a long time at the beginning of self-observation and observation of others while using the guidelines and schematics of this system, observation must of necessity be done by the lower centers themselves. The instinctive and intellectual centers begin this work, with the instinctive center receiving the various impressions, while the intellectual center is busily classifying and labeling them and filing them under their definitions. Since the emotional center operates much faster than the other centers, they are only able to record the residue of its functioning. For example, imagine that the person trying to observe himself is talking with two colleagues in the office where he works. A fourth person walks up to them and shortly afterward the self-observer is aware of an excess of adrenaline in his bloodstream and the impulse to walk away from the group. This he does, making a trip to the water cooler while the others continue talking. He can observe the sensation of adrenaline circulating. He can certainly observe his moving center walking away from the others while they continue talking, but he is unable to see the emotion that was stimulated when the fourth person joined the group. Was it fear? Jealousy? Attraction? It may take many observations of the relationship he has with this other person before enough data is recorded for any conclusion, even a tentative hypothesis, to be reached.

Notice in the previous example that observation would cease if judgment or the attempt to change intervened. If, for instance, the observer thought, "Why does George always have to butt into our conversations?" or, "It's silly of me to avoid George. I'm not going to do it any more," that would preclude any opportunity to continue to observe what is actually occurring in his emotional center. It is very important, particularly when trying to see the emotional mind at work, to avoid judgment and justification as much as possible—and of course to observe them when they occur. Observe as impartially as possible. Gurdjieff suggested that we try to observe ourselves as though we were an interesting stranger—which is very difficult to do since we constantly identify with what we observe, and then observation stops.

The visible manifestations of the functioning of the emotional center are ambiguous and can be deceptive. We can smile whether we like the person we are smiling at or not, and we can feign indifference when we are passionately attracted to someone. Of course the emotional center can, to a certain extent, communicate directly with another person's emotional center and thus know at least when the other person's manifestations (such as a smile or frown) are accurate representations of that person's feelings.

But while the emotional center can tell when a manifestation is a false indicator of the actual emotional functioning, it may not be able to tell what the actual condition is. It sees, for instance, that another person is only pretending to be indifferent to someone she is with. What lies behind the feigned lack of interest is not easy to know. Is it a strong attraction she is afraid to show for fear of being rebuffed? Is it anger that she thinks is not appropriate to manifest in public? All the emotional center of the observer can tell is that the emotional condition the moving center is pretending to is not the real one. And as actors demonstrate effectively every time we go to the theater or the movies or watch television, people who are practiced in emotional deception can convince us that emotional manifestations are genuine when they are not.

The emotional center is also difficult to observe because it has no negotiable language in the sense that the intellectual center does. While it is true that certain words may have a strong emotional association for nearly every speaker of a given language, there is no controlling what that association might be. The word "mother," for example, will almost always have strong connotations, but they will differ markedly from one person to the next. For one they may evoke positive feelings of security, for another fear or guilt, for another revulsion, and so forth. The emotional meaning of a word cannot be controlled in the same way as its intellectual meaning, its definable content, is controlled by agreed upon definitions which are recorded in dictionaries.

The emotional center communicates with symbols in the form of images more than with symbols in the form of words. Music, the visual arts, and poetry communicate emotions much more effectively than the clumsy attempts of the intellectual center to describe the emotions. As poet Archibald MacLeish demonstrates in "Ars Poetica," "For all the history of grief/An empty doorway and a maple leaf./For love/The leaning grasses and two lights above the sea—/A poem should not mean/but be."[1] The image communicates the emotion, not the words. In the visual arts images convey the emotions directly, without the intervention of words, and so we know Van Gogh through the images of his bedroom at Arles in a way that we could not have had we been in Arles and talked to him. And with music it sometimes seems as though emotion has become pure sound and sound pure emotion.

Some of the other animals, dogs particularly, seem to have rudimentary emotional centers that have feelings distinct from instinctive emotions (i.e., the likes and dislikes predicated on the queen of clubs' desire for comfort). Dogs, in fact, have been known to demonstrate loyalty and devotion that can override their instinctive concern for survival, just as humans sometimes do. As with the other types of intelligence, however, the emotional mind in humans seems much more highly organized than that of other animals that may have such a function.

The mechanical part of the emotional center contains all the automatic responses that we produce in relationship to others. It is in this part of the human makeup that cultural attitudes and rituals are stored, and they are deeply rooted and difficult to ob-

---

[1]Archibald MacLeish, *New and Collected Poems* (Boston: Houghton Mifflin, 1976), p. 106.

serve. In fact, the best way to be able to see the programming of the mechanical part of the emotional center is to live and work in another culture for a while. It soon becomes painfully apparent that the responses we make automatically are not appropriate in the new setting. Volumes have been written about this phenomenon, commonly termed "culture shock," and about the myriad differences in the ways members of different cultures handle time, personal space, relationships to family members or to strangers, business transactions, dining, and all the other complex interactions of social life.

We learn these mechanical responses by imitation when we are very young, long before we are even aware that we are absorbing certain ways of reacting to other people. To use a very ordinary and obvious example of how young we are when such responses begin, consider the way Russians and Americans alter or do not alter their facial expressions when looking at a stranger. The Russian tends to keep the face motionless and impassive while the American will smile or grimace in some way to acknowledge the stranger's direct gaze. This difference can be observed in infants as young as one or two months old. When a stranger looks at a Russian infant, it looks back impassively, but an American baby will usually smile or make some sort of grimace when a stranger looks at it. Small wonder that these mechanical responses remain invisible to us when they are learned so early.

This imitative aspect of the jack of hearts—and of the mechanical parts of all of the centers—is one of the main ways to distinguish between the jack and the queen. That is, many of the emotions typical of the queen also appear to be occurring in the jack. The difference is that they are merely being imitated and are much less intense. They pass as soon as our friends and acquaintances lose interest.

The mechanical part of the emotional center, the jack of hearts, is also the repository of crowd emotions. Large groups of people will be swept into the same emotional response at concerts, sporting events, political rallies, or during disasters. This automatic imitation of the emotional tenor of the group, whether restrained or violently demonstrative, is one of the most characteristic manifestations of the jack of hearts. This part of the emotional center can be sentimental and affectionate, but it can just as easily be coldly rejecting and even cruel, depending on the stimulus. Loyalty to the team can turn into violence against the other team, and has done so repeatedly at soccer matches in various parts of the world. Political violence has become such a commonplace that it is taken for granted.

The jack of hearts also dictates the aesthetic tastes of the members of a culture. Walk into any apartment in central Athens, any working class flat in London, any bungalow in a suburban subdivision in the U.S.A., and chances are very high that you will find it decorated in exactly the same way as all the other dwellings in that area. The furniture, the wall decorations, the floor coverings, the miscellaneous artifacts, the choice of colors will all be of a similar type. Again, the jack of hearts operates by imitation, and wants for its environment the same mass-produced articles it has seen in the homes of friends and relatives.

Like the mechanical parts of the other centers, the mechanical part of the emotional center has a useful function to perform. Under ordinary day-to-day conditions the jack of hearts provides the social lubricant necessary to keep interactions from degenerating into instinctive hostilities. Between members of the same culture the familiar greetings and pleasantries offset the instinctive wariness of encountering strangers, at least enough so that the ordinary business of living can continue without interruption. (This, of course, is exactly what is missing between members of different cultures, so the instinctive hostilities often take over.) These gestures and verbal formulas are exchanged without attention being given to them and are categorized as "courtesy" or "manners" by the participants in the rituals, which can be very complex, as they are in Japan, where a different form of address must be used for persons of different rank and relationships, or very casual as they are in the U.S.A. where a brief "Hi," along with a smile, will cover most situations.

The person whose center of gravity is in the mechanical part of the emotional center usually has a friendly, gregarious manner—unless for some reason the automatic emotional responses have been the result of negative programming. In the latter instance the result might be a person who reacts with fear or suspicion when meeting people. The typical jack of hearts type, however, is cheerful and positive in social situations, seeming to be warm and caring in most relationships. This type is attuned to the little social conventions of friendship. You can expect greeting cards on your birthday and most holidays, thank you notes for any favors or gifts, get-well-quick cards for any illnesses, and condolences for any misfortunes. This person knows exactly what is appropriate attire for any occasion, so if you are in doubt, just ask the jack of hearts type what she will be wearing.

Beneath these conventional expressions of emotion, however, this type is likely to be shallow and insensitive. Since the mechanical part of the emotional center functions without attention, it is likely to be aware of only the surface manifestations of emotion, to mimic the prevailing emotional tone without any deeper awareness of what might be occurring. This part of the emotional center is automatically concerned with people and relationships, and is fond of gossip without awareness of what harm might be done by talking indiscriminately about what others have done.

The taste of those centered in the jack of hearts is also conventional. Sentimental movies and love songs, artificial flowers, stuffed animals, greeting card verse, escape fiction, soap operas, little china knickknacks and other mass produced decorative items appeal to this type and will be found in abundance in her surroundings. The male of this type will enjoy telling jokes, be loyal to a particular team, and wear clothing with the team's colors and logo, enjoy sports that a group participates in together, and have a favorite tavern where he socializes and drinks with a few good buddies.

When functioning from the negative half of this part of the emotional center, the person with a center of gravity in the jack of hearts can be petty and spiteful and have a tendency toward jealousy and vindictiveness. His specialty is cruel remarks disguised as humor, such as nicknames that emphasize a flaw or weakness in another person—calling an overweight friend

"Lardo," or a short person "Runt." Because these insults are disguised as friendly humor, the victims seldom have the courage to object, but the hurt feelings are real, and the jack of hearts intends them to be.

Considering the energy that the emotional center can produce, and the importance of the way humans relate to each other, it is rather curious that we leave the programming of the jack of hearts almost entirely to chance, while we lavish so much attention on the programming of the jack of diamonds. We do not educate the emotional center through any deliberate or intelligent planning. Rather this is left largely to happenstance and individual family situations. In a great many instances, then, the automatic programming of the emotional center occurs through brutality, neglect, and deprivation. Thus there are many persons in our populations whose mechanical emotions are negative and dangerous to others. When children leave homes where their emotional reactions have been imprinted with negative emotions, they go to schools where the emphasis is entirely on the programming of the jack of diamonds. In schools the emotional center is not only ignored but is suppressed and prevented from manifesting so that the mechanical emotions are never even examined, and little effort is made to educate this important type of intelligence. Because we do not make an effort to educate the mechanical part of the emotional center, it produces people whose automatic emotional responses are indifference, rudeness, derision, or even more violent forms of negativity. This is one of the most obvious indicators of the breakdown of cultural unity, which in turn causes the culture to decline even more rapidly in a snowball effect that seems impossible to reverse.

The programming of the mechanical part of the emotional center may be useful, or harmful, or neutral as far as its effect on other people and on society, but the difficulties encountered with this division of the emotional center are small in comparison to the havoc created by the emotional part of the emotional center. This part of the center, the queen of hearts, is emotional about emotion. It enjoys emotion for its own sake, and values those experiences and impressions that create emotions. The queen of hearts enjoys negative emotions as much or more than positive emotions—the only requirement being that the emotions be as intense as possible. Where the jack of hearts likes or dislikes, the queen loves or hates passionately. Where the jack is pleased by something it considers beautiful, the queen is ecstatic. And where the jack is relatively consistent in its reactions, the queen is unpredictable, liable to violent mood swings from positive to negative responses, from adoring someone to loathing him for little or no reason. It is the queen of hearts that falls in love, and the queen of hearts that commits the domestic homicides reported in the newspapers. Any time we experience intense, out-of-control emotions, we are being controlled by our queen of hearts, and that part of us has its attention held by some object. Since the emotional center is concerned with relationships, the object by which the queen of hearts' attention is held will usually be a person or a group of people.

The emotional part of the emotional center is the location of some very harmful manifestations. It is the part of us that is identified with other people, that loses the sense of our own worth in our concern with what others think of us. It is also the part of us that judges others. The emotional part of the emotional center is greatly interested in what other people are doing, particularly in what they are doing in their emotional and sexual relationships. And this part of us almost never approves of what other people are doing. It is greatly concerned with conventional morality and whether others are living up to the tenets of moral behavior. If they are not, and the queen is usually certain that they are not, then she wants to see them punished. The queen thus creates constant havoc in public affairs, prying into the private lives of public figures, avidly sniffing for any whiff of scandal, and creating a great hue and cry when she finds any misstep or wrongdoing. In this manner the emotional part of the emotional center is able to keep most democratic institutions from functioning effectively—or sometimes from functioning at all.

People seem to enjoy these emotions, particularly when they can safely be directed at public figures. Outraged indignation at the behavior of celebrities, such as film stars, the British Royal

Family, politicians, and star athletes, keeps the books and magazines and television talk shows much in demand when they are devoted to this material. And when the queen of hearts cannot find enough to hold its attention in public affairs, it turns to soap operas, romantic novels, horror films, and other forms of entertainment that serve as a type of emotional masturbation, allowing the queen to experience strong emotions about imaginary objects.

The havoc caused in public affairs and the energy lavished on artificial stimulation is exceeded only by the emotional part of the emotional center's rages and ravages in that most private of institutions, the family. It is here that identification with other people is the most intense and the possibilities for judgment, outraged indignation, anger, jealousy, possessiveness, and other negative emotions most prevalent. Domestic violence is the leading cause of homicide. Child abuse is usually perpetrated by a parent or close relative. All of these familiar facts are illustrations of the problems caused by the queen of hearts.

But the queen of hearts is also the part of the human emotional mind that experiences what we consider to be noble or altruistic emotions. Religious emotions are lodged here, as are philanthropic and charitable impulses. It is the transport of intense religious devotion and piety that turn into the slaughter of heathens, infidels, or anyone else who doesn't happen to share the belief in the particular deity or prophet or creed that is commanding the attention of the worshiper. It is the fervor to save the lives of the unborn that changes into the murder of the long-since born at abortion clinics. We would do well to observe ourselves closely at any time strong urges for social justice grip us. The passion for justice has a consistent habit of suddenly turning into injustice.

Those who have the emotional part of the emotional center as a center of gravity are subject to pronounced changes of mood due to the tendency of the queens to flip from the positive to the negative half of this part of the center and back again. In the emotional center, this shift is obvious because of the intense energy involved. The queen of hearts thrives on extremes and moves between ecstatic enthusiasm and bleak despair, seldom finding a moderate middle ground.

Like persons centered in the queens of any of the other centers, those with their center of gravity in the queen of hearts have a very low tolerance for boredom. In fact, they have less tolerance than the other queens. Having the attention held by an object, and the object always being emotional, the queen of hearts would rather experience any emotion, no matter how painful, than no emotion at all. This means that this part of the emotional center will provoke an argument or any type of emotional exchange simply in order to have an emotion to experience. For people with this center of gravity, there is always someone in the immediate environment to love, and always someone to hate. If the person the queen has selected to hate is removed from her daily life, she will soon find someone else to hate, even if it is the person formerly loved. The purpose, of course, is to allow her to continue to experience strong emotions—it has little to do with the people involved or what they did or did not do. The queen of hearts can also turn this alternating positive and negative intensity inward, fluctuating between self-love that is arrogant and overbearing and dark depressions that result from self-loathing.

People centered in the queen of hearts usually attract friends from among types who have difficulty in experiencing their own emotions and therefore enjoy absorbing the emotional energy that radiates from the queen. Usually these types who have low emotional responses, frequently those who have the mechanical part of the moving or intellectual centers as a center of gravity, are dismayed by the negative manifestations of the queen of hearts. They don't realize that it is impossible to expect the energy to be positive all the time.

From the above discussion, it may seem that there is no correct or useful functioning for the emotional part of the emotional center, and that is true, unless the queen of hearts is controlled by the king of hearts. The queen does, however, have an incredible amount of energy which she can command. We need only remember the occasions on which we have fallen in love to know what feats of endurance and foolishness we are capable of when in this condition. We can dance all night, lose forty pounds, fight duels, or elope. And the negative half of the queen can use the same mad energy to hijack airplanes or capture hostages. (It is the intemperate squandering of energies that makes the queen of hearts deeply disliked by the king of clubs.) If anything of value is to result from the intense energies of the queen, they must be placed in the service of the intellectual part of the emotional center.

Lewis Carroll has given us a wonderful portrait of the queen of hearts and the king of hearts in *Alice in Wonderland*. The Queen of Hearts is in a rage at everyone in her entourage, incessantly screaming, "Off with their heads!" The mild little King of Hearts is following at a distance, murmuring, "You are all forgiven. You are all forgiven."[2]

Unlike the demonstrative and highly visible emotions of the queen of hearts, the emotions of the intellectual part of the emotional center are silent and inward, Forgiveness, compassion, empathy, and forbearance are emotions of the king of hearts. This part of us is capable of external consideration—considering what is best for another—rather than inner consideration, being concerned with what others think of us and worrying lest they not give us enough respect. Where the queen of hearts wants to be understood, the king of hearts wants to understand. Where the queen of hearts wants to be loved, the king of hearts wants to love. The emotions of the intellectual part of the center require awareness and directed attention.

The king of hearts is the location of a properly formed magnetic center, that part of the human psychological makeup which is attracted to higher possibilities, the possibilities of development and evolution. According to this system, it is the magnetic center that begins to recognize the traces of a higher intelligence than that of ordinary humans, a level of consciousness beyond that which most people experience. These traces are encountered in various sources. The world's great religions and the sacred works

---

[2]Lewis Carroll, *Complete Works* (New York: Vintage Books, 1976), p. 88.

they have produced contain such traces. Some of the greatest art and literature and music contain such traces, as do some works of philosophy and metaphysics. The intellectual part of the emotional center may become extremely sensitive to these remnants of higher consciousness when it encounters them, and may begin actively to seek their source. This search may lead the person to a school which has a direct connection with higher intelligence through the agency of a conscious teacher. This is the function of the magnetic center.

But whether a magnetic center develops there or not, the intellectual part of the emotional center is the location of emotions that are capable of genuine concern for other people in a disinterested way. (The instinctive emotions of the queen of clubs are concerned with others, but only as those others are directly connected with pleasure or procreation.) The emotions of the king of hearts require efforts—as do the functions of the intellectual parts of all the centers—and can easily descend to the lower parts of the emotional center when those efforts cease. As an example, we may help a friend by taking care of her young child while she is ill, and at the time we are doing this it is out of compassion for a family that is experiencing difficulty. Later, however, when the difficult period is past, the memory of our assistance may form resentment in us because we feel our help wasn't appreciated enough—in other words, the emotions of the queen of hearts may usurp the emotions of the king once an intentional effort to avoid these lower responses has ceased. The queen of hearts will attempt to appropriate the actions of the king.

The king of hearts is also the location of aesthetic discrimination, the part of us that is sensitive to beauty and to refinement of impressions. The intellectual part of the emotional center is capable of seeing that there are finer creations than the ones which may be attractive to the lower parts of the center. A person may enjoy popular music, rock and roll, or folk music, and still understand that Bach's fugues are a much higher form of music. He may like Maxfield Parrish prints but know that Rembrandt's self-portraits are art on a different level. In other words, the discrimination of the king of hearts does not mean rejection of the pleasures and appreciations of the lower parts of the center, only an understanding that there are various levels of refinement and different kinds of energy available in different types of art. The king of hearts understands that drinking coffee—the same coffee—from a styrofoam cup, a pottery mug, or a fine porcelain cup are quite different experiences, and that the latter is higher, or more refined, than the former. Nonetheless, the king of hearts also understands relativity, and when the styrofoam cup is the appropriate one, that is the one the king of hearts will drink his coffee from.

People who have their center of gravity in the king of hearts may be difficult to recognize as being emotionally centered. They frequently seem to be cool and unapproachable, and their more detached emotions may be mistaken for an absence of emotion. Also, the king's concern for aesthetics can cause an impatience with the chaotic and messy presence of people. I remember discussing this with two friends at the Trevi Fountain in Rome. One of these friends had his center of gravity in the king of hearts, and the other had hers in the queen of hearts. We were there in the late afternoon when the square was packed with tourists in addition to noisy Italian families whose children were splashing in the water, and bands of young Italian men ogling the pretty blond German girls in shorts and backpacks, all of the noise and clutter and movement of a major tourist attraction on a hot summer afternoon. My king of hearts friend expressed the wish to see the fountain without the distraction of all the people. My queen of hearts friend, quick to judge him of course, was indignant and launched an impassioned defense of the scene as it was, declaring that the people and the color and the noise were an essential part of the entire impression and how greatly impoverished we would be to have only the fountain without its surrounding gaiety and life and so on. The three of us then discussed this difference in the way the several parts of the emotional center experience the world, and it was apparent that the differences in ways of perceiving and reacting that exist between the divisions of a center can be almost as great as those between the different centers.

One very large difference between the three divisions of the centers is in the connections among the centers. The intellectual parts of all four centers, the kings, can combine their different varieties of intelligence and bring to an experience or a problem the understanding that can only result from all of the intelligences operating simultaneously and with mutual awareness. It is virtually impossible, therefore, to isolate the king of hearts' aesthetic sensibilities from the king of spades' awareness of effective design and satisfying proportion. The king of diamonds' ability to apply scale and relativity in thinking requires the king of hearts' capacity to examine possibilities without identification.

The king of hearts is the gateway to the higher centers that are dormant or undeveloped in people in their natural condition. Because the king is the only part of us that is capable of understanding that there are higher possibilities than are represented by the lower functions, and the only part that can control the other parts of the functions which have no interest in attaining more awareness, the king of hearts needs to be strengthened by anyone who is seriously interested in working on himself or herself. Of the techniques that can be used to increase the power of the king of hearts, the most important is the effort not to express negative emotions. This effort requires being intentional about emotions, observing them, and monitoring their manifestations. This weakens the lower parts of the emotional center and gives energy to the king. Another way of strengthening the king of hearts is the effort to surround ourselves with fine impressions as often as possible. This of course means keeping our environment at as high a level as possible, but also making the efforts to experience the finest music and art at good concerts and art museums, to read good literature, and to study the ideas of the great minds of the past.

None of these efforts are easy. They are in fact the most difficult work a human can undertake. As soon as the attention is not controlled—and the controlling of attention requires a great deal of energy which the instinctive center does not want to release—the emotional and mechanical parts of the four minds reestablish themselves. While the kings work together, the queens do not, although certainly they exert a strong influence on each other. When the queen of clubs is tired or hungry, the queen of hearts is much more likely to fly into a rage over some small matter. When the queen of spades becomes fascinated by scuba diving, the queen of diamonds is stimulated to start reading about barrier reefs and tropical fish, and the queen of clubs looks for recipes for cooking abalone.

The kings work together, the queens influence each other, but the jacks are almost entirely unconnected. Since the mechanical parts operate without attention, they are operating in the dark. There is no awareness of the automatic functioning that goes on, so even though all four centers might be manifesting, they are unaware of each other.

The effort to be more conscious is the effort to be more intelligent, and the effort to be more intelligent is the effort to be unified, and the effort to be unified is the effort to have will, to be able to do, and to love. This work of observing ourselves and of dividing our attention between our inner states and the impressions of the world around us, of trying to see which of our manifestations come from what part of our centers, is not trivial. The understanding of types, which are the result of people having different centers of gravity and different dominant endocrine glands, is not for the purpose of operating more effectively in the activities of life in the world, although this may in fact be a side effect. The understanding of types and how they act and react and relate to each other is a necessary beginning move in the Master Game[3], as one Fourth Way teacher termed the transformation of the four natural types of human intelligence into a higher form of intelligence.

I have discussed the effect on a person's type that is caused by the person having a center of gravity in one of the four functions. Gurdjieff and Ouspensky called these types Man No. 1, in whom either the instinctive or moving function is dominant; Man No. 2, in whom the emotional function is dominant; or

---

[3]Robert S. De Ropp, *The Master Game* (New York: Delacourt Press, 1968).

Man No. 3, in whom the intellectual function is dominant. These three are all on the same level, are all asleep, and have great difficulty in understanding each other since they perceive the world differently and react to their experiences with different kinds of intelligence.[4] Now we need to turn to another factor that keeps people from being able to understand each other—their body types, which are determined by the endocrine glands.

---

[4]See P. D. Ouspensky, *The Psychology of Man's Possible Evolution* (New York: Alfred A. Knopf, 1974), pp. 53–56.

CHAPTER 9

RECOGNIZING CLASSIC TYPES

In describing and discussing each of the seven human types, we will begin with a physical description. This is always the place to begin in determining body types. Great Danes do not look like cocker spaniels. English setters do not look like Boston bull dogs. Just as the different breeds of dogs do not look alike, the different types of humans do not look alike. The same planetary influences and the same endocrine activity that produce a distinctive psychology and specific habits and tendencies in humans also produce a particular configuration in the structures of the body. This is pronounced in the classical types, that is, people who are nearly centered in one type and have one dominant gland in the endocrine system that has governed their development. Saturns do not look like Venusians. Jovials do not look like Mercurials. Sometimes it is possible to make an accurate type determination simply on the basis of a photograph.

I remember on one occasion speaking with a teacher who is very experienced in recognizing human types. We were having a conversation about Shakespeare and the teacher said, "Yes, Shakespeare was a Jovial-Lunar."

Amazed, skeptical, and envisioning some deep textual analysis of Shakespeare's plays and poetry that would have revealed the psychological tendencies of the Jovial-Lunar type, I asked, "How could you possibly know that?"

The teacher said simply, "I've seen portraits of Shakespeare."

A part, a large part, of the difficulties we have in observing, is that we get lost in theories, definitions, explanations, and words, words, words—and we forget to just look out of our eyes and see what is obvious.

Because human beings form much more complicated and confusing personalities than other animals do, it may be extremely difficult to determine which psychological tendencies are a part of a person's essence, and which are a part of personality. The personality, that complex combination of learned behaviors that has been acquired from parents, teachers, friends, relatives, the whole intricate web of social interactions, may or may not be much like the essence of a person. A Saturn may act like a Venusian. A Jovial may act like a Mercurial—and may even swear vehemently that these actions represent her deepest being. But a Saturn is not going to look like a Venusian. And a Jovial is not going to look like a Mercurial. Even with the tortures of stringent dieting, hours of daily aerobic and body-shaping exercises, even with plastic surgery and liposuction to remove some of the rounded forms, a Jovial is not going to look like a Mercurial. Human personalities are amazingly adaptable and malleable. We have an almost insatiable need for acceptance and love, and a corresponding deep fear of rejection. We need each other and we are afraid of each other: this is one reason for our ability to learn, and even become very good at, behaviors that may not be suitable for, and may even be harmful to, our particular essences.

This adaptability and malleability is why it may be extremely difficult to determine the psychology that is a part of a person's essence. And it is also the reason why it is crucial for us to know what we essentially are. There are few examples of waste so sad as unlived lives, lives that might have been productive and joyful but are, instead, merely endured gray day after gray day, grinding away at the wrong job, married to the wrong mate, trying to force the children to become something they have no inclination to be— and so perpetuating the whole grim cycle of waste.

Determining one's psychological type may take years of self observation. Type is not likely to be identified by taking a twenty-question quiz in a magazine, or by reading a book (including this one). There are no quick fixes, no instant pre-packaged solutions to the problems we face. C. G. Jung discussed one reason for the difficulty:

> [I]t is often very difficult to find out whether a person belongs to one type or the other, especially in regard to oneself. In respect of one's own personality one's judgment is as a rule extraordinarily clouded. This subjective clouding of judgment is particularly common because in every pronounced type there is a special tendency to compensate the one-sidedness of that type, a tendency which is biologically purposive since it strives constantly to maintain the psychic equilibrium. The compensation gives rise to secondary characteristics, or secondary types, which present a picture that is extremely difficult to interpret, so difficult that one is inclined to deny the existence of types altogether and to believe only in individual differences.[1]

The process of determining one's type, and the types of family members, friends, children, work associates and colleagues, can be a long and difficult process. (And sometimes it is not. Occasionally a classical type will have developed a quite healthy and suitable personality, be in an appropriate job, have married a congenial partner, and be so obviously and happily who he is that determining his type is easy.)

In ancient Greece, in Apollo's temple where the Oracle of Delphi dispensed wisdom, this simple and profound injunction was inscribed: "Know Thyself." Then and now it forms the foundation that must underlie any successful human life. It is the basis for the most profound wisdom. It is echoed in the Socratic statement, "The unexamined life is not worth living." It is

---

[1]C. G. Jung, *The Essential Jung* (Princeton: Princeton University Press, 1983), p. 130.

converted to metaphor in New Testament parables such as building one's house upon rock (essence) and not on sand (personality), and becoming as little children—who of course are in essence—in order to enter the Kingdom of Heaven. And in Shakespeare's *Hamlet* it appears in Polonius' advice to his son, "This above all: to thine own self be true, and it must follow, as the night the day, thou canst not then be false to any man."[2]

Because identifying type correctly is so important, and because it is sometimes difficult to separate essence characteristics from the characteristics that are in personality, it is a good idea always to begin with a close observation of physical characteristics. It may not be possible to conclusively determine type on the basis of the physical body alone, but it is usually possible to eliminate some of the types on that basis, that is, to narrow the possibilities. This method of proceeding, eliminating the types that are extremely unlikely to be the essence type of a particular person, is a reasonable way to begin. And, as was mentioned before, always begin with a close examination of physical characteristics. It is very easy to deceive ourselves and others, even without intending to, about psychological tendencies. But it is very difficult to deceive ourselves and others about the size of our hands and feet, the amount and texture of the hair on our bodies, our height, the measurement of our hips, and so forth. We may dislike these things. We may struggle to conceal or change these physical characteristics with diets, depilatories, elevator shoes, exercises, padding, wigs and toupees, waist-cinchers, girdles, thigh cream, hair dye, and cosmetics. The huge industries supported by our efforts to be something other than what we are testify to the human energies devoted to changing rather than accepting what one essentially is.

But no matter how successful we may be in the illusions we perpetrate—and usually we just look silly, like the balding men

---

[2]Wm. Shakespeare, *Hamlet, Prince of Denmark*, in *Shakespeare Arranged for Modern Reading*, Frank W. Cady and Van H. Cartmell, eds. (New York: Doubleday, 1936), p. 871.

who comb three pathetic long strands of hair across their bald heads instead of accepting that their baldness is right and attractive for their type—the facts of our physical bodies remain facts.

In each of the descriptions of the seven basic human types, I have begun with a description of the typical physical characteristics of the type. By comparing your own body's configuration with these descriptions you should be able to, at the very least, eliminate some of the types as possibilities for your essence type. Or, if you are trying to recognize the type of someone else, you should be able to determine what type or types she or he definitely is not. Since the purpose is to determine fact, to work through the veil of illusion and imagination created by wishes and dreams, by assumptions and artificially created social or cultural ideals, a good place to begin is with a close examination of the body. For some people this may be difficult. If you have been a victim of the self-deprecation, self-improvement cycle in which your body has been observed only in order to criticize it, camouflage it, paint it over, starve it, rearrange it, hide it, or completely ignore it and form an imaginary picture of it that bears little or no relationship to your actual body, it may be hard for you to simply look at your body closely and dispassionately.

Nevertheless, the effort is necessary. If you can't do without some form of imagination, this might be a good opportunity to use some directed creative imagination (as opposed to the automatic self-deceiving type of imagination we usually employ). Take on the role of an artist standing in front of a nude model about to make a charcoal figure drawing, or a sculptor considering the model for a sculpture he has just been commissioned to do. Stand naked before a full-length mirror and look with a clear, careful, observant eye, without judgment or vanity, at what you actually see.

How tall are you? If you are a woman over 5'9" in height, or a man over six feet tall, you are probably not one of the active, negative types, since both of those types, the Mercurial and the Martial, tend to be comparatively short. So, with one fact you have narrowed the possibilities to five instead of seven.

How thin are you? And how hard is it for you to stay that way? If you are slender, it is unlikely that you have made large efforts to gain weight, since we live in a time when the ideals of beauty promulgated by the fashion centers of Paris, New York, and Rome assure us that it is impossible to be too thin. If you are slender, and have no difficulty remaining slim even though you eat as much as you want whenever you want, it is virtually certain that you are not one of the passive and positive types. Both of these types, the Jovial and the Venusian, are fleshy, rounded, and have to watch their diet carefully if they do not want to put on weight. (If you are one of these types you can determine which one by observing where the bulk accumulates—Jovials carry their weight high, Venusians carry theirs low.) So, with one more fact you have eliminated two more possibilities, and you now have only three types to consider. You are quite tall, so it is unlikely that you are a Mercurial or a Martial. You are naturally thin, so is unlikely that you are a Jovial or a Venusian. This leaves three possibilities: you might be a Lunar, a Solar, or a Saturn.

Now is the time for more detailed observation. Notice your hands and feet, the articulation of bones in your joints—the wrists, ankles, elbows, and knees. Notice the line of the jaw, the cheekbones, the brow. Are the bones relatively prominent, the hands and feet large, the joints rather knobby, the jaw protruding rather than receding? On the basis of these facts you can at least tentatively eliminate the delicate Solar type and the relatively amorphous Lunar, who would more likely have a receding chin. At this point you have a working hypothesis: you may be a Saturnine type. Of course it will take much more observation and experimentation before you can be relatively certain about your type. The important point, however, is that you should always begin your observations with an impartial scrutiny of the structures of the body.

You cannot, of course, make such close observations of the bodies of others. You may be more easily deceived by their efforts to change the characteristics they don't like. (Does your boss wear a toupee or is that hair natural? Better not ask.) On the other hand, it will probably be easier for you to be objective about your observations of other people's bodies since you aren't as identified with them and concerned with changing them. Unfortunately, people sometimes invest quite a bit of effort in trying to change the appearance of their mates or children, but perhaps, with a better understanding of types, this sort of mistaken and largely destructive effort will be eliminated.

After the physical description of each type in the following chapters, there will be a short description of the celestial body which is believed to influence that particular type. According to the esoteric tradition of the Emerald Tablets of Hermes Trismegistus, one of the laws of interrelated cosmoses is, "As above, so below." This idea of different systems on different scales being models of each other is an interesting one. And the correspondences between the celestial bodies and the human types are so revealing of tendencies and characteristics of the several types that such a discussion seems useful even though there is no empirically valid way of verifying that there is a direct connection between planets and people of a specific type. The discussion of the endocrine gland which governs a particular type is considerably less theoretical, since it is based on a wealth of scientific information that has been accumulated by endocrinologists, psychiatrists, and psychologists in this century. The information about how the different endocrine glands affect human development and behavior can provide insight into why the different types look and act the way they do, and why, in fact, they could not possibly be different than they are.

The characteristic attitudes, actions, tendencies, preferences, and aversions of each type will be discussed in an attempt to understand the psychology of each. This will refer to those tendencies found in essence rather than in personality, which may be difficult to determine without individual work and observation. Most of us, when we begin self-observation, have many ideas about ourselves that simply are not accurate. We may think we like music because we come from a family where music was highly valued and many family members were musicians. We may, however, have very little appreciation for music in our essence. It may come as an enormous relief to realize that it is fine to prefer silence to constantly having music playing.

One very large obstacle to self-observation is the fact that when we are acting most mechanically, that is, from the natural tendencies of body type and center of gravity, we are too asleep to make any observations. What we observe and remember, therefore, tends to be those behaviors which are atypical. Only when normal patterns have been somehow disrupted are we awake enough to create a memory of what has occurred. As a result, most people only have memories of times when they were not acting according to their mechanics.

In any culture, there are abilities that are valued more highly than others. The types that excel at culturally approved activities receive more praise and admiration than types who are good at less-valued activities. And of course the same is true of individual families. Some parents expect their children to be academically talented, other families want athletes, and still others prefer artists. The effect this may have on the developing child can be great. In the family I grew up in, for instance, athletic prowess and a military career were expected of the boys. For one son, a Saturn-Mars type, fulfilling the parental expectations was no problem. Indeed it was a pleasure. The other, a sensitive, feeling-oriented Lunar, suffered very real torments. He could neither disappoint the father he loved and respected nor find any pleasure in the rough sports of football and wrestling, or the rigid discipline of a military academy. He did play football, and even exceled at it, but he confessed that he would throw up in the locker room before every game, so much did he dread the ordeal.

Sex roles were quite rigidly delineated in my family. Not only was the gentle, passive Lunar boy expected to be a star athlete and prepare for a military career, but a girl who was a rough and boisterous Martial type was frequently admonished for not being nice and quiet and docile as was expected of female children. The sense of inadequacy children feel when they are, in their essence characteristics, not the type that their parents and teachers prefer whether because of gender roles or for other reasons, can have long-lasting and very destructive effects. Lack of self-valuation can cause many harmful attitudes and behaviors, including addictions, unsatisfactory personal relationships, criminal acts, and perpetuation of the whole cycle of poor parenting skills for the next generation.

Without careful self-observation, many people are able to convince themselves that they do in fact like activities for which they have no natural inclination. After years of controlling and denying the desires of essence in order to please others, the person may no longer be aware of what those preferences actually are. For this reason it is best to be cautious in evaluating your own essence characteristics. It can take a long time to work through the painstaking process of separating what is in essence from what is in personality. This is the task that Venus (love) set for Psyche (the soul)—the separating of the seeds. Do not be in a hurry. In trying to determine one's essence type, it is important to observe without judging or in any way evaluating what is observed. Try to observe yourself as though you were an interesting stranger. Above all, do not try to change what you observe. Again. This is extremely important: *do not try to change what you observe*. For many, perhaps most people, essence has been so suffocated and stifled and stunted by the development of personality, that it is extremely fragile. In many cases it has not developed beyond a very early chronological age. When essence begins to emerge, it may well be as vulnerable and sensitive as a 3- or 4-year-old child—and as barbaric and uneducated. Such an essence has already suffered a great deal from efforts to control it, change it, punish it, ridicule it, or otherwise try to get it to be something other than it is. If you allow your personality to continue this abuse of your essence (sometimes referred to as "the child within"), you will gain nothing and you will certainly not be able to determine your actual type. Later, after your essence becomes strong and sound of its type, there may be things that it will be possible to modify, but this will require the help of others. Meanwhile, just observe, observe, observe.

It is, oddly enough, easier to observe which characteristics are coming from essence and which from personality in another than in yourself. There is a wonderful childlike genuineness to essence characteristics in another person that is unmistakable once it has been experienced. There is a wholesomeness, a rightness, about actions that originate in essence. The guileless openness, enthusiasm, and charm that so attract in babies and small children will suddenly sparkle forth from an adult with the same purity. Essence is unmistakable once it has been experienced, but it is easier to see in another than in yourself. Your own personality, echoing the voice of a parent or teacher, is quick to criticize essence: "Why can't you be more like your brother?" "Nice girls don't do that." "Only sissies study music." These voices from the past intrude on the present, obscuring your ability to observe without praise or blame.

As we discuss each type, its tendencies, characteristics, strengths, and weaknesses, it will be easier to mention what career choices are most satisfying for that type. I will keep as a basic assumption the precept that it is better to enjoy life on a daily basis, than to labor grimly in the hope of enjoying some imagined future that may never arrive. You may, of course, occasionally decide to defer your pleasures for a while in order to achieve some legitimate aim. For example, a college student may have to take general education courses she is not interested in so that she can have a career in nursing, a field that she is admirably suited for. But this would be very different from a person choosing a career in nursing because it seemed practical and stable employment when she is an instinctively centered Mercurial and not suited for nursing at all. There is a large difference between engaging in activities that are not appropriate for essence for a year or two, and enduring them for forty years. The number of people who take advanced university degrees in subjects for which they are totally unsuited because of parental pressure or because of illusions about what they like is quite astonishing.

In talking about the characteristics and tendencies of each of the classic types, I will consider how the center of gravity of a person affects and modifies the way the type appears and behaves. Venusians are a very slow type, for example, but Venusians who are moving centered may appear more active than Venusians who are intellectually centered, since the intellectual center is the slowest of the functions. Saturns are usually very controlled and deliberate in their actions, but a Saturn whose center of gravity is in one of the lower parts of the emotional center might seem quite spontaneous and impulsive with a group of friends. Sometimes characteristics may double up, as it were, so it is hard to tell whether a particular manifestation is coming from one's type or one's dominant function. The Lunar type, for instance, is very cautious and wary in new situations. The king of clubs, the intellectual part of the instinctive center, is also very much aware and careful when encountering unfamiliar surroundings. A Lunar type who is centered in the king of clubs would have cautious responses coming from both center of gravity and body type, and would therefore be more wary than if only one factor were operating.

Each type has a characteristic failing or weakness called a chief feature. Frequently this weakness, the main obstacle to personal development, is closely related to the strengths and virtues of the type. Saturns, for instance, have the ability to consider many possible courses of action and to select the one which is for the common good. This type very often does know what is best for all of the people concerned in a given situation. But when Saturns go one step further, as they frequently do, and try to control others, to exert pressure on people to do whatever the Saturn has decided is the wisest thing, they have fallen victim to the feature of dominance. Jovials, as another example, are likely to be quite good at whatever they attempt. They have natural gifts for language, for the arts, for intellectual pursuits, and they are good with people, making friends easily. The weakness of the Jovials occurs because they can't help but notice that they are superior to others. The chief feature of the Jovial type is likely to be vanity. Benjamin Franklin, a typical and brilliantly accomplished Jovial, has recorded his efforts at self-improvement in his *Autobiography*.[3] He did well with all of his weaknesses except one. He despaired of ever controlling what he called his pride. If he ever

---

[3]Benjamin Franklin, *The Autobiography of Benjamin Franklin*, Kenneth Silverman, ed. (New York: Penguin Classics, 1986).

succeeded in being humble, he confessed, he would be proud of his humility.

It is important to understand that the chief feature is a characteristic of personality, the axis around which personality revolves. What we see in essence are certain mechanical tendencies (or weaknesses) which predispose a person toward a certain feature. Whether or not people will actually develop the feature that is characteristic of their type depends on their early experiences, the family they are born into, and many other factors.

Quite aside from chief feature, there are, for each type, things that they are not particularly good at, or have difficulty with. Both of the active negative types, Mercurials and Martials, need to be able to move. They need challenge and they need change. For either of these types to be restricted to a desk, or confined in a limited space, particularly if the job requires repetitive routine, is to make their lives almost unendurable—and, I might add, the people who have to work and live with them won't be having a lot of laughs either. At the same time, these active and negative types wouldn't be doing the job very well. A Lunar, on the other hand, would probably be very comfortable in a job that made active types miserable. The same Lunar would be terrified at the prospect of having to go out every day to meet strangers and to try to sell something—a prospect the Mercurial would respond to with enthusiasm. We have each been designed to serve certain purposes in the work of humanity, and will do better and be happier if we are true to the natural design.

For each of the types there are certain other types to which they are particularly attracted. They feel comfortable with these other types, and their interests and abilities and tendencies complement or reinforce each other. They marry this other type, or have good friends that are of this type, or choose business partners or colleagues of this type. These maximum attractions find each other easy to get along with and fun to be with. There are still other types that react neutrally to each other. There is no strong attraction, but neither is there any difficulty when they need to work together. They may become friends under the constraints of proximity—if they work at adjoining counters in the same store or are waiters in the same restaurant—but would probably not seek each other out under other circumstances and will not remain close if their situations change.

There will also be types that have considerable difficulty with each other. Problems can arise when two types are so different from one another that there is no common meeting ground on which to establish an understanding. Either their speed is so different that one whizzes by before the other gets started, or their ways of interpreting experience and their understanding of correct action is so at variance that they can never agree. More likely, however, the problems occur because there are too many similarities. When different types fulfill similar functions in relationship to others, when they occupy the same space as it were, they can be very irritating to each other. The two parental types, for example, Jovials and Saturns, are both positive types who genuinely enjoy helping others, but in quite different ways. When they both turn up in the same family or organization, there can be competition and misunderstandings between them.

In discussing each type separately in the following chapters, mention will be made of the types each is naturally attracted to. There will also be suggestions about how each type can understand and get along with those types to which it may not be easy to relate. We don't have much latitude in deciding what people we are going to have to live with and work with. We can choose our friends (but not our friends' friends who may show up with them). We cannot choose who will be in the family we are born into—Martial babies don't get to request Venusian mothers. If the Martial baby gets a Mercurial mother, well they're pretty much stuck with each other for a while. We cannot choose who we will have to work with, what type the boss will be, what type our colleagues will be. Let us suppose that an enterprising young Saturn receives a promotion to vice president as a result of excellent organizational skills and a brilliant new plan for a system of inventory control. He finds that the man he must now work the most closely with, the vice president in charge of sales, is a Jovial. Now the Jovial is a brilliant sales manager whose sales team has provided the company with a profit margin that is making many things possible—a new factory is being built, new products developed, and so forth. In fact, that's why the Saturn has gotten the promotion, because with all this expansion, inventory control is badly needed. Of course, one of the reasons the Jovial has become so successful is by giving the customers what they want when they want it, and the sales force does, too. This means that they are frequently in and out of the warehouse, picking up a crate of widgets or a few cartons of doodads when a customer needs them. So, at this point the Saturn thinks the main problem is inventory control, i.e., ensuring that the new system is followed by everyone, and in a way it is. But the real problem is not inventory control, it's Jovial control. To put it more accurately, the Saturn's problem is learning how to work harmoniously with a Jovial.

The problems that different types have working with each other are not going to go away just because they are understood. Lunars are not magically going to function at the speed of Solars, and they will always experience fairly intense feelings of resistance if anyone tries to pressure them to move faster. Martials are not going to relax and enjoy a cup of coffee while the Saturn takes seventeen more factors into account before making a decision. Martials will always want to get on with it and start work now, just as they always have wanted to do. They'll have the same rush of adrenaline in their system and it will make them just as impatient as it always has. Understanding doesn't change the way things are. It only helps us accept the way things are because that's what truth is, and truth just is. It isn't good or bad, it just is. Once you have a good clear look at it, you can begin the job of accepting it. You can stop taking personally a lot of the behavior of others that isn't in any way directed at you.

This acceptance includes accepting yourself as you are, and no longer beating yourself up about things you can't possibly be expected to change. And it means accepting others in the same way without expecting them to change. The issue is this: in order to get where you want to get, you have to walk through a mine field. Looking at the surface of the ground—it's a pleasant meadow full of lovely wildflowers; the sun is shining; the sky is blue—there's no way to tell where the land mines are. But the mines are there. Lots of them. So the question is, would you rather walk across the field with a map that shows where the mines are buried, or just take your chances?

Particular mention will be made about parenting practices that will be the most successful for each type of child. It makes much more sense to start nurturing essence in appropriate ways before it has been damaged and bruised by pressures that are harmful to it than to have to undo all the negative aspects of an inappropriate personality structure and go through the necessary healing process before development and education of essence can begin. The vision of a community in which all of the members are sound and healthy examples of mature development of their types is quite a dream. Meanwhile, helping just one child to grow into the best he or she can be is a very worthwhile effort.

Each chapter describing a particular type will conclude with an extended example of a person of that type, since the best way of understanding the different essence types and how they behave is by direct observation of examples of each type. That, of course, is the only way to verify whether these descriptions are accurate. Not as satisfactory, but still a way to approach specific examples rather than dealing exclusively with generalities, is considering well-known historical or contemporary individuals who were of a particular essence type. What we know of the appearance, abilities, accomplishments, and interests of such people can help to form the understanding of types that will be a foundation for our own observations of the people around us.

CHAPTER 10

THE LUNAR TYPE

The Lunar type is the only passive and negative type. This is also the only human type whose governing celestial body is considered to be a satellite. Lunars are probably as prevalent as any other type, but their determination to be inconspicuous keeps this from being obvious. There is quite a lot of variety in the physical appearance of Lunars, but most will have several of the following characteristics.

Whether the Lunar is tall and thin, as is sometimes the case, or short and slightly rounded as is more common, he or she is likely to have an awkward, unfinished look. The Lunar body has a frail, partially developed appearance, like a child's body There is frequently a lack of physical coordination that intensifies the impression of being incompletely formed. Outlines are indistinct, the skin pale and a little puffy, like underbaked pastry. Lunars frequently stoop or hunch over in their effort not to be noticed, as though they were trying to disappear entirely. They are likely to select dark or neutral colors for their clothing, which seems chosen to be as inconspicuous as possible.

Lunars are likely to have round moon faces, pale with rather large and sometimes slightly protruding eyes that can give them an owlish appearance. Since many Lunars need glasses to correct their vision, this impression of owlishness is increased. The eyes are usually downcast or prone to look away rather than to make

eye contact. Most Lunars have weak chins; indeed most of the facial features are softened and not clearly delineated. It would be
unusual for Lunars to have prominent cheekbones or a distinct
jawline. Their hair is likely to be thin, fine textured, and of a
mousy color, light brown or dishwater blonde. Like children, Lunars have almost no body hair, and what they do have is also pale
and fine-textured. If Lunar males attempt to grow facial hair, as
they sometimes do, the resulting beard or moustache is usually
thin and patchy. A sparse goatee is about the best that can be
expected.

Before describing the psychological tendencies of the Lunar
type, consider the celestial body that is believed to influence Lunars and the endocrine gland thought to be their dominant
gland. Although it is not possible to produce evidence of the
Moon's influence on this type, the ancient esoteric principle of
"as above, so below" is appropriate here, and knowledge about
the Moon is applicable, metaphorically at least, to an understanding of the Lunar type.

The celestial body associated with the Lunar type, the
Moon, has an ambiguous status in the solar system. When compared to the other large satellites of the Sun's planets, such as the
four largest satellites of Jupiter and the satellites of Saturn and
Neptune, it is found to be of similar size. However, when we
consider the size of those satellites in relationship to the gigantic
planets that they orbit, we see that the Moon is very large to be
the satellite of a relatively small planet like the Earth. When we
compare the Moon to the smallest of the inner planets, Mercury,
we find that it is not much smaller.

Furthermore, the Moon, which has a diameter about one
fourth that of the Earth, does not actually orbit the Earth. The
Moon and the Earth both revolve around a common center of
gravity. Since the Earth is larger than the Moon, and they are
quite close to each other (when the enormous distances between
planets are considered), that center of gravity is within the terrestrial globe. Because of these anomalies, many astronomers consider that it is more accurate to see the Moon and the Earth as a
double planet system rather than as a planet and a satellite. But

LUNAR: The Lunar Type is passive and negative. It is a young-looking type, frequently frail-seeming and awkward. The Lunar does not like crowds or being the focus of attention, preferring solitude to socializing. Lunars frequently have weak eyesight and prefer dim lighting to bright lights or direct sunlight. Because their dominant endocrine gland is the pancreas, they frequently have digestive problems. They are good with details but sometimes have difficulty seeing the big picture. The chief feature of the Lunar is likely to be willfulness, although fear is also a typical feature.

whether the Moon is called planet or satellite, it is undeniably Earth's closest neighbor, and the celestial body about which the most information is available.

The Moon always keeps the same face toward the Earth, so not until the beginning years of space exploration did scientists have any idea what the back side of the Moon looked like. Since then, the entire Moon has been photographed, measured, and analyzed to such an extent that there are now better maps of the entire Moon than there are of some areas on the surface of the Earth. The Moon is not a perfect sphere, but is a bit awkwardly formed. It has a slight egg shape, with the small end of the egg toward the Earth, possibly because it was affected by the stronger gravitational pull of the Earth. Although the Moon is complex, it is probably the most colorless of all the bodies in the solar system, planets or satellites. All of the Lunar landscapes are covered by a layer of fine powder and broken-up rubble between one and twenty meters thick. This layer is called the Lunar soil, although it is totally different than the soil formed on Earth by the action of wind, water, and organic life.

The Lunar soil was formed over billions of years of bombardment by large and small meteorites, most of which were so small they would have burned up if they had entered Earth's atmosphere. These meteorites formed craters when they hit the Moon. Tiny particles of cosmic dust produced microscopic craters only a micron across, while the much less frequent impact of larger objects blasted out craters that could be miles in diameter. Each of these blows shattered solid rock on the Moon's surface, scattered material around the crater, and stirred the soil. But the soil is more than ground-up rock. It is the boundary layer between the Moon and space that absorbs matter and energy coming from the Sun, the planets of the solar system, and the rest of the universe beyond. Tiny bits of cosmic dust and atomic particles constantly hit the Lunar surface. As it is buffeted by the solar wind, the Moon has these particles mixed with its soil.

After the Moon landings of the Apollo program between 1969 and 1972, the instruments placed on the Moon by Apollo astronauts operated for as long as eight years. Seismometers recorded the tiny vibrations caused by meteorite impacts on the surface and by small moonquakes deep in the interior. Because these vibrations provide clues about the material through which they pass, scientists are able to speculate about what the inside of the Moon may be like. The outer part of the Moon is much colder, thicker, and more rigid than the outer part of the Earth. Moonquakes occur very much deeper than earthquakes, 600 to 800 kilometers beneath a thick, dense mantle. The deep interior of the Moon is still unknown. Some theorize that it may be partly molten inside, and may possibly have a small iron core at its center as the Earth does.

As is usual in scientific endeavors, Moon explorations left many questions unanswered, and some questions that had not previously been thought of presented themselves. One baffling phenomenon was the magnetism discovered in many of the old Lunar rocks. Since the Moon itself does not now have any detectable magnetic field, what caused the magnetism in the rocks? Although many theories have been proposed, the Moon retains its mystery.

The Moon's relative quiet made it possible for the Apollo instruments to register the impact of meteorites as small as grapefruit anywhere on the Moon's surface. The detectors registered between 70 and 150 impacts per year for the eight years they were sending data. Some of these impacts came from clusters of small meteorites traveling in groups. The detection of such events provides information about the distribution of meteorites in the solar system.

Just as scientific investigation has learned about certain features of the Moon, it has also learned a lot about one aspect of the endocrine gland, the pancreas, that the Moon is believed to stimulate. The motivation for the interest in the functioning of the pancreas, as was mentioned earlier, is that the endocrine portion of this gland produces insulin. Insulin is produced in the Islets of Langerhans, which are cell structures making up only two to three percent of the pancreas. Insulin is needed by almost all of the cells in the body because it enables them to absorb glucose, which is the cells' main energy source. When blood glucose levels rise after a person eats sweets, the pancreas is stimulated to release insulin and the body is stimulated to produce proteins and fats. If this mechanism doesn't work right, when there isn't sufficient insulin, the cells are unable to use the energy. The resulting disorder, diabetes, is a common and dangerous disease—and the reason why so much attention is focused on the pancreas.

Insulin is not the only hormone known to be produced by the Islets of Langerhans, however. This endocrine gland also produces the hormones glucagon and somatostatin. Glucagon, like insulin, is concerned with the energy available to the body's cells. It stimulates the liver to break down stored sugar for use. Without this hormone a coma would result when the brain ran out of energy. Somatostatin is a messenger hormone that controls the secretion of intestinal hormones of digestion such as insulin and gastrin. It also affects the release of the growth hormone from the pituitary. Since somatostatin can now be synthesized, it is possible to treat the problems caused by excess gastrin production: ulcers. It is also possible to treat problems caused by excess insulin: hypoglycemia. The problems which occur from excess growth hormone can also be treated with somatostatin.

Another part of the pancreas, called Aselli's pancreas, is composed of an assemblage of lymphatic glands and appears to be concerned with the circulation of lymph. This nearly colorless liquid is crucial to the body's immune system. Lymph circulates through the spaces and vessels between tissues and organs, removes bacteria and certain proteins from the tissues, and transports fat from the intestines. It also supplies lymphocytes, the infection-fighting white cells, to the blood.

The Lunar type, pale and cool, is governed by the pale cool Moon. The Lunar is silent and secretive, as the Moon keeps one side turned always away from Earth and hides the secrets of its interior deep in the center, under a dense mantle. These aspects of the Moon seem perfect metaphors for the psychology of the Lunar type, which is both reflective and withdrawn. Lunars are very private people, who prefer solitude to being in groups, and who avoid parties and social gatherings. Or, if unable to avoid such events, the Lunar will probably be found sitting in a corner or standing by a wall, observing but not participating in the activity or conversation. If pressed to join in, the Lunar declines, and may even leave.

Since the Lunar is the only passive and negative type, it is useful to explore the implications of this particular combination in order to have some understanding of how the Lunar experiences the world. First of all, the orientation of passive rather than active means that the person sees the outside world as something that acts upon him or her rather than something to be acted upon. In other words, while active types think of their environment and the people in it as something to be changed, rearranged, organized, improved, or in some way dealt with, passive types react to the environment and the people in it as something over which they have no control. For the passive and positive types, the Venusians and Jovials, this seems fine. Venusians just accept things and go with the flow, and Jovials see most situations as either a party or an excuse for planning one. Lunars, on the other hand, see the external world as threatening, something against which they need to defend themselves. Like the Moon out on the dark edge of space, unprotected by an atmosphere, bombarded with meteorites and cosmic particles, Lunars see no option but to develop a hard shell as defense against the bewildering onslaught of impressions and experiences that confront them.

I have mentioned the idea of the four functions, or types of intelligence, that people have. Each of these four functions has a positive part and a negative part. For the intellectual function, the positive part is yes, correct, true; the negative part is no, erroneous, false. For the moving function, the contrast is between movement and rest; for the instinctive function between comfort and discomfort. And for the emotional function, the positive part likes and the negative part dislikes. In the positive types, the positive parts of the functions are more fully developed. This means that any impression or experience is more likely to register as positive—these parts of the functions present a larger target. In negative types it is the other way around. The negative parts of centers are more developed and present a larger target so that any impression or experience is likely to be received as negative. No.

I don't want to move. No, I'm uncomfortable. I don't like it. No. Positive types are the-glass-is-half-full people. Negative types are the-glass-is-half-empty people.

For the three negative types, the response to any stimulus is much more likely to be no than yes if the stimulus is an idea; more likely dislike than liking if the stimulus is emotional, and so forth. The active negative types, Martials and Mercurials, see the stimulus they receive as negative, as something to change. They feel they need to act, and both set out to make the change they feel is necessary, each in his own way. The Lunar type, however, sees only that the stimulus is a negative thing, something to ignore, or hide from, or deflect, or refuse, or, if necessary, to escape.

To give a specific example of Lunar behavior that is consistent and predictable, imagine that you want to see a particular movie that is playing at a theater in your neighborhood. On your way you think of a good friend whose company you would enjoy and who you think might enjoy the movie, too. Since your friend lives nearby, you stop at her house, knock on the door, and when she answers you suggest that she go with you to the movie. The Lunar will say no. She doesn't want to. She has heard that the movie got bad reviews. She's busy. No.

The habitual nay-saying of the Lunar can be very frustrating for friends and family, to the extent that they may give up asking and just leave the Lunar alone. This may be all they can do, no matter how active and determined they may be. The more a Lunar is persuaded, pushed, begged, reasoned with, bribed, cajoled, threatened, or otherwise urged to do something, the more stubbornly he will refuse. The only possible way to get a Lunar to change his mind about something is not to make an issue of it. Simply accept the first negative response and let it go. If the Lunar does not have someone or something to oppose, there is a chance he might change his mind on his own, given sufficient time and space to come around.

If you want a Lunar to do something, it is necessary to be very circumspect in approach. You must understand that the Lunar type cannot—actually physiologically cannot—act quickly. Remember that the digestive hormones produced by the pancreas have the effect of dampening the adrenals. No one gets riled up after a good meal, and most of us hardly want to move at all. Without the galvanizing effect of adrenaline, there is no impetus to action. The Lunar says no. Therefore, you don't want to approach the subject of what you want to do at anywhere close to the time you want to do it. Let's go back to the example of the Lunar friend whom you asked to the movie. If you really wanted her to go, you should have thought of calling her in the afternoon and just mentioning it, saying that you wanted to go, saying that another friend had highly recommended it, and then changing the subject. Then allow her a couple of hours to get used to the idea before you call a second time and actually invite her to go along. This approach of preparing the Lunar, softening him or her up a little before actually making a suggestion, won't work every time. But it will work sometimes, and making suggestions abruptly will never work at all.

This actual physiological inability of the Lunar type to act rapidly or to become excited can be very useful in crisis situations. Lunars do not panic and do rash or dangerous things. Their coolness and calm response to emergencies in which everyone else is hysterical or incapacitated with fear can be quite remarkable. For all their usual timidity and passivity, they can be heroes in a disaster because they actually, chemically and physiologically, cannot become excited rapidly. For this reason they are ideally suited to be on medical teams in emergency rooms, on bomb demolition squads, or in other activities that require calmness in the face of critical situations.

Lunars are night people, and can tolerate working the graveyard shift more easily than other types. They can be found as night desk clerks in hotels, as short order cooks in all-night diners, as night auditors for businesses, as night nurses and orderlies in hospitals. In the daytime Lunars tend to keep the blinds down and the curtains closed. Dim interiors suit them much better than strong sunlight. A friend of mine, a Lunar, always steps inside a building lobby or entry while waiting at a bus stop rather than standing in the summer sun on the streets of St. Petersburg.

The Lunar is well-suited for work requiring careful attention to detail. Exacting and tidy, this type has no tolerance for imprecision. Accounting, data entry, most clerical positions, library science, medical record-keeping, legal research, all are occupations the Lunar would enjoy and do well. They all require detailed and precise work, and they all can be executed with a minimum of interaction with other people. They all require a tolerance for solitude and sustained concentration. For the Lunar these conditions are more than tolerated, they are preferred.

The interests of Lunars, as is true of the interests of any of the types, will be affected both by type and by center of gravity. The function with which they are most likely to relate to the world, the type of intelligence they prefer, will be an important factor in deciding what activities they enjoy, and even what work they choose. Moving-centered Lunars will enjoy combining their concern with precision with their pleasure in movement and spatial relationships. One moving-centered Lunar I know has had a successful career in ballet, and another is an expert on the joining techniques of classical Chinese furniture of the Ming dynasty. Both of these persons applied the persistence and dedication typical of the Lunar to become experts in their fields. Other moving-centered Lunars may be mechanics or technicians.

Lunars with their center of gravity in the instinctive center will be greatly interested in food. Or perhaps it is more accurate to say they are interested in digestion, since it is the effect of food on the body that concerns them, more than the taste. Since the Lunars' dominant gland, the pancreas, is the source of the digestive hormones, it is not surprising that this type, and particularly the instinctively-centered members of the type, are greatly concerned with food. Lunars can be very good cooks, making up in consistency what they may lack in adventuresome experimentation. If you have an apple pie that a Lunar has made, and it is delicious, you can be sure that the next one will also be delicious. The Lunar will not vary the recipe or the process at all. Lunars may be vegetarians, or may go on regimens of brown rice, or decide to fast for a week drinking only lemon juice and water with a teaspoon of blackstrap molasses.

Intellectually-centered Lunars are the world's slowest people. They may have brilliant minds and be able to think the greatest thoughts, but they don't operate rapidly. The Lunar is the most passive of the types, and the intellectual center is the slowest of the functions, so the combination of the two makes for a most deliberate and contemplative sort of person. They are the world's scholars, mathematicians, philosophers, and inventors. They can be found on university campuses the world over, isolated, shy bachelors or spinsters, pursuing with relentless precision some abstruse specialty in quantum physics, or philology, or Medieval history, at which they have become so expert that only two other people in the whole world have the slightest idea what it is they are doing.

The emotionally-centered Lunar can be very creative. The timidity and sensitivity of this type may be hidden beneath an apparently indifferent exterior, but the Lunar is capable of the depth of feeling that produces great art. Emotionally-centered Lunars may be painters or musicians. They are very frequently writers. Again, this type has the tolerance for solitude that the perfection of an art form requires, and the persistence to master the techniques of the art. The private inner world that remains protected from most outside influences may reveal itself in poetry or film. Woody Allen is an example of a Lunar who has capitalized on the discomforts and awkwardness of his type to write very funny films about the bleakness of the human condition and the difficulty of human relationships. Lunar humor is dark humor, but it can be exceedingly funny.

Emotionally-centered Lunars may also be drawn to the monastic life. If interested in spiritual development, the way of the monk will appeal to them because the isolation, the hours of meditation and prayer, are nourishment for the Lunar spirit. St. Theresa was of this type, as many of those religious contemplatives who have so enriched the literature of spirituality have probably been.

The strengths of the Lunar type are the sensitivity, the persistence, the careful attention to detail, the loyalty demonstrated to a friend or a cause, and the enjoyment of solitude that are characteristic. This type can also have weaknesses that are related to its strengths and which can be seen as extreme manifestations of the same tendencies.

The Lunar's sensitivity, when extreme, can result in a strong feature of fear if the timidity is overwhelming. This can lead to paranoia and morbidity. When the Lunar withdraws from contact with others and becomes preoccupied with his own dark imaginings, a dangerous and self-destructive pathology can result. Sometimes the dim and slightly skewed view of the world that the Lunar's cynicism produces is something widely enjoyed, as in the work of cartoonists like Gary Larson, Graham Wilson, and Charles Addams. There is an apocryphal story about Addams, who was for years a contributor to the *New Yorker*, that every once in a while his editor would receive some of his work, look at it, and pick up the phone. "Go get Charles," he would tell the psychiatrist who was in charge of the mental institution Addams occasionally visited. Whether the story is true or not, it illustrates the tendency Lunars have of losing touch with the rest of the world. To a certain extent we are charmed and delighted with the off-beat vision, the wacky perspective on things that Lunars can bring us. But then one day they may go farther than we would care to follow, and they may need help coming back.

The chief feature, or chief weakness, of the Lunar type may also be willfulness. When pushed, the Lunar resists; when urged, he declines; when dominated, he rebels. When active features such as power and dominance compete with willfulness, willfulness wins. The Lunar can say "no" longer than any of the other types can say "yes," and his stubbornness can withstand any amount of force or coercion.

Another feature that the Lunar type may exhibit is called lunatic. This feature is characterized by an inability to realize when a particular interest or activity is not important enough to deserve the amount of time and energy being lavished on it. Because Lunars tend to get bogged down in details, they can lose any sense of scale or proportion. A Lunar may allow all of his energies to be consumed by some relatively trivial hobby, such as collecting baseball cards or working crossword puzzles. Where another type might use a hobby like this for relaxation, the Lunar can become obsessed by it and virtually give his life over to the activity. These small, closed worlds of stamp collectors, bird watchers, duplicate bridge players, evidently seem safe and familiar, and the contact with others who share the same interest provides some minimal social contact that is not threatening.

Although Lunars do not enjoy social activities and prefer being alone to being with a lot of other people, they do form strong and durable friendships. Lunars are loyal and consistent friends of the sort that can go for five years without seeing you when geographical separation occurs, and then resume a conversation in midsentence from wherever you left off. In the context of family life, Lunars can be content, particularly when the choice of a mate has been a suitable one.

The maximum attraction for the passive and negative Lunar is the active and positive Saturnine type—the Lunar is at the midpoint of femininity and the Saturn at the midpoint of masculinity. This is independent of the sex of the individual. Extremely effeminate-looking Lunar men may have a totally heterosexual orientation and be very good lovers, husbands, and fathers. It is also true, however, that there is a greater tendency toward homosexuality among male Lunars than among other types. And by the same token there is a greater tendency for female Saturns to have lesbian tendencies than there is for other types.

This pair of maximum attractions, Lunars and Saturns, have relationships that are more like parent and child. The fatherly Saturn guides and protects the passive and childlike Lunar. For this reason the combination is excellent for managers and employees in businesses. The Saturn has the overview and the planning ability, and the Lunar is quite content to be left to tend to the details. Although Saturns and Lunars do marry, and can have stable and enduring marriages when they do, they will be likely to have quite different interests and activities and not spend much time together. Usually the Lunar will be the homebody, and the Saturn more likely to be out organizing the world, or that part of it in the immediate vicinity. It is also quite usual for Lunars to marry each other. One wonders, sometimes, how either one of them ever got around to suggesting it, but it does seem to happen frequently. The attraction of being understood, of being allowed plenty of space and silence, and of having a mate who operates at the same slow pace seems to more than compensate for the lack of surprises or zest or color or passion in the relationship.

The Lunar may have some difficulty with the two other negative types. And they may have difficulty with him. The problems can stem from two areas. The first is the difference in the speeds with which the types operate. The Lunar is not able to, and doesn't want to, move as fast as the Martial and Mercurial types move. This applies to decision making, physical and mental activities, and development of relationships. And just as the Lunar cannot speed up, the other two types cannot slow down. So if there is going to be friendship here, it is going to require quite a bit of understanding of one's own and the other person's limitations.

The other area that can cause problems for the Lunar in relationships with Mercurials and Martials is the play of features. Features evoke features, and the feature of power, which both of the active negative types are likely to have, evokes willfulness. The Martial pushes and the Lunar digs in to resist. The Mercurial manipulates and the Lunar refuses with contempt. It takes a great deal of good will on both sides for these types to get along well together.

The two passive and positive types cause the Lunar no particular problems, although the Lunar would just as soon not go to the Jovial's parties. If the Lunar needs to work with either of these positive types, he will be able to, but he probably won't choose to socialize with them—but of course he doesn't socialize much anyway. The active and positive Saturn, as has been mentioned, is the Lunar's maximum attraction, so they get along very well, as long as the Saturn is not overly dominant. The other active and positive type, the Solar, is likely to be annoying to the Lunar with their unmitigated positive attitudes. Since the Lunar sees almost exclusively the dark side of experience, and the Solar is virtually incapable of seeing the dark side, it is difficult for these two types to have a meeting of minds or hearts.

If you have a Lunar in your life, the care required in relating to him or her is well compensated by the benefits of the relationship. In the first place, if you have a Lunar in your life, it is because you have been granted the relatively rare privilege of being allowed into a life that is carefully guarded. You have been granted an honor not offered to many. This is true, at least, if the Lunar is your mate or friend. If the Lunar is a family member, you need to remember that you have not, in fact, been chosen, except by fate. It is up to you to respect the Lunar's privacy and need for solitude.

If you have a Lunar child, it is particularly important to use great care not to force the child to be other than he is. Since Lunars are timid and shy—qualities usually not valued in boys—and do not like to be the center of attention, efforts to force him to be more bold and outgoing, to participate in sports, to enjoy parties and group events are doomed to failure. Not only will the efforts fail, but these pressures can have very bad results. The Lunar type is extremely sensitive, and the tendency toward pessimism combined with the tendency toward introspection can combine to produce extremely low self-esteem. You cannot change the Lunar to be what you want him to be, but you can make him bitter and vindictive and vicious by trying.

Of all the types, Lunar children probably need the most supportive and loving environment despite the fact that of all the types, Lunar children may seem the least lovable and affectionate. For these children the support needs to be in the form of understanding that they cannot be hurried, that they do not like surprises, that they need protection and safety more than other children, and probably do not want a hug. It is hard for Lunars to accept anything, and that includes themselves, so having parents and teachers who clearly accept and love them is crucial. Since many Lunars are among the most sensitive writers and poets, we have ample evidence of what a horror childhood can be for this type. One such Lunar poet, Rainer Maria Rilke in his *Notebooks of Malte Laurids Brigge*, has left a record of a Lunar childhood that was made miserable by parents unable to accept the reality of the child they had.[1]

Rilke was born in Prague in 1875 to a mother who was temperamental and emotionally unstable and who treated her son like a daughter. His father, Josef Rilke, had been frustrated in his own desire for a military career, and was a harsh martinet determined to force his son to lead the life he had not been able to lead himself. The marriage was a battleground with the boy the spoils of war. When he was 9, the young Rilke's parents separated and he was forced to go to a military school that he hated. He suffered acutely under nearly every aspect of the school, the strict regimen, the enforced living in close proximity with rough boys who tormented him, the harsh punishments for any infraction of the rules. But he was recognized for his writing ability, so he had that to sustain him.

Rilke's early writing, in the 1890s, was not very successful, as he, himself, was very aware. But he had the Lunar quality of persistence in full measure, and his patient perfection of his craft was to produce poetry that won a place, not just in German literature, but in world literature of all the ages.

Rilke's intimate relationships did not endure—his marriage to young sculptor Clara Westhoff did not last, nor did his affairs with other women—but while the sexual relationships ended, his friendships with the women did not. Most of the women in Rilke's life remained his close friends and confidants throughout his life.

One close woman friend of Rilke's, Princess Marie von Thurn und Taxis-Hohenlohe, invited him to her castle at Schloss Duino near Trieste during the winter of 1911–1912. Rilke lived in Trieste alone between December and April, and from that period of solitude came the *Duino Elegies*. It is the *Elegies*, and Rilke's other mature poetry, that gives his readers the still, intense inner vision that is both characteristic of the subjective world of

---

[1]Rainer Maria Rilke, *Notebook of Malte Laurids Brigge*, Stephen Mitchell, trans. (New York: Vintage/Random House, 1990).

the Lunar type and universal in its profound and moving depiction of the isolation and vulnerability of the human condition. These lines from "The First Elegy," written at Duino, convey the wonder and strangeness of the solitary who

> . . . begins to espy a trace of eternity.—Yes, but all of the living make the mistake of drawing too sharp distinctions. Angels (they say) are often unable to tell whether they move among living or dead. The eternal torrent whirls all the ages through either realm for ever, and sounds above their voices in both.[2]

Understanding and respecting the Lunar type is, as with any of the types, understanding our common humanity with all its difficulties and possibilities. Lunars, with their secretiveness and the cool distance they keep between themselves and others, do not make this easy, but with their loyalty and sensitivity they make it very much worth the effort.

---

[2]Rainer Maria Rilke, *Duino Elegies,* Stephen Garmey and Jay Wilson, trans. (New York: Harper & Row, 1972), p. 37.

CHAPTER 11

THE VENUSIAN TYPE

While it is possible to describe the typical appearance of the Venusian type, it is also true that Venusians are like chameleons in their ability to take on the physical appearance of other types, particularly of other types that they prefer to their own.

Venusians in their natural state are large, tending toward bulkiness. They are sometimes tall, with a comfortable overstuffed appearance, like a favorite armchair. Their faces, while seldom angular, are more pleasingly proportioned than are the faces of Lunars. Indeed, Venusians can be very attractive. They very frequently are dark, with brown eyes that make direct eye contact and thick black or dark brown hair. Venusian men can have luxurious beards if they wish, and may have a five o'clock shadow or the currently fashionable unshaved look if they don't actually have a beard.

Venusian women, and many of the men as well, may be very sensuous, with seductive curves and soft pillowy flesh. Venusians carry their weight low on their bodies, having wide hips and heavy thighs beneath a relatively high waistline. This configuration gives the body a pear-shaped contour.

Since Venusians are lovers of comfort, they frequently choose loose flowing clothing: caftans or mumus for the women, large Hawaiian shirts for the men. Sometimes this type may appear rumpled and careless of their appearance. Their neckties may attract gravy spots, the fronts of their blouses stains from the spaghetti sauce.

Samoans seem frequently to be Venusians, as do the other South Sea Islanders painted by Gauguin. This type is also frequently found among the North and Central American Indians and among the peoples of the Mediterranean countries.

Again, however, it is useful to remember that Venusians can change their appearance deliberately, particularly if they think that this will please other people. Venusian contours are not admired in our time when thin is in. A Venusian woman's determination to please could well extend to bleaching or dying her hair and dieting strenuously to have a slender body. Venusian men, already having a large body, may go in for bodybuilding and weight lifting exercises to be more muscular. In either instance, the Venusian tendency toward sensuous pleasures and comfort would be overshadowed by the desire to please people or the wish to emulate another type which the Venusian admires.

Earth's closest neighbor in the solar system, except for the Moon, is the planet Venus. This planet is also the brightest object in our skies except for the Sun and Moon. Venus appears as the brilliant morning and evening stars, the brightness due partly to being an excellent reflector of light and partly to being a comparatively large planet. Venus has a diameter almost as large as the Earth's and a similar mass. Venus is closer to the Sun than Earth is, with an average distance of 67 million miles. When closest to the Earth in its nearly circular orbit, it is only 25 million miles away. Given that Venus is among the brightest and most visible objects in our sky, and that it is our closest neighbor—very close considering the scale of interplanetary distances—we might assume that a lot is known about this planet. Wrong.

Unfortunately, when Venus is closest to Earth it cannot be seen at all because the dark side is turned toward Earth. This planet appears brightest when at the crescent stage with about 30 percent of the daylight hemisphere turned toward us. At this stage, the planet is closer than when it is fully illuminated because then it is all the way on the other side of the Sun, about 160 mil-

VENUSIAN: The Venusian Type is passive and positive. It is an earthy type, usually large and fleshy, and broad in the hips and thighs. The Venusian is a born follower, preferring to live through others. Venusians are warm and nurturing, fond of creature comforts and familiar surroundings. They may be slothful and untidy. Venusians sometimes have bad teeth since the dominant parathyroid gland's hormone causes the release of calcium into the bloodstream. The chief feature of the Venusian is frequently nonexistence.

lion miles away. Because Venus looks so spectacular to the naked eye when it is closer, we might assume that with a good telescope we could see a lot. Again, wrong. All that can be seen is a bright almost blank disk, the upper layers of a deep cloud covering.

Probes sent up in the late 1970s added little to our knowledge of the planet since their cameras were as unable to penetrate the dense cloud cover as the telescopes had been. Then, in 1978, the Pioneer Venus spacecraft was placed in orbit around Venus to return radar soundings. The resulting topographic maps indicate that 60 percent of the surface lies within 500 yards of the most common radius, and only 5 percent lies more than a mile above it. The range of the elevations is thus comparable to those on Earth's surface.

Venus rotates only once every 243 days, and in a retrograde direction—if you could see a sunrise from Venus, which you couldn't because of the clouds, it would be in the west. Sunset in the east would occur so many months later you would have forgotten about it anyway. The upper atmosphere rotates very much faster than the surface of the planet, whirling around in only four days and moving from equator to pole. Winds on the surface seldom exceed a rate of about forty inches per second, but reach gale force close to the cloud tops.

There are no oceans on Venus because it is too hot. The deep and dense cloud cover creates a greenhouse effect that keeps the entire surface of the planet literally boiling hot. In fact, lead would melt at the surface. Any water or other familiar liquid is therefore vaporized and becomes a part of the atmosphere. Because of this mixture of gases, the atmospheric pressure on the surface is 90 times greater than that on the Earth's surface.

If relatively little is known about the planet Venus, neither is there much known about the endocrine gland that the planet is said to activate, so in that sense at least the idea of correspondences holds true. The mysterious parathyroid glands have traditionally been thought to counteract the action of the thyroid glands and inhibit the thyroid hormone. But exactly how that might be accomplished is not clear. If, in fact, this is one of the functions of this gland, then the body type affected by it would be slow, mellow, and vegetative, which is a fairly good description of the Venusian. The parathyroid glands, supposed to be under the influence of the planet Venus, are located on either side of the thyroid gland, close to the windpipe. They vary in shape and size from person to person, but most people have four of them. The only hormone they are presently known to secrete is called simply the parathyroid hormone, which makes up in easy reference what it lacks in originality.

The only known function of this hormone is to regulate the blood calcium level. If the level of blood calcium is low, the parathyroid secretes its hormone and the hormone causes bone to partially dissolve to add the calcium into the blood. The parathyroid hormone also causes the kidneys to excrete the phosphorus normally bound to the calcium. The calcium is then freed to circulate in the blood. As the blood calcium level rises, the hormone secretion of the parathyroid glands is inhibited. The overactivity of the parathyroid glands results in too much of the hormone being secreted. This can cause a gradual weakening of the bones. The effect of high calcium levels in the blood is to produce symptoms of lethargy, fatigue, and weakness. If blood calcium levels become extremely high, the person becomes drowsy and confused.

Like their planet and their dominant gland, Venusians can be baffling. What are Venusians like, exactly? What do they think? How do they feel? What do they want? What do they like to do? It is quite unsettling to others to realize that the answers to these questions may be: nothing much.

Venusians are passive and positive. This means that the status quo is fine with them. They think pretty much what the people around them think. If the people around them think that the current political and economic situation is unbearable and it's time for violent armed revolution, then Venusians will go to the barricades. They are not passive in the sense of being opposed to violence or strong action, but in the sense of not thinking and deciding for themselves. There is nothing lacking in Venusian functions. They can understand and repeat, even heatedly, the most complex philosophical theories, and champion extensive reforms which they can explain in minute and plausible detail. But these aren't their own ideas. They are not leaders or organizers, no matter how passionate and dedicated they seem to be. Venusians are born followers.

How does the Venusian feel? Well, how do you feel? She feels pretty much the same way. Naturally she wants you to feel better because then she will feel better. If you are stressed out or tense, anxious or frightened, angry or frustrated, she will listen to you for hours if need be. She will absorb all the details of the continuing saga of your domestic problems, your difficulties with your boss, your physical ailments, your financial troubles. From time to time she may interject comforting or encouraging comments into your monologue. She will not, as some irritating people do, give the impression that she is only listening to your problems so that she can have a turn and tell you her problems. She doesn't seem to have any. She just wants to feel what you feel, even when it's negative, because that is better than not feeling anything at all. When you're done talking and leave, she'll turn on the television and feel what the characters on the soap operas are feeling.

What do Venusians like? Well, there is a bit more evidence about this. Venusians like it here. Planet Earth, with all its obvious problems and perils, suits them. Maybe because Venus is so similar in size and topography to our planet, Venusians are comfortable here, and they very much like being comfortable. What they like to do is what they are already doing, and even if they don't really like what they are doing all that much, they like continuing to do it more than they like the effort it would take to make a change. If they happened to begin their working days in an occupation that does suit them—gardening, working in a nursery, in one of the health care occupations, cooking—then they are really comfortable where they are. But if they got into a job that they don't like much—inventory control in a big warehouse, a factory assembly line, office work—well, at least it's steady.

Maybe the Venusian's apartment isn't as large as he needs now that he has a wife and two children, a dog and three cats. It isn't as large as he could afford now that he's been working at the same job for fifteen years and has made some good investments.

But it's home. It's familiar. It's comfortable. Maybe next week he'll think about finding a larger place, but this weekend there are a lot of good programs on television and on Sunday they're going to visit his mother (as they do every Sunday).

Venusians like people. They like their families so much they may not get around to starting one of their own. If, when she grows up, her brothers and sisters have moved out of the family home, the Venusian may be the one to stay with the aging parents, content to enjoy family life vicariously through nephews and nieces rather than having children of her own. If she does marry and have children of her own, she tends to live through her husband and her children.

What do Venusians want to do? They want to do whatever you want to do. If you want to go bungee jumping, the Venusian wants to go bungee jumping. If you want to lie on the beach and get a tan, the Venusian wants to lie on the beach and get a tan. If you want to go out dancing, the Venusian wants to go out dancing. If you want to be alone for a while and have some time for yourself, the Venusian . . . Hey, wait a minute! What are friends for? Friends are to be with, right? If you want to be alone and have some time for yourself, then the Venusian will find someone else to do with whatever the friend wants to do.

The Venusian blends in, goes with the flow, doesn't make waves. In a group, this type tends not to be noticed. Dressed like his friends are dressed, talking about what his friends are talking about, doing what his friends are doing, he gets lost in the crowd. If you go out with a group of friends, and can remember that there were eight of you sitting at the table in the pizza place but can only name seven, chances are the one you can't remember was a Venusian. If three couples order dinner at a restaurant, and all of them have to wait because the waiter forgot one of the orders, chances are the forgotten order was the Venusian's. The Venusian just doesn't make a distinct impression.

The strivings, anxieties, problems, and concerns of the other types don't seem to perturb the Venusian, although of course he is very willing to listen to others complain about them, and comfort them if he can. This is a vegetative type that doesn't have much urge to move around. He may putter about in the garden sometimes, pruning the roses a little, or raking a few leaves for the compost heap that will nourish the plants he enjoys tending, but that's about it. Venusians can be slothful, oblivious to the dust in the corners, the dishes in the sink, the dirty clothes spilling out of the laundry basket. Instead of cleaning the house, the Venusian might prefer watching the soap operas on television—the lives of the characters taking the place of a life of her own. Whether it's television characters and personalities, or friends and relations, the Venusian easily loses himself in others and tends to live through others. He is a warm and sympathetic listener, always willing to hear about problems without either judging or offering advice. Venusians make good bartenders, barbers, and therapists.

This willingness to live through others can make Venusians deceptively difficult to recognize since they frequently take on the characteristics of the people to whom they are close. And of course with their passivity they attract active types and are themselves drawn to active types. Whether the active type is a husband or wife, a business partner, or a good friend, with Venusians it's Pete and Repeat. It is not unusual to find supposedly lethargic Venusians playing football, basketball, baseball, tennis, and golf. How can this be? Their best friends like sports so they like sports, too. Scuba diving? Sure. Sky diving? Sure. Anyone for bridge? Poker? Sure. Venusian mothers are content to live through their children, showing up faithfully for the P.T.A., volunteering to be classroom aids. They pack wonderful lunches, sew the kids clothes, go to all the school activities, and bake great cookies. And when the children grow up, well maybe there will be grandchildren. Or if not, there's always the soap operas.

Venusians are very loyal, and they don't like change. This may actually be only one characteristic rather than two—they may be loyal by default, keeping the same job, friend, or home rather than making the effort to find a better one. The jobs they are best at are occupations that enable them to use their warm, accepting nature. Venusians are natural healers, making good steady nurses and paramedics. They may not have the ambition to withstand the rigors of medical school, but if they do they make good general practitioners and pediatricians.

Whatever the dominant function in the Venusian type, it may be difficult to determine which part of the center is the center of gravity. This is because the low energy level of the Venusian does not lend itself to either the enthusiasms of emotional parts of centers or the effort required to control the attention needed by the intellectual parts of centers. Venusians who are instinctively centered, are probably content to remain in a vegetative state. Blood is circulating, food is digesting, toenails are growing, but that's about all that is going on. If Venusians are hungry, the leftovers in the refrigerator will do fine; they won't bother going out for pizza or get a sudden craving for ice cream that's strong enough to warrant a trip to a café.

Venusians who are moving centered have a tolerance for repetitive actions, could work as typists day after day, week after week without getting restless, could be bakers, kneading, rolling, forming bread and rolls. Jobs that would otherwise cause great frustration for the queen or king of spades may be tolerated when those parts of the moving center are combined with the steadiness of the Venusian type.

Intellectually-centered Venusians may be very good at accumulating facts and storing information, but are unlikely to be original thinkers since this type tends to absorb the ideas of others. They may enjoy research. The process of finding sources and precedents could make them good legal research assistants, but they probably wouldn't have the agile thought processes and quick reactions required of lawyers.

Emotionally-centered Venusians have the prefabricated emotions that their culture has programmed into them. They like conventional greeting card verse, the celebration of traditional holidays, family reunions, and everybody's birthday. They are content to exchange pleasantries with co-workers and inquire about co-workers' families. They like being members of a crowd or social group and don't much care what the group is doing as long as they are in the middle of it. Spectator sports—cheering for the home team, wearing a hat or jacket proclaiming an affiliation—

make Venusians feel involved and part of the action, and that's what they need. There is so little of their own emotional life that they need to tap into the life of a group.

Sometimes the impression of individuality in Venusians is so weak that it seems there's no one there at all. You can have the sense of being alone in a room while Venusian types are with you. It is quite an eerie sensation to realize that what you thought was solitude is in fact being shared with another human being, or at least another body. It is as though the other body were uninhabited. This characteristic is the Venusian's chief feature, or weakness—nonexistence.

Nonexistence, as the word implies, means a failure to exist, to be aware of the surroundings and events around you. At the same time there is a lack of interior activity as well. Other types may not be aware of their surroundings because they are engrossed with their inner worlds, with their thoughts and feelings and imaginings. The Venusian, however, is aware of neither the outer nor the inner world. There is no awareness in the state of nonexistence.

The strengths and virtues of the Venusian result from the warmth and tolerance of this type, and the willingness to comfort and help others. The Venusian may be bland and lack sparkling conversational skills, but there are times when bland is beautiful, and silent acceptance the most blessedly healing balm one could wish for. The dependability of the Venusian endears itself to employers, family members, and friends. You can count on the Venusian to be there for you, even if it's only because he or she couldn't think of anywhere else to go. If you have a Venusian in your life, count yourself fortunate. You have a warm friend, a loyal supporter, an uncritical partisan. Venusians get along well with all of the other types. They may be slightly less likely to attract Jovial friends because the two passive and positive types are more likely to be home waiting to receive guests than to be out being one.

But while Venusians get along with all types, they are particularly attracted to the active and negative Martial. The passion, energy, and drive of the Martial can make the slow, lethargic Venusian come alive. The sensuality of the Venusian attracts the excessive sex drive of the Martial irresistibly. This pair of maximum attractions, the Martial and the Venusian, is the most explosive and passionate of the sexual relationships between types. The forces that draw these two together are powerful, and the volatility of the combination can blow the relationship apart just as powerfully. An example of a Martial-Venusian love affair on the grand scale was the relationship between Richard Burton and Elizabeth Taylor. Their stormy marriages (three or four) and bitter divorces, followed by romantic reconciliations, and then more battles, made news all over the world. The sexual attraction is so intense, and the basic psychology of the two types so different—they see the world so differently, operate at such different speeds, and have such different values—that they seem able neither to live without each other nor to live with each other.

If you have a close friend or family member who is Venusian, it is tempting to just accept the Venusian as a tag-along cheering section, a confidant whose confidences you don't have to listen to in return, a giver who makes no demands. But this type of relationship isn't very useful for the Venusian. She already knows how to follow and listen and give. What she doesn't know is how to make decisions for herself, how to talk as well as listen, how to take as well as give in a relationship. It may be difficult, particularly if you are an active type with plenty of ideas and opinions and preferences, to slow down and wait for the Venusian to think of something that he wants to do. Once in a while leave the plans open: "Shall we go to a movie or to a concert?" The Venusian will probably say, "Whatever you want to do is fine with me." Don't let him off the hook that easily. Have him decide.

If you have a Venusian child, it is very easy to let her remain unnoticed, particularly if there are other children in the family who present problems or clamor for attention. The Venusian child is well-behaved, easy to please, and quiet. She will be content to follow her older siblings around and passively watch them play, or to sit for hours in front of the television set lost in the prefabricated dreams of cartoon characters or situation comedies. At school the Venusian child is likely to be the one the teacher never notices, and when it's time for grade cards to be sent home, the teacher may not even quite remember the child's face that goes with that name, much less have any observations to share with parents. Watch out for noncommittal remarks like, "Tanya is showing progress." Be sure the teacher knows who Tanya is—in a room full of 35 children, Tanya may have gotten lost in a blur of faces.

The Venusian child needs to be encouraged to make decisions. Have the child select the clothing he will wear. Spend time reading to the child, of course, but also have the child read to you, or answer questions and make predictions about the story you are reading. In other words, make sure your little Venusian is actively involved rather than just passively receptive to whatever is going on. Give the Venusian chores to do, and follow through to be sure that he does them. Ask him his opinion about what to fix for dinner, and let him help prepare the food.

Remember also that Venusians can have trouble with their teeth, both because they are likely to overindulge in sweets and because the active parathyroids can rob the teeth and bones of needed calcium. Watch the diet carefully to be sure it contains calcium-rich foods, and provide calcium supplements if needed. It is particularly important for this type to form good habits early and to be consistent with them. If they don't, the Venusian tendency toward indolence can cause problems.

It is difficult to think of any famous Venusians to discuss as examples of the type. In fact, the phrase "famous Venusians" is probably an oxymoron. There probably are some well-known Venusians, but if there are, their very efforts in whatever field they excel in would be atypical of Venusian tendencies or would be the result of their imitating some other type. There is, however, a very accurate dramatic portrayal of the Venusian type in Paddy Chayevsky's play, *Marty*. This play was originally written for television, but was also made into an excellent movie starring Ernest Borgnine in the title role.[1]

The main character in the film is a Venusian, a middle-aged butcher who lives with his mother in the family home. His father

---

[1]Paddy Chayevsky, *Marty*, in *The Collected Works of Paddy Chayevsky: The Television Plays*, Vol. 2 (New York: Applause Theatre Book Publishers, 1994).

is dead, his brothers and sisters all married, leaving him to care for the aging mother. The issues that the family are concerned about are whether the big house should be sold now that it is nearly empty and whether the mother's sister should come there to live. Marty's mother is against both of these possibilities and contends that she and Marty are doing just fine.

Marty's social life, such as it is, revolves around a group of unmarried cronies who hang around on the street corner trying to decide what to do in the evening. Marty and his closest friend, Joey, have long aimless conversations which consist of asking each other what they want to do: "What do you want to do, Marty?" "I dunno, Joey, what do you want to do?" Usually they either do nothing, or go into the pool hall and shoot a game or two of pool and then go home. Occasionally they decide to go to a dance at a big dance hall, but if they do go they just stand on the side and watch the dancers. Neither is attractive, and if they ask women to dance they are usually refused.

One night, however, Marty overhears a plain woman crying, and asks her what's the matter. She was left alone by a blind date who had gone off with another partner. Marty consoles the woman and asks her to dance. The two of them start talking and enjoy themselves so much they go out for coffee afterward and stay up most of the night. Marty takes her by his house to get something before taking her home, and his mother comes down and meets her. When Marty parts with the woman he met at the dance, he tells her that he will call her on Sunday and they will go out.

At that point the battle is joined. Everyone in Marty's life, his family and friends, unite in trying to end this relationship before it goes any further. Marty's friends who saw the woman with him at the dance make fun of her. "She's a dog, Marty," Joey says. "You don't want to go out with no dog." Marty's mother asks, "What kind of a girl would go to a man's house when she doesn't even know him?" Marty's sisters and brothers, worried that they would have to share the responsibility for their mother if Marty weren't there to do it all, join in to urge him not to see the woman again.

Sunday comes and Marty doesn't call her. The woman is shown at home—she also lives with her parents—watching television in the living room. Marty and Joey are at the pool hall and Joey is reiterating that Marty is doing the right thing because the woman is a dog.

But Marty finally takes a stand. In the midst of Joey's questions about what they should do that evening, Marty suddenly says, "All right, she's a dog. And I'm a fat ugly little man, and I'm lonely, and I like talking to her." He gets up abruptly and goes to the pay phone in the pool hall to make the call. The whole tension in this very effective drama comes from the question of whether a Venusian can live his own life.

There's a good possibility that Ernest Borgnine, who starred in the film *Marty*, is a Venusian. He is fleshy, and has the gap between his upper front teeth that is typical of the Venusian type. This actor has, of course, played a number of roles successfully, bad guys and good guys, tough guys and tender guys. While this would be in keeping with the Venusian ability to assume diffferent personalities, it is not possible to determine an actor's type with assurance without knowing him personally.

Acting is, however, a profession that would attract Venusians. Lacking a clear sense of their own identity, Venusians may find a sense of existing in the roles they play. Like the planet with its madly whirling upper atmosphere and its very slow surface rotation, Venusians may be able to use the turmoil and frenzy of show business as a cover for their own lack of inner certainty or sense of self.

The Venusian type is one that other types would do well to find within themselves—all of the types are there in each of us to some degree. Their warmth and acceptance of this difficult life, and most particularly of other people, is a characteristic in short supply. Their ability to find pleasure in the small comforts and familiar routines of everyday existence can serve us all in good stead. With this type, as with all the others, the mechanical tendencies which may be obstacles or shortcomings for the Venusian may be virtues to be practiced intentionally by others.

CHAPTER 12

THE MERCURIAL TYPE

Mercurials are the smallest type. They are short with wiry well-formed, well-coordinated compact bodies. Mercurial men have relatively broad shoulders and deep chests tapering to slender waists and narrow hips. Mercurial women are petite and small-boned, with delicate hands and feet. This type retains a youthful, childlike appearance well into maturity, frequently looking ten or fifteen years younger than they are.

The Mercurial is usually dark haired, frequently with thick curly hair that fits close to a well-shaped head. Mercurial men invariably look good with a neat mustache, and may have a well-trimmed beard also. Called the sunshine people, Mercurials have dazzling smiles that flash brilliant, even, white teeth that could be in a toothpaste commercial. Their eyes are bright and sparkling, intensifying the impression of charm and friendliness.

The deep melodious voice of the Mercurial can be a shock, coming as it does from such a small body. We may be surprised to notice that the basses and baritones at the opera are so slight in comparison with the frequently rotund and imposing tenors. Deeper voices are likely to belong to Mercurials.

Mercurials are restless. They are in almost constant motion. Even when they stay in one room for a while, they will move from one chair to another, get up to look out the window, cross the room to straighten a picture. But for all their moving around,

Mercurials never seem to get mussed or rumpled. They have a natural neatness. Their clothes always look as though they had just been ironed. Somehow, the tidy Mercurials can sleep in their clothes and rise looking like a fashion advertisement while other types may spend a lot of effort ironing clothes and still look like they slept in them.

This smallest of the human types, the quick, childlike Mercurial, is under the influence of the planet closest to the Sun. Mercury, the smallest and innermost of the planets of our solar system, was recognized by ancient peoples long before the beginning of history. They knew this bright point of light could not be a star; sometimes seen in the western sky just after the sun had set, it moved too fast and could only be a planet. Later it was realized that the similar planet seen sometimes in the east was the same planet. Small wonder the ancient Greeks named it for that most elusive and deceptive of the gods, the swift wing-footed messenger, Hermes. The Romans changed his name to Mercury when they adopted this god into their pantheon.

Mercury is hard to catch sight of—virtually impossible for city dwellers—since when this planet can be seen by the naked eye, it is always very low in the sky. Even with sophisticated equipment, Mercury is not easy to observe, and there are more theories than facts about it still. It is very small, not a great deal larger than the Moon and smaller than some of the satellites of the outer planets. For a long time, well into this century, it was assumed that the apparently erratic orbit of Mercury indicated that some other inner planet was affecting Mercury's path. After Einstein developed his theory of relativity, however, it was realized that the apparent shift in expected position was caused by the bending of light and not by the gravitational pull of an unknown body. This was only one of the many problems astronomers encountered in trying to learn more about Mercury.

Since this planet is so close to the Sun—an average distance of 36 million miles in its elliptical orbit—it is very hard to observe. Furthermore, Mercury revolves once on its axis in exactly the same time that it takes to go once around the Sun, about eighty-eight of our days. This means that one hemisphere is

MERCURIAL: The Mercurial Type is active and negative. The activity is obvious but a brilliant smile and sparkling eyes usually conceal their negative perceptions. Mercurials are small and wiry, rapid in movement and well-coordinated. They frequently have deep, melodious voices and are natural entertainers. Mercurials can be deceitful, using their quick perceptions to take advantage of the unwary. The chief feature of the Mercurial is likely to be manipulative power.

turned permanently toward the Sun while the other is in perpetual darkness. There is no day or night for Mercury, only the blazing light and scorching heat of one side and the utter darkness and unspeakable cold of the other (there is no atmosphere to mitigate the extremes). If Mercury's trip around the Sun were at a constant speed, the hemispheres would be divided exactly half and half, but things are never simple with this deceptive little planet. Because of its elliptical orbit, its velocity changes. When it is closer to the Sun it travels faster; when it is farther away it travels slower. But its axial revolution is constant, so the Sun must wobble in the Mercurial sky. And there is a fairly wide twilight zone where the Sun will rise and set between the hemispheres of permanent day and everlasting night.

Since Mercury always has its dark side toward Earth, except for the brief periods when it is about to disappear behind the brilliance of the Sun, not much is known about its surface features. The only chances to observe the elusive little planet have occurred either when Mercury passes in transit across the face of the Sun, or when there is a total eclipse of the Sun and we can see the planet at the edge. Total eclipses are rare, of course, and when they occur attention is focused on the Sun itself. Because Mercury's orbit is inclined to ours at an angle of seven degrees, transits are also irregular. Furthermore, few of the observations that have been made are in agreement with any of the others. About the only point of agreement is that Mercury has almost no atmosphere. This is known because when it does pass across the face of the Sun, it appears as a small, sharply defined spot. If there were a layer of atmosphere, the edges would look fuzzy.

Even the space probes have found out very little information about Mercury. Mariner 10's flyby reconnaissance of Venus and Mercury in 1974 didn't reveal much, although it did return images of about 35 percent of the planet's surface. Geologic mapping reveals steep scarps believed to be the result of regional or perhaps global compression—Mercury has a very high density. There also seems to be some evidence of volcanic activity. Aside from these few indications, Mercury's secrets remain concealed.

Although relatively little is known about this rapidly moving little planet, quite a bit is known about the endocrine gland it triggers. The thyroid gland and the hormone of the same name which it produces have obvious effects on human metabolism that have long been recognized by the medical profession. The thyroid hormones control metabolic rate—a healthy body will produce more thyroid in response to low temperatures so that the body keeps warm. Since a higher metabolic rate converts food to energy more efficiently and faster, thyroid controls weight, burning off the body's caloric intake.

The deficiency of thyroid has the opposite effect, causing the body to store calories in the form of fat deposits rather than converting the calorie intake to energy. Doctors frequently prescribe thyroid supplements for their patients with weight problems. Metabolism is a complicated affair. There is a complex monitoring system in the hypothalamus and the anterior pituitary that checks the amounts of thyroid hormone in the bloodstream and sends the necessary signals to the thyroid gland. The thyroid hormone then released affects respiration, heart rate, and blood pressure by determining the rate at which cellular energy is burned.

There is also growing evidence of the effect of the thyroid hormone on the brain. A deficiency of thyroid in the fetus can seriously retard brain development, causing cretinism. Depression, apathy, and intellectual deterioration in cases of thyroid insufficiency have been recognized for a century, and have been successfully treated with sheep thyroid tissue for almost as long. Supplementing the body's thyroid supply in such pathological cases has typically improved mental and psychological functioning. The fact that mental aberrations disappear with thyroid replacement is convincing evidence for their hormonal basis.

An excess of thyroid hormone produces quite different symptoms. Patients with this problem are hyperactive, nervous, irritable, and have difficulty concentrating. They may also experience rapid mood shifts. When these symptoms are pronounced, they are pathological and need to be treated; when they are merely tendencies, they are indications of the Mercurial type.

Mercurials are active and negative. With their high metabolic rate, they are the fastest of the human types, just as the god whose name they bear was the fastest and most cunning of the Olympians. Not only are Mercurials quick in movement, but their minds also function very rapidly. Mercurials are extremely perceptive. This mental acuity makes them very observant.

When a Mercurial enters a room, she notices everything: the cobweb in the corner, the titles of the books in the bookcase, the worn spot in the carpet. She makes rapid calculations about the probable value of the porcelain cups in the china cabinet and figures you just moved the furniture because there are indentations in the rug where the sofa used to be along the side wall. And all the time she's wearing a bright cheerful smile and engaging in light, humorous conversation.

Mercurials are the sunshine people. Like the little planet that always has one side in full sunlight, they sparkle with warmth and humor. Indeed, it is difficult at first to understand that Mercurials are a negative type, although it is certainly obvious that they are active. Like the planet, they have a dark side that is hard to see— nonetheless it is there. Mercurials always have four or five projects going at once.

Not long after your new friend has inspected your living room, she'll check her watch and ask to use the phone. But instead of the one call you assumed she'd make, she'll make three or four, and then explain that something unexpected has come up and she has to dash to meet an important client. With a shrug and engaging grin as an apology for her brief stay, she's out the door and gone. Maybe you'll see her tomorrow, maybe next week, but don't expect to see her for long.

The high metabolic rate of the Mercurial type makes them prone to insomnia and sleep disturbances. They wake easily. Teenagers with a Mercurial parent may well despair of being able to sneak in after curfew without being caught. And if Mercurials are unusually sensitive to outside stimuli, they are equally aware of all their own interior bodily functions. Mercurials tend to be hypochondriacs, always suffering from real or imagined aches and pains, or, worse yet, terrible maladies that have no symptoms at all but are almost certainly fatal. Mercurials may spend at least a portion of their considerable energies investigating one after another of a series of special diets, miracle cures, revolutionary new treatments, and faith healers.

With their quick minds and perceptive senses, Mercurials notice more, and frequently understand more, than the people around them. (Since this is the fastest type, everyone except other Mercurials really is more slow-witted.) It is difficult for them not to take advantage of this fact. If they see an advantage to be gained, they are likely to take it. If they understand a way to get a better business deal than the next person, they'll probably get it. There is a definite tendency toward deception and sometimes outright dishonesty in this type. Mercurials make excellent salesmen, advertising executives, commodities traders, and lawyers. In fact, any business or occupation in which quickness of thought processes and competitive spirit pays off is likely to attract Mercurials.

It is in the inner world of the Mercurial that it becomes clear that this is a negative type. The cheerful exterior masks a complicated labyrinth of doubt and insecurity that can easily develop into paranoia. The Mercurial's thinking is so rapid that hardly has one concept been formulated than its opposite pops up as a possibility. Used to the quick changes of his own thoughts, the Mercurial assumes that others are having the same kaleidoscopic shifts of thoughts, attitudes, ideas, and intentions. Aware that he himself is always looking for the advantage he might gain over you, he naturally expects that you are looking for the advantage you might gain over him. Seeing the dip in your hemline and the grime on your cuff, she assumes that you are inspecting her clothes for any flaws as well. All of these anxieties weigh on the already high-strung constitution of the Mercurial.

Convinced of your critical attitude toward him, believing that you are about to make some attempt to get the best of him, the Mercurial must think even faster to prevent you from succeeding. He smiles more winningly, tells a funnier story, invites you to lunch sometime next week (the details of this invitation are not clear), and excuses himself abruptly before you can put your diabolical plan into action.

The intellectually-centered Mercurial will be slowed down somewhat by this slowest of the functions, but will still be very rapid in contrast with others having this center of gravity. In research work or academic areas, the Mercurial can capitalize on the sudden flash of insight, the brilliant perception, the intuitive leap that opens whole new fields of inquiry. Not for him, however, the painstaking experiments carefully recorded over decades of laboratory work, or years of tracking obscure facts through dusty library shelves. Leave that sort of thing to the Lunars. The Mercurial frequently pays for his quickness of perception and his mental agility with a lack of depth. The ideas snap and crackle, but they also may fizzle from lack of real substance.

The instinctively-centered Mercurial lives in a torment of doubt about her health and personal safety and that of her family. If she goes to a restaurant, she just has to get a look at the kitchen to be sure it's clean enough. The food might be tainted. They might all get food poisoning. And for that matter she can't be all that sure about the food in the supermarket. How fresh is the meat? How old are the eggs? Did they spray the vegetables with pesticide? Adequate clothing provides more worrisome decisions. Is it going to rain? Will the children be warm enough wearing sweaters or do they need their jackets too? And of course there are germs everywhere. Who knows what sort of diseases the people on the metro might be carrying.

The moving-centered Mercurial is in almost constant movement. It seems as though the negative half of this center, rest, doesn't exist at all. He fidgets, drums with his fingers, paces around the room, participates in seven or eight sports and plays the fastest video games. In this age of supersonic global transportation, he may show up anywhere. Travel can become almost an obsession, as though any part of the planet that remains uninspected were a personal affront.

The emotionally-centered Mercurial moves as rapidly from person to person as the moving-centered one moves from place to place. She has intense but relatively brief friendships because it is very hard for her to make long-term commitments. Also, it is hard for her to believe that people really like her. The inner doubts and insecurity about her own worth are a torment, every scowl or raised eyebrow—and she notices them all—are taken personally, and finally the discomfort of constantly wondering whether her friend really is a friend causes her to try someone new as a confidant. After all, the best way to avoid being abandoned is to leave first.

Having a Mercurial friend is a little like trying to sleep with a mosquito in the room. No sooner do you get comfortable, relax, and begin to doze than the frantic high-pitched buzzing invades your ear. Startled awake, you swat wildly at your own head, landing several smart blows at least one of which you hope will have solved the problem. Silence. You get comfortable again, only to have the frenzied buzz return. So it is with your Mercurial friend. You are relaxing at home after a hard day, feet up, your favorite television program on, a cup of tea next to you, comfort at last. But no. The phone rings and it's your friend who has just gotten two tickets to the best concert of the season and is determined that you should meet and go together. No, you say. Thanks very much but you are too tired. No. Absolutely no. Not tonight. Some other time. After listening to all the reasons why you should go to the concert, three times around for each reason (the *real* reason you don't want to go, your friend thinks, is that you don't like her, so she has to convince you so she will feel good about herself), you finally say no for the twenty-seventh time and say goodbye.

Back to the sofa and your now lukewarm tea. You are just beginning to figure out what happened during the part of the television program you missed while you were on the phone, when the phone rings again. That's right, it's your Mercurial friend. Since you're not going to the concert, she isn't either. But she just bought this dress and she doesn't know if it's the right length or if she should shorten it. Could you possibly help her decide? It won't take a minute. She could just run over to your place, and as long as you're too tired to go out, would you mind?

At this point your choice is fairly clear. You are either going to sacrifice your evening of relaxation or your friendship. If you say no, the Mercurial will decide that you were never her friend anyway, that all the things you've done together or for each other were just self-seeking duplicity on your part. Her quick mind will think of dozens of instances when you took advantage of her, or tried to, and manipulated her for your own selfish interests. In fact all of the things she might well have considered will be projected onto you. You might at this point think that it would be fine not to have such a friend. You want to remember, however, that you aren't always going to be tired, and that there will be times when you do want to go out on the spur of the moment, do something new and interesting, try a new jazz club. You won't ever find a more charming and amusing companion than a Mercurial. You also want to remember that if you don't want a Mercurial for a friend, you certainly don't want one for an enemy. Better just tell her to come on over, and spend the evening hemming up her new dress.

Of course the Mercurial would never do any direct harm. He would not openly criticize someone he disliked or with whom he was angry. In fact, he would probably make favorable observations about the person. "I see that Peter is sober today," he might mention just as the boss is walking by. Of course Peter is sober everyday, but it wasn't something the boss had ever thought about before. Now he wonders whether he has been watching Peter's performance as carefully as he should have been. The innuendo, the supposedly innocent but damaging remark, the seemingly unintentional revelation—these are the Mercurial's tactics when he's displeased or angry. The open confrontation is not his style. Perhaps because of his short stature and slight physique, the Mercurial does not launch direct frontal attacks. Like the quick little planet always disappearing just as you catch a glimpse of it, the Mercurial is master of the evasive maneuver and the tactical advantage. His quick movements and cleverness in turning any opponent's mistakes into his advantages make him a formidable foe, whether the arena is a bantam-weight boxing ring or a courtroom.

The Mercurial does very well in any occupation that provides an appreciative audience because this type likes to be the center of attention. Insecure and plagued by self doubts, a Mercurial needs the admiration of others to convince him of his own value. These quick and agile charmers make great performers. They are dancers, singers, actors, comedians, jugglers, musicians, acrobats, clowns. Any act where agility and a quick wit will enhance the performance is likely to allow the Mercurial to shine. The late Sammy Davis Jr. was an example of the talent and versatility of this type at its best. He could sing, dance, act, and tell jokes. There seemed to be no aspect of show business that Davis did not master.

The Mercurial facility for language, for story telling, for perceptiveness makes them good teachers. The Mercurial quickness in noticing the mistakes of others and turning them to their own advantage makes them good lawyers and politicians (although occasionally a politician like Richard Nixon, who earned himself the nickname Tricky Dick, may try one too many deceptions and get caught at it).

The Mercurial is miserable in jobs where sustained attention and predictable routines are required. Mercurial hell would be a position as a bookkeeper or a job on a factory assembly line putting the same widget on the same bolt day after day, week after week. Mercurials need change, movement, and variety with the same intensity that Lunars need stability, peace, and comforting predictability in their lives. These two types are admirably designed to drive each other crazy if they have to live or work together. But if the quick impulsive Mercurial has difficulty with the slow, stubborn Lunar, it is nothing compared to the problems he has with the Martial.

The two active and negative types, the Mercurial and the Martial, have difficulty in their interactions. They are the two fastest types on the enneagram, so it is true that they can appreciate in each other the ability to make quick decisions and act on those decisions rapidly. The problems arise because neither one can understand the other's approach to a given situation, and both want to control the outcome. The Mercurial would never think of using the Martial's direct and open way of confronting issues. In fact, he can't even really believe the Martial is actually being direct and open. The Mercurial wonders what the Martial is hiding, what his ulterior motive or hidden agenda is. Of course the Martial isn't hiding anything. It didn't occur to him to hide anything, and if it had occurred to him he isn't clever enough to get away with it, so he wouldn't try. He can't for the life of him understand why the Mercurial doesn't just come right out and say what he wants instead of playing all those time and energy consuming games.

Ultimately these two types baffle and frustrate each other to the point of hostility—open hostility on the part of the Martial, covert hostility on the part of the Mercurial. This may be nature's way of protecting everyone else, since if the two active and negative types could join forces, the energy and zeal of their efforts would be likely to overcome all obstacles. And the boundlessness of their ambitions would be likely to reduce the surface of the planet to rubble.

The Mercurial is a bit of a magpie in her pleasure in collecting things. Quick to see a bargain, to recognize the good antique hidden under a pile of junk in the corner of the garage, to spot the good cut glass vase amidst a clutter of dime store dishes, the Mercurial can't resist buying. And of course having bought, she expects to get the best possible price when she sells, and is willing to wait for the best opportunity. Things pile up, until it is time to have a garage sale, or to take some of these priceless items to the flea market and convert them to cash.

And the truth of the matter is that some people are not as careful as they should be with their belongings. Lunars are, of course; Lunars are very careful to lock up what belongs to them. And Saturns have everything organized and under control. But then there are those others. The careless, sometimes even sloppy Venusian can't be bothered, or can't even remember where she left her purse. It never occurs to the Martial that people would take tools that don't belong to them, so of course he doesn't put them away before he takes the truck he was working on for a test drive. The generous, hospitable Jovial wouldn't think of depriving a guest of anything, and the naive Solar doesn't think anyone would commit a crime.

Sometimes the temptation is just more than a Mercurial is able to resist. With his superior powers of rationalization and justification, it can be very hard to determine just where the line between "getting a good deal" and "stealing" actually is. With his charm, his ability to persuade others, and his quick wit, it can be just as hard to tell the difference between *caveat emptor* and a swindle, between a clever deal and fraud. In brief, Mercurials have a tendency to be dishonest.

At best Mercurials have brilliant perceptive minds and great personal charm. Because they understand others intuitively, they are able to entertain and to serve. The maximum attraction of active and negative Mercurials are the passive and positive Jovials. They bring out the best in each other, and have a lot of fun doing it. This pair of maximum attractions is like an indulgent mother with a charming child—it is not the passionate and stormy relationship that Venusians and Martials have. Jovials love to have parties and make people feel welcome and at home. Mercurials love to entertain and be the life of those parties. Both types are drawn to the arts—you can see them at the opera, the ballet, the theater, parading at intermission to show off the clothes they both love. The large, colorful Jovial lady in her mauve and purple flowing caftan edged with ostrich plumes, escorted by the dapper Mercurial in impeccable tuxedo are clearly having a fine time.

With their quickness and excellent coordination Mercurials make good athletes and graceful dancers, their business acumen makes them excellent corporate strategists, their verbal capacity and ability to think on their feet make them great entertainers. Their annoying qualities would include the impatience they demonstrate toward anyone not as quick and clever as they are— and of course almost no one is. They are impetuous and impulsive, often rash in their tendency to act before they have completely thought through the consequences of their actions. Their insomnia and hypochondria can make them whine and complain a lot, and their insecurity can cause them to constantly seek reassurance. Their egotism and desire to be constantly the center of attention can be tiresome. At worst Mercurials can be devious and deceitful. Able to trick others, they can be manipulative opportunists, gold diggers who use their attractiveness and childlike appearance to exploit people with no concern about those people's feelings. Or Mercurials may be criminals, using agility and stealth to plan robberies, or their understanding of human weakness combined with their natural charm to con the unwary.

The Mercurial's chief feature is frequently power, a manipulative power that attempts to get others to do what he wishes by stratagems rather than by force. Because of the drive for power and the desire for attention, there are many famous, and infamous, Mercurials. The charismatic Adolf Hitler, whose mesmerizing speeches led a Jovial nation to extremes of cruelty and madness on a scale the world had never seen before, was Mercurial. Legions of scintillating performers are Mercurial: Sammy Davis Jr., Frank Sinatra, Cantinflas, Marcel Marceau, Holly Hunter, Demi Moore, and scores of ballerinas, including the great Margot Fonteyn who danced Juliette to Nureyev's Romeo when she was old enough to be Juliette's grandmother.

If you have a Mercurial in your life, you may not be comfortable, but you won't be bored. Keeping up with him or her may be exhausting, and it's probably better not to try—just enjoy the fun and excitement when it's available, and rest up in between. Don't be confused by the Mercurial's breezy manner, sparkling eyes, and big smile into thinking that he doesn't have a care in the world. He may be in big trouble and still put on a confident facade. Try not to be disappointed and disillusioned if your Mercurial mate or friend lets you down. He didn't mean to—it's just that he has so much going on that he can't quite keep up with himself. He is not insensitive. If anything, he is too sensitive and is probably suffering as much from having disappointed you as you are from being disappointed. It is important to remember how insecure and in need of a calm and generous reassurance the Mercurial is, however cheerful he may appear on the outside. And don't expect the Mercurial in your life to be completely open and candid. He can't be.

If you have a Mercurial child, your work is cut out for you. From earliest infancy there will be fretfulness, sleepless nights, colic, and demanding squalling. Just be glad the baby has a mellow crying voice and not a high-pitched squeal, because you'll have to listen to a lot of it. As a toddler the Mercurial will be into twice as much mischief as other toddlers, which may seem impossible, but it isn't. Child-proofing the home is a task for a genius, but at least the young Mercurial is wary and on the lookout for danger. If not it seems unlikely any of them would grow up—their insatiable curiosity gets them into all manner of difficult situations. Be sure that you give this child plenty of opportunity to run and climb and exercise, for both of your sakes. The energy of this type is almost inexhaustible in childhood, and the child needs to expend it in wholesome ways.

When your Mercurial children reach school age, you will need to be their partisan and advocate, supporter and defender. In short, they probably will not be the teacher's favorites (unless they happen upon a very mellow, calm Jovial teacher who values their quickness enough to overlook their activity level and short attention span). The schools, with their large classrooms, overworked teachers, and limited facilities, teach to the middle. Mercurial children are not likely to be in the middle. They are smart, mischievous, and bored, bored, bored. They are into trouble most of the time. Be very, very careful if you are told that these children are behavior problems, that they are hyperactive, have an attention deficiency disorder, or whatever fancy terminology may currently be fashionable. Of course there are children who do have serious problems of this kind, but probably there are many more who are simply normal, healthy Mercurials who need understanding more than they need to be drugged into a submissive apathy so the teachers won't be bothered by them. Mercurial children didn't choose to be Mercurials, but if they are, then they need extra amounts of love, reassurance, and guidance.

Some areas in which Mercurials will probably need help are in being consistent and in following through on commitments. Mercurials have many different ideas and feelings that are so chaotic and rapid, it is hard for them to sort it all out and to understand which are important and which are not. This is where the understanding of a patient but firm parent is going to be essential. Of course these children are going to use any devious methods they can think of to avoid detection or punishment if they have made mistakes, so it is up to the parent to be consistent and clear about what the rules are and what the consequences are. Don't be manipulated—it's worse for the children than for you in the long run—but on the other hand, don't make an enormous issue about total honesty as the ultimate virtue. It isn't really, and it will be much more effective if little Mercurials see that fibs just don't work rather than trying to categorize them as mortal sins.

There are, as was mentioned, many well-known Mercurials in show business, sports, and politics that might serve as examples of this type, but in this instance we can look at the recent history of an entire and very successful nation to exemplify some of the typical Mercurial attributes. I refer to Japan. Of course, not all Japanese are Mercurial, but the values of the Japanese culture, and the way this culture has operated seem to be Mercurial values and stratagems. Perhaps the most striking attribute the Japanese have demonstrated in the last fifty years is the ability to act quickly and intelligently, and to change tactics almost immediately when a previous approach didn't work.

After their successful surprise attack on Pearl Harbor in 1941, the Japanese hesitated. Unable to believe their basically Martial target, the United States, was as unprepared to retaliate as it actually was, the Japanese did not press their advantage. Quite possibly the whole issue rested on miscommunication of the sort that frequently occurs between Mercurial and Martial. Be that as it may, Japan lost the war. To the astonishment of the Americans, the Japanese people turned on a dime and began learning everything they could about manufacturing processes, electronics, corporate structures, business and finance, and other areas in which the United States had formerly excelled. Now it is the Japanese who excel in these areas, and the United States is complaining that they don't play fair. They do not, of course, play the same way. The Japanese play to win, and employ market manipulations that involve selling their products for less than it costs to manufacture them—for a while. Then, after the competition from other nations has been effectively destroyed and the Japanese corporations are in control of the market, they can set prices that do make a profit.

There are other parallels as well that suggest that the Japanese culture is strongly influenced by Mercurial psychology. The very strong value placed on appearances whatever the inner reality may be—"saving face"—seems to be in keeping with the tendencies of this type. The efficiency, quickness, and tidiness of the Japanese people also seem like Mercurial traits. This is definitely not to suggest that an entire nation or culture is of a single type. It is to suggest that the values of a particular type may become the values operating within an entire culture, and may affect the members of that culture no matter what the types of individual people may be. There are Lunars, Saturns, Jovials, all the types among the population of Japan, just as there are all the types represented in all nations. Nonetheless, I would contend that Japan has a Mercurial culture in that its values and tendencies are in keeping with those of the Mercurial body type.

CHAPTER 13

THE SATURN TYPE

Saturns are one of the easiest types to identify on the basis of appearance. They are tall, with long, strong bones, in a solidly connected, well-articulated skeletal system. The joints, hands, and feet are large, the fingers and toes long. The Saturn's sturdy, elongated frame supports firm muscles. This type is not easy to ignore.

If a Saturn is in the vicinity, everyone will notice. Not only does the Saturn have a large, solid body, but he has a large, solid presence to go with it. The Saturn's head is likely to be long and thin like the rest of his body, with prominent brow, cheekbones, and jaw. The Saturnine type has no typical coloring and may be blonde or have dark hair, with blue or brown eyes. The Saturn's eyes look out at the world with a level, thoughtful gaze, whatever their color. Saturnine movements are slow and deliberate. Indeed, this type may move infrequently, preferring to sit, or to stand motionless, observing. The Saturn seems aloof and distant like the planet he is named for.

Saturn was the outermost of the planets known to the ancient world. When compared to its brilliant and colorful neighbor, Jupiter, its yellowish almost beige hue makes it appear drab and leaden. It moves rather slowly. Saturn is best known for its rings, which are such a prominent feature that they can actually be seen from the Earth with a good set of binoculars when

SATURN: The Saturn Type is active and positive. This type is the largest, being both tall and of heavy bone structure. Saturns frequently occupy positions of leadership, directing or managing others, just as their dominant gland, the anterior pituitary, regulates the other endocrine glands. Saturns may not at first seem to be either active or positive since they are slow to act and serious—they are active in that they act upon their environment rather than being acted upon, and positive in their confidence in their own abilities. The chief feature of the Saturn is often dominance.

SATURN: The Saturn woman is an active, or masculine, type. This does not affect her sexuality or attractiveness. Saturns are, in fact, the current ideal type of feminine beauty. Their prominant bone structure, height, and slenderness make them photogenic and preferred as fashion models. Saturn woman have the same capacities for leadership as Saturn men and frequently hold responsible positions.

viewing conditions are just right. The rings tend to divert attention from the globe itself. The surface details are not easy to make out. Although Saturn has cloud belts and spots as Jupiter does, there seems to be less activity. It is a quieter world than its flamboyant neighbor.

Saturn has a diameter of about 75,000 miles. The average distance from the Sun of its orbit is 886 million miles, and its orbital velocity is so slow that Saturn takes 29 years to complete one revolution. The axial rotation, however, is very rapid: it takes a little more than ten hours to spin around. This means that a year on Saturn would contain about 25,000 days. This exceedingly long year could not be divided into lunar months very easily (as is the year on Earth) because Saturn has nine moons instead of one. Creating a calendar to keep track of time on Saturn's surface would be such a complicated task it would take a Saturn to do it.

There are some odd paradoxes about Saturn's size. The globe is large enough to contain more than 700 Earths, but its density is less than that of water. Its mass is 95 times as great as that of Earth, but its gravity is not. A person who weighs 140 pounds on Earth would weigh only 60 pounds on Saturn. (In fact, with the exception of Jupiter, there is no planet on which a human would feel uncomfortably heavy.) Of course such speculations are silly, since the gaseous surface would be impossible to stand on anyway. In fact, both Saturn and Jupiter are so very different from the four inner planets—which is what our conception of "planet" is based on—that any sort of comparison is difficult.

Saturn is very much more remote than Jupiter, but what has been seen by telescopes and photographed by flyby probes indicates that there is much less activity on Saturn than on Jupiter. The equatorial zone is usually a brighter cream color than the overall dull yellowish beige of the rest of the planet. Occasional lighter spots have appeared, but not often and not lasting long. Whatever the perturbations Saturn may experience, its lower temperatures seem to make them considerably less dramatic than the colorful eruptions on Jupiter.

The ring system of Saturn is unique in the solar system. There are several rings with gaps between them. The innermost ring does not touch the planet's surface. All of the three principal rings lie in exactly the same plane and have a total diameter of 170,000 miles, more than twice the diameter of the planet itself. The rings are very thin, probably not much more than ten miles deep. If Saturn were a globe with a diameter of five inches, the ring span would be one foot but the thickness only one fifteen hundredth of an inch. When the rings are exactly aligned toward us, they almost disappear. When Saturn's equator is tilted in relationship to Earth's orbit, however, the rings appear solid because of their reflective brilliance. The rings are composed of small solid particles, and each revolves around the planet in its individual orbit. This fits all the known facts, including that the inner parts move around Saturn more rapidly than the outer. The gaps in the ring sections are explained by the orbits of some of Saturn's satellites, which sweep clear some sections of the particles by zooming through them.

Of Saturn's nine known satellites, the most important is Titan. Much more massive than our Moon, Titan is of planetary dimensions, larger than Mercury but smaller than Mars. Although Titan is large, it is so far away from us that its surface details are hard to make out. Its distance from Saturn exceeds the 750,000 miles of the rings' diameter and its color is yellowish. The remaining satellites are considerably smaller and fainter. The five inner ones have diameters ranging from about 300 to 1,000 miles; it is their orbits that break up the continuity of the rings. Outside of Titan's orbit are two more satellites, one very small and the other second in size only to Titan, very far out—over 2,000,000 miles. It is only a little smaller than our Moon and has a revolution period of 79 days. Even further out is a tiny satellite with an estimated diameter of only 150 miles. It is so far from Saturn, over 8,000,000 miles, that it takes a year and a half to complete one revolution. Like Jupiter's outer satellites, it moves in a retrograde or wrong-way direction and may be a captured asteroid rather than a regular satellite.

The Saturnine system is complex, remote, and magnificent, with so many different complicated and interrelated features that comparison with the other planets is difficult. Turning to what is currently known about the endocrine gland which this planet is thought to stimulate, we find a comparable complexity. The anterior lobe of the pituitary gland produces six hormones of established functional significance. Most of these hormones have exceedingly complex multi-syllabic names, so they are referred to by letters or by their functions. Many of these functions involve stimulating or repressing the action of other endocrine glands to either release or retain the hormones associated with them. The anterior pituitary, then, is the gland which monitors and controls the amount and ratio of much of the hormonal content of the blood stream.

The hormone designated as ACTH is associated with the stimulation of the adrenal glands and therefore with the production of adrenal steroids in response to stress. Numerous types of stimuli, both physical and psychological, are known to provoke the secretion of this hormone which carries its instructions to several parts of the body. In addition to the biological actions exerted through the adrenal glands, ACTH produces direct effects upon the brain. It affects endorphin secretion which in turn affects learning and memory, and is suspected of many other specific functions in different parts of the brain.

Another hormone produced by the anterior pituitary gland is designated TSH because it is a thyroid-stimulating hormone. Just as ACTH controls the activity of the adrenal glands, TSH controls the activity of the thyroid gland. It stimulates or inhibits the synthesis and secretion of the thyroid hormones affecting the body's metabolism. In laboratory animals, TSH secretion was increased when they were cold and needed a higher metabolic rate. In humans, exposure to heat was found to depress the thyroid function. The psychological conditions associated with an excess or a deficiency of thyroid have responded to treatment with TSH as well as to thyroid hormone.

Yet another hormone produced and released by the anterior pituitary is called simply the growth hormone. As its name implies, it is the hormone that stimulates growth, particularly bone growth. Its secretion is particularly high in adolescent children. An excess of this hormone causes gigantism and acromegaly, diseases in which bone growth is excessive, resulting in very tall stature if the bones have not fully formed and in widening and coarsening of the bones if they have.

Still other hormones in the anterior pituitary control or monitor the production and release of sex hormones. The onset of puberty in both girls and boys and the level of sexual activity in adulthood is stimulated by hormones produced in the pituitary. The anterior pituitary has been termed the master gland as a result of its function of producing and releasing the hormones that stimulate the other endocrine glands to produce and release their hormones. This complex messenger service uses the blood stream as its method of transportation and is constantly adjusting and readjusting the hormonal content of the blood in the process.

The Saturnine body type is governed by the anterior pituitary gland, and is as complex in its psychology as we would expect from the above brief consideration of the functions of this gland. Saturns monitor and control the other types, just as the pituitary monitors and controls other glands. In fact control—of themselves, of others, and of the environment—seems the primary characteristic of Saturns.

This type is active and positive, although both may initially be hard to understand about Saturns. It seems at first that the Saturn doesn't move often enough or fast enough to be considered an active type, and yet it occupies the central position of the three active types. Saturns consider carefully before they take any action, and are sometimes so slow and methodical in their deliberations that the time for any action has passed before they come to a decision. It is not that they decide not to act, but rather that they think about what action they are going to take for so long that the action is irrelevant to the new situation which has formed. And of course, then the Saturn has to begin deliberating about the new situation. Remember that the distinction between active and passive is not based on how fast a type acts but on the degree to which that type acts on the world as opposed to being acted upon by it, and it becomes clear that the Saturn is indeed an active, or masculine type.

If it is difficult to see that Saturns are active, it is even more difficult to see that they are positive. This is a ponderous and somber sort of person, not given to humor and certainly not to frivolity. The Saturn is not a party animal; life is far too serious a matter for this type to waste any time on trivialities. In fact this type is given to asceticism and self-denial. Saturns prefer order above all else, and are virtually incapable of spontaneous or impulsive action or speech.

The activity of Saturns is an inner activity. They will consider all the factors in any situation, consult with others, research similar events, and try to evaluate the relative importance of all the relevant details. Only when they are sure of all of the facts and their significance will they plan a course of action. As a result of this cautious decision-making process, the plan the Saturn arrives at will be as sound as human rationality can make it. It will certainly be well considered. Furthermore, whatever proposal Saturns come up with will be for the common good and not just for their own self-interest.

I was once traveling in a group that included a Saturn and a very active Martial. We were in Paris, and getting around by public transportation. None of us spoke French, so the labyrinth of the Paris subway system, the Metro, occupied our attention. On the first day the Martial glanced quickly at the map on the gleaming white tile wall and plunged into the crowd heading for the trains, arriving at our destination a good twenty minutes ahead of the rest of the group. The Saturn was the last to arrive. On the second day, however, the Saturn was the first to arrive at wherever we were going. She had studied the Metro map until it was thoroughly mastered and thereafter wasted no time getting on the wrong trains or the right trains heading in the wrong direction. By the third day the other members of the group simply followed the Saturn instead of thrashing about on their own. This, basically, is how Saturns operate. The initial seeming inactivity is deceptive. The time spent thinking things through before acting pays off over the long haul in much greater efficiency. The Saturn is likely to complete a demanding and complicated job far ahead of the fast starters, and do it much better.

These careful planners, once they have arrived at a decision, can more clearly be seen to be active types. Saturns are forceful and determined in seeing their objectives realized. They will modify their strategy if new information comes to light, and they will listen seriously to the ideas of others. But as long as a particular course of action seems desirable, Saturns will pursue it and do everything in their considerable powers to convince others to pursue it.

That Saturns are positive is not demonstrated by charm and wit. It is demonstrated by the virtually boundless confidence they have in their own ability to determine what is important and to see that it is accomplished. Saturns not only believe in the good, the true, and the beautiful, they believe they are uniquely qualified to determine these qualities and to defend and uphold them. As a Saturn explained to me, "Because I understand more objectively, it is my responsibility to act on my understanding." This rather smug self-confidence can be irritating at times, but it is quite often justified. I don't know about the "more objective" part, but Saturns are usually right in their appraisals because of their careful deliberations and insistence on considering all the relevant facts, and quite a few that may not be relevant as well.

Saturns feel qualified not only to determine the best course of action for themselves, but also for those around them. They are selfless in their concern for the welfare of others, and they will do whatever they can to ensure that others conduct themselves in ways that are in their best interests—as they see those interests. Some other types may have the mistaken idea that fun and relaxation are occasionally in their best interests. The Jovial, for instance, may imagine that rich food and good wine are among the pleasures that make life worth living. Saturns will patiently explain about the deleterious effects of high cholesterol, and the harm inflicted on the liver by alcohol consumption. Somehow, by the time they're done, the party isn't nearly as much fun.

Parties and recreational activities are not the Saturn's best venue—although the type may be attracted to the kind of sports that are basically endurance contests. Mountain climbing, cross-country skiing, marathon running, activities in which control over the body during long grueling ordeals is required, may appeal to the Saturnine tendency toward mortification of the flesh. But the Saturn's natural sphere of action is business, education, science, medicine, administration, any endeavor in which organization and careful planning, overview and order are the keys to successful outcomes. Saturns make good gamblers, except that they don't gamble. Rather they invest, and their investments pay off. They have the patience to understand economics, to study all of the complex factors that influence market economies, and to make judicious choices on the basis of unhurried deliberation. They may well be investment brokers, giving the same careful attention to their clients' capital as they would to their own. They may be bank presidents, or chair the boards of multi-national corporations.

It is uncanny how Saturns seem to rise to responsible positions in whatever professions they undertake. If they are teachers, they soon find themselves in administrative positions. If they are scientists or technicians, they soon find themselves planning and monitoring the projects. I remember a Beetle Bailey cartoon in which several officers were deciding which enlisted man to promote. One of them said, "We'll consider all of their qualifications and then pick the tallest one." Quite often it seems that either method will result in the same choice. The tallest one is the Saturn and the one with the best qualifications is more often than not going to be the Saturn, too.

Like the planet Saturn, the Saturnine type is likely to have many satellites. Saturns enjoy having others depend on them and are willing to devote themselves tirelessly to large families, businesses, groups, religions, political parties, or whatever organizations need their services. Their management abilities enable them to evaluate and use the abilities of others effectively. Just as the hormones of the anterior pituitary gland seek out and regulate the other hormones produced by other glands, Saturns know how to use the other types to the best effect. Saturns with their broad overview and genuine concern for others sense at once that a Lunar will do well taking care of the details of business—the bookkeeping, the inventories, the weekly schedules of production. Furthermore, Saturns know that the Lunar will be happiest in those positions where attention to detail is required. The positions that call for quick perceptions and fast action are for Mercurials, and Saturns will find one for the job. And those that require energy and endurance are for Martials. In other words, Saturns seem to have an intuitive understanding of types and how to bring out the best of each.

The type of group or organization Saturns will be in charge of is likely to be dictated by center of gravity. If the function which is most used is the intellectual center, then the institution the Saturn serves is likely to be an educational or research institution. In other words, the field of interest will be governed by the center of gravity—and the intellectual center might be drawn to nuclear physics, or applied linguistics, or philosophy. Because of type, however, the Saturn will probably be the dean of the academic department or the project administrator. It is not likely that Saturns could be involved in any pursuit without having many ideas about how it could be organized better, and since they are an active type, it won't be long until they put their ideas into action. Soon after that, they are in charge.

Instinctively-centered Saturns, on the other hand, may concentrate on home and family. These are the people who would design and build their own homes; in fact they may be architects in professional life as well. Saturns' homes are likely to be a reflection of their psychology—austere, efficient, spacious, with high ceilings and tall windows. The activities they are involved with are likely to be environmental concerns, and they will enjoy taking the family on wilderness trips, backpacking into the mountains or white water rafting or fly fishing down isolated streams. They may be scout leaders, or coach a little league team. Again, the center of gravity causes them to be oriented toward home and family, but the body type ensures that they will be active organizers of activities.

The moving-centered Saturn is the one mentioned previously who enjoys sports of the sort that require endurance and physical stamina. A century ago this type was in their golden age in the period of the great exploration expeditions. Up the Amazon, down the Nile, into the jungle, off to the North Pole, conquering Everest or whatever mountain presented the greatest challenge—these were the visions of the moving-centered Saturn. They are still at it, of course; it's just that technology has taken the former great feats of endurance and made them summer outings for retired Jovial elementary school teachers. Oh well, there's still marathon running and cross-country skiing.

Emotionally-centered Saturns might be attracted to any number of careers, but these will involve either working with people or in one of the arts. Orchestra conductors are frequently of this type, as are curators of art museums. The Saturn might be, as C. G. Jung was, concerned with psychology as a therapist or psychoanalyst.

The Saturnine type's many strengths are obvious, but like all types, they have weaknesses to which they are prone. One of these weaknesses is the result of the very thoroughness of their thought processes. Saturns can take far longer than a situation warrants in making a decision. And they can be far too cautious and conservative as a result of having taken into account everything that could possibly go wrong. If a major decision is being made—where to locate a new factory, when to move a military battalion into position, how to invest a large inheritance—by all means be sure a Saturn is involved in the planning. On the other hand, if the decision is where to have a picnic on Sunday afternoon, when to move the patio furniture into the garage, or what kind of doughnuts to buy for brunch, be sure not to have Saturns involved in the planning. They will invest the same solemn deliberation whatever the scale of the undertaking.

The chief feature of the Saturnine type is usually dominance. This feature is sometimes quite obvious, as when you are sitting in a room reading and the Saturn comes in and turns the light on so that you will have the proper lighting to read by, whether you want it or not. At other times the feature is felt more as a psychological weight. A Saturn can merely pause for a moment and watch what you are doing, and you know that somehow you are not doing it right even though no word has been said. The Saturn, when in this feature, seems to be operating according to a doctrine of assumed incompetence. Whatever is going on, this attitude implies it should be going on in some better way—and the Saturn knows exactly what that better way is.

In their relationship with other types, Saturns are usually very successful if they keep the feature of dominance from being too oppressive. Since this type is very frequently in positions where they have authority over others, the feature may be appropriate to a work or family situation. Managers do have the position of setting standards for other workers; parents do have the responsibility for setting reasonable rules for their children; administrators do have the obligation of planning school curricula. It just comes with the territory. The problems are likely to arise when Saturns are dealing with others on an equal footing. It is in situations like this—or worse, when the Saturn is not the boss but under the authority of someone else—that difficulties may arise.

Saturns may have difficulties with the other active types if their dominance evokes power in the Martial, Mercurial, or Solar. All of the active types have a penchant for trying to improve the environment, and of course they each think they have the best ideas about what improvements are needed. Of the passive types, the Saturn's maximum attraction is the Lunar, so they usually get along well—unless the Saturn's dominance is too strong. If it is, it is likely to evoke willfulness in the Lunar. The Venusian is a problem for the Saturn only when this passive type won't do much of anything. The Jovial is probably the type with which the Saturn has the most difficulty. The Jovial vanity is likely not to be very interested in what the Saturn thinks should be done, and certainly the Jovial has very little patience with the restraint and austerity of the Saturn.

Saturns, even more than Lunars, are likely to prefer their own type when choosing friends, associates, and marriage partners. Certainly they are much concerned with other types, in a paternal and responsible way, and are likely to have a complex variety of satellites. When it comes to an association of equals, however, Saturns prefer . . . well, equals. And, in the Saturnine view at least, the only possible equal for a Saturn would be another Saturn.

If you have a Saturn in your life, you will know it. The Saturn is not easy to ignore. In fact, she is likely to be the hub around which the rest of the family revolves, the one who makes the plans for the whole group. Most of the time, it is a good idea to do what the Saturn suggests, unless for some reason it is clear that your own best interests are being jeopardized. If that is the case, simply explain what your view of the situation is, and she will no doubt consider your opinion carefully. Remember that this type is genuinely concerned with what is best for everyone involved, and is usually willing to make whatever arrangements are necessary. On the other hand, if there are factors which you have not considered, she will be glad to point them out to you.

If you have a Saturnine child, sometimes the most difficult problem is to remember that he or she is a child. Saturns are so competent, even when very young, that they are sometimes given more responsibility than a child should have to shoulder. I have a Saturnine friend who told me how her parents had left her to live in an empty house when the rest of the family moved to another city when she was a teenager. She had not wanted to leave her friends at school and had talked her mother and father into leaving her with a sleeping bag and a few essentials to stay until either the house was sold or the school year was over. I can understand how the parents might have been convinced by her arguments and her competence, but the desolation she felt while alone was proof that she was, after all, just a teenage kid and not ready for the experience of being on her own. One time not to follow the advice of the Saturn is when you are the adult and the Saturn is a child.

Although, as mentioned before, no national or ethnic group consists homogeneously of a single type, it is true that some cultures seem to consistently produce examples of the classic types. Furthermore, there are cultural ideals, admired archetypes that obviously conform to one of the planetary types. For the British, the ideal type is clearly the Saturnine. The current monarch, Elizabeth II, chose a Saturnine consort and produced a Saturnine heir, Prince Charles. He in turn consistently chooses Saturnine women. That the British idealize the Saturnine type and espouse its values is clearly indicated by their attempts to colonize and dominate as many of the world's people as possible. At least one of Britain's former colonies, the United States, has continued the tradition. Uncle Sam, the U.S.A. mascot, is a classic Saturnine figure, as was the greatest American president, Abraham Lincoln.

Although Lincoln's greatness clearly transcends type, there is much in the way he approached and solved the momentous problems he faced that is typical of the Saturnine psychology. He was, to begin with, almost entirely self-educated. Lincoln had less than a year of formal schooling and filled the lack by reading widely and studying on his own. This accomplishment—he was a widely read and thoroughly well-educated man—indicates not only a strongly disciplined person, but one with an active mind capable of determining the relative importance of ideas and values without assistance. He was also educated in the school of hard knocks. His family was very poor and as a child and young man Lincoln was accustomed to bone-grinding hard labor as a farmer, woodcutter, and bargeman. At 19 years of age he took a barge to New Orleans, and shortly after that he opened his own business, a store which failed, leaving him heavily in debt. He enlisted in the army and was commissioned as a captain in the Blackhawk Indian Wars, although he never actually saw battle.

After that war he studied law, using almost everything he earned to pay back the debts he felt morally obligated to pay from his bankrupt business. He was elected to state office in Illinois, and nearly bankrupted the state with the improvements he felt were necessary. In 1846 he was elected to the United States Congress as a representative from Illinois, but his unpopular stand against the Mexican War—which he felt was based on greed for territory—cost him the next election. At that point he felt that his political career was over. It is pleasant to remember that Lincoln and his family, his wife and young sons, had ten happy years in Illinois during which Lincoln practiced law with a partner who was also a good friend. The Lincoln family lived in a large comfortable home, and had a social life which they enjoyed. Lincoln's law partner during this period observed that Lincoln's genius as a lawyer was the result of his ability to concede all nonessential matters to the opposition while relentlessly insisting on what he called the nub of the case.[1] When those ten halcyon years of success and comfort were over and Lincoln's great battle was joined, it was exactly that ability—to concede the nonessential while never losing sight of or wavering on essential matters—that won his great victories, the preservation of the union and the abolition of slavery.

It is here that we can see the particularly Saturnine qualities of Lincoln's political genius. He stood alone. Distrusted and frequently vilified by all factions, Lincoln equivocated, compromised, waited, changed directions, and outright lied. Karl Marx, who observed the American scene with interest, said, "All Lincoln's acts have the appearance of mean, hedging provisos, which one lawyer puts to his opposing lawyer."[2]

Lincoln avoided the abolitionists and did everything he could possibly do to reassure the Southern slave owners that he would not interfere with their system. His attempts to preserve the union of the states and avoid war drew the abolitionists' contempt. He held together an unruly coalition of diverse factions under the aegis of the fledgling Republican Party by promising everybody anything they wanted. When the southern states seceded from the Union and the United States was plunged into civil war, Lincoln employed every stratagem he could to win that war. Plagued with ineffectual generals, he remonstrated with, ridiculed, and then replaced them. Finally, after Lincoln had about despaired of finding the military man who would lead the Union to victory, that man appeared.

General Ulysses S. Grant was a Martial who had risen rapidly through the ranks to a position of command. Lincoln recognized

---

[1] Gary Wills, "Dishonest Abe," in *Time Magazine*, October 5, 1992.
[2] Gary Wills, "Dishonest Abe," p. 42.

when they met that this was the military leader he had waited for and prayed for. One familiar story about the two men claims that there were complaints about how much whiskey the hard-drinking Grant consumed. Lincoln's reply was to inquire about the brand of liquor so he could send a case to all his generals. Whether true or not, the story points up a consistent practice of Lincoln's. When he found what he felt was the right man for a job, whether in the army or in government, he delegated authority to that man and gave him his total support. Lincoln talked to people, and, more important, he listened to people. He was flexible and pragmatic, and, most astonishing, considering the pressures he was under and the loneliness of facing them entirely by himself, he was patient. Lincoln felt deeply that the United States, with all its problems and failings, was "the last, best hope" for all of humanity because of the high ideals stated in the documents the nation considered sacred, the Declaration of Independence and the Constitution. To uphold them both, to reconcile the statement that "all men are created equal" with the determination of the southern states to continue the institution of slavery, seemed an impossible task. When Lincoln moved to the White House in March of 1861, there seemed no possible way both to preserve the Union and to eliminate slavery. When Lincoln was assassinated four years and one month later, both tasks had been completed. Marx, who earlier had criticized Lincoln's "mean, hedging provisos," understood, as the world understood, what Lincoln had accomplished by "inflexibly pressing on to his great goal, never compromising it by blind haste, slowly maturing his steps."[3]

Lincoln personified both the appearance and the psychology of the Saturnine type at its finest. This type has the ability to direct others effectively, just as the dominant gland directs the activities of the other endocrine glands. At the same time, Saturns have the ability to stand alone against tremendous pressures and resistance from others once they have determined, to their own satisfaction, the right course of action.

---

[3]Gary Wills, "Dishonest Abe," p. 42.

CHAPTER 14

THE MARTIAL TYPE

The Martial is typically of average (or shorter) height and sturdy build, compact and powerfully built rather than fleshy. With wide shoulders, well-developed chest, and strong arms, Martial men look like the warriors they were meant to be. Martial women are also sturdily built but more slender. Both men and women are well coordinated and can be excellent athletes, particularly in sports requiring endurance. They may be slightly bow-legged, although the legs are strong.

Martials have round heads. Their skin may be ruddy and freckled, and is likely to burn easily and be easily irritated, subject to rashes and inflammation. They frequently have red hair, or unusual hair color for their ethnic background. Their hair is thick and can be unruly, and they have thick beards and abundant body hair although of a pale, probably reddish color. Martials may have pug noses and round cheeks, and usually do not have refined features. Their hands and feet are blunt and square. They probably will have visible scars since they are frequently hurt.

Even though the planet Mars is further away than Venus—35 million miles is as close as it gets—much more is known about its surface features than is known about cloud-covered Venus, our nearer neighbor. Mars is comparatively small, having little over one tenth the mass of the Earth. A day on Mars is approximately the same length as a day on Earth, since the axial rotation of the two planets is nearly the same. A year on Mars, however, is nearly twice as long since the distance from Mars to the Sun averages out to 141 million miles. It is difficult to observe Mars because its orbital velocity is so similar to the Earth's that oppositions (times when both planets are in the same vicinity) occur only every 780 days or so, instead of every year, and because Mars' orbit is eccentric, the planet is sometimes very far away even at the closest point.

Even though there are such long periods between oppositions, when the opportunities present themselves, astronomers are able to study the solid surface. There is some atmosphere, but not much. There are some features of Mars, such as polar caps, that indicate the presence of water. Mars is called the red planet because of the reddish-ochre color typical of its surface area. There is volcanic activity: in fact Mars has the largest volcano in the Solar system. Mariner and Viking space probes have photographed the planet, and two of the Viking spacecraft landed on the planet's surface and sent back thousands of pictures. Dust storms, volcanic activity, and cyclones indicate that Mars has legitimate claim to its nickname, "the angry planet."

The two small satellites of Mars are the most unusual in the solar system. They are named Phobos (Dread) and Deimos (Terror) after the two attendants of the war god of Greek and Roman mythology. They are very small. Phobos is about ten miles in diameter and Deimos only five. They move in a very strange fashion. Phobos, the odder of the two, is very close to the surface of Mars, only 3,700 miles out, and circles the planet in one third of the Martian day. To someone watching from the surface, Phobos would rise in the west and set in the east, crossing the sky in four-and-a-half hours. In this brief time it would pass through more than half its phases—if it rose as a crescent, it would be nearly full before it set. Meanwhile Deimos, which is much farther out at 12,500 miles, orbits Mars in 30 hours, which is only slightly longer than the Martian day. So while Phobos is zipping around, Deimos almost keeps pace with the revolving planet, falling behind only gradually. It remains above the horizon for

MARTIAL: The Martial Type is active and negative. Although not tall, Martials are usually powerfully built, with well-developed torsos and broad shoulders. The activitiy of Martials is goal-oriented, and they are quick to respond to any stimulus. Frequently their response is negative. The dominant gland for the Martial Type is the adrenals, and the abundance of adrenaline in their bloodstream governs the fight or flight response. The chief feature of the Martial may be destructiveness or power, although it also may be fear.

two-and-a-half days at a time, passing through its cycle of phases twice.

Quite a bit is also known about the endocrine glands thought to be influenced by Mars, and about the action of the hormones which they release. The adrenal glands produce the adrenal steroids, adrenaline and noradrenaline, which have long been known to affect strong emotional and instinctive reactions in humans and other animals. These hormones can elicit rage, violently aggressive behavior, and intense fear. This has been termed the "fight or flight" response. Noradrenaline is associated with active, aggressive action and adrenaline secretion with apprehension and anxiety. The adrenal glands also produce hormones regulating sexual response and melatonin, which affects skin pigmentation.

Knowing that the dominant glands in the Martial type are the adrenals tells us a lot about the psychological tendencies of this type. The Martial is an active and negative type, quickly ready for action whether that action is an attack or a rapid retreat. Anyone who has ever experienced the sensation of adrenaline circulating through the body is aware of the power of this hormone to incite action. Martials have an excess of adrenal steroids and are quick to respond to any provocation, frequently without stopping to consider what sort of response would be the most effective in achieving a desired aim. Martials are blunt, direct, and honest, tending to blurt out exactly what they are thinking regardless of the consequences. They definitely are not good at diplomacy, tending to polarize disagreements rather than to diminish them. Martials are idealists, willing to uphold the noblest principles with a loyalty and unflinching determination that may miss the subtleties of a situation but never fails to defend the highest values as they perceive them. Of course, in a tavern brawl the highest value the Martial may be able to perceive is whose turn it is to buy the next round of drinks, or who might have made a rude remark to the barmaid that the Martial thinks needs defending. This is not, in brief, a refined or naturally civilized type.

Because they are an active and negative type, Martials frequently overestimate the amount of opposition or resistance they will encounter. Therefore they tend to exert more force than the situation warrants. One result of this tendency is that Martials tend to break things, including their own skin and bones. In trying to open a stuck window, for instance, the Martial may give it a good yank which results in shattering the glass and cutting her hand. In pruning trees, the Martial might be too vigorous in lopping off limbs, not noticing that he's sending the biggest one crashing through his porch roof. This type is goal-oriented, with the kind of tunnel vision that does not see anything but the immediate aim. If other things or people get in the way, he may not notice until it is too late. If his own thumb is in the way, he also may not notice until it is too late. The Martial type, spurred on by the adrenal hormones in his blood, lives in an almost constant state of activity, directing his considerable energies to rearranging the exterior world.

Once embarked upon a project, the Martial will work tirelessly until the task is completed, and then start another one. A large percentage of Martials would probably be classified as workaholics by their friends and families because of their single-minded intensity when pursuing a given objective. When a Martial encounters obstacles or objections to his plans or ideas, he simply redoubles his efforts. Where another type might quit, or modify the plan, or employ some stratagem to circumvent the opposition, the Martial forges straight ahead. The image that comes to mind is of a battery operated robot toy: when it comes to a wall, it keeps making the same walking motion even though any forward motion has been completely stopped. The Martial is so straight-line oriented that he will continue trying to walk through a wall when there is a door only a few feet away. Rather than change direction or modify his plans, he will expend the energy to break down the wall if that is what is necessary to achieve the aim.

The high energy level and direct, forthright nature of the Martial makes him the ideal soldier or law enforcement officer. He has a devotion to duty and commitment to principle and law that make him easily stirred by patriotic or humanitarian causes. And once he has committed himself to such a cause, he is selfless and loyal in his defense of it. The Martial has little patience with bureaucratic paper shuffling or even with negotiations. His approach is direct, open, and forceful. If you need someone to cut through labyrinthine complexities and get to the heart of the matter in one clean stroke, you want a Martial. He may hurt people's feelings with his tactlessness, he may make enemies with his contempt for anyone less committed to principle than he is, but you never need to worry that he has ulterior motives or hidden agendas. Everything that the Martial thinks and believes is available for scrutiny, even when you'd rather not know.

Like the features of the small red planet that lends its name to this type, the Martial's motives, opinions, allegiances, and affections are clearly in view. If you have a Martial friend, you may have difficulty not being hurt by her frank criticisms and appraisals, but you can be sure that they won't be made behind your back. If she thinks that the new dress you are wearing looks tacky, she'll say so. If she disapproves of the way you discipline your children, she'll say so. But she will never speak a disparaging word about you to other friends, and she won't hear anyone else criticize you without defending you staunchly. Suffering her frankness and candor is the price you pay for a loyal and devoted partisan.

The Martial type is down to earth and practical, and when left to his natural inclinations his tastes are likely to be unsophisticated and even coarse. If he enjoys athletics, he will prefer contact sports like American football or rugby. And he is definitely a participant rather than a spectator. If he does find himself in the role of spectator, it will likely be in a tavern where he may soon be involved in his own personal contact sport if anyone criticizes his favorite team. Martials would, in fact, be well advised to steer clear of taverns and the alcohol they sell. The active adrenals and the stimulation of alcohol can lead to trouble, and many a brawling Martial has woken up the next morning with a hangover and a good collection of bumps and bruises, or in a jail cell, or both.

The Martial type has the greatest intensity of sexual energy of any of the types, which causes considerable conflict for them. Both men and women have strong ties of loyalty to their families, while at the same time they feel powerful sexual attractions to many members of the opposite sex. If the person to whom the Martial is attracted is a willing sex partner, and the situation presents itself, the temptation is likely to overwhelm even the Martial's strong principles. Then, of course, Martials feel obliged to be loyal to the new partner, and to tell everyone concerned exactly what has occurred. This can cause a great deal of suffering in their personal lives, and cause suffering for their families as well.

The Martial is also plagued by an explosive temper. When surprised by unexpected events, the adrenals start pumping out inordinate amounts of the hormones that propel the Martial into action. And since the Martial is a negative type, that action may well be aggressive and even violent. The Martial tends to attack first and ask questions afterward. Or, if the hormonal stimulus is of another variety, the Martial may flee first and ask questions afterward. Either way, the reaction is likely to be both strong and unpredictable, like the erratic orbit of Mars which sometimes brings it close to the Earth and sometimes sends it spinning off to the far side of the Sun for two years before it reappears. So the Martial can be a strange mixture of solid dependability and single-minded action with unpredictable outbursts of anger or anxiety or erratic behavior.

The typical day in a Martial's life probably doesn't begin too early, since he is likely to have worked late the night before, or to have been out enjoying himself, which for the Martial is likely to be as vigorous as his work anyway. So, it's late, and he's off and running with no time for more than a cup of coffee which he takes with him in the truck. Whatever job he goes to is definitely not going to be behind a desk or at any other location which restricts his freedom of movement. The Martial might be in agricultural work; he might be in forestry, or run a ranch. He could well be a firefighter, or a policeman. He might be in the armed services. He might work on an oil rig, or be a commercial fisherman. He might be a scientist, but not in a laboratory. Geology or oceanography would be far more likely.

Martial women would be just as likely to have one of the above careers as the men. Martial women are more likely than any other type to be satisfied having an active, interesting job and foregoing family life. All Martials can have a tendency to be loners, but the women in particular can find it hard to accept the wifely and motherly responsibilities of caring for and nurturing others. A Martial woman enjoys male companionship, and she definitely enjoys an active sex life, but she may find it easier to do without a husband than either to take a subservient role to an active male or to respect a passive one.

Whatever job the Martial has, she can be counted on to work hard at it. She may arrive late, but once on the job she gives it the full benefit of her considerable energies. If she's a physical education teacher, the administration would do well to schedule her preparation period for the first period in the school day, and not notice when she gets there a little late. She'll also be there far longer than she's required to be, coaching the girl's basketball team. Her students may complain that she pushes them too hard, but they won't really mean it if they value being the best they can be. They know their coach won't accept any less.

When the regular workday is over, and on weekends, the Martial probably has several other projects that seem more like hard work than his job does. He may be building his own cabin, or cutting wood for the winter, or diving for abalone, or piloting a small plane. She may be training horses, hang gliding, or pruning apple trees. There's also a good chance that the Martial may be doing some kind of volunteer work for a cause that he believes in. He may be campaigning or demonstrating for an environmental issue. She may be involved with feminist politics. But whatever they are doing, you can be sure that they won't be sitting around watching videos, or any other vicarious living. Martials are doers.

The intellectually-centered Martial is likely to operate from the mechanical or emotional part of that center. Martials simply don't have the patience for the slow and painstaking operations of the intellectual parts of centers. The Martial whose center of gravity is in the mechanical part of the intellectual center runs the danger of being rigid and insensitive. This part of the intellectual center operates by definition and association; it has a pat response for every situation with little awareness of factors that might mitigate or modify a particular instance. When this is combined with the tunnel vision and "damn the torpedoes, full speed ahead" mentality and the energy of the Martial type, the results can be the frightening intensity of the zealot, blind to everything except whatever ideology has been seized upon. When the Martial values ideas above human beings, as the intellectually-centered are prone to do, and destructive and punitive force serves these ideas, a dangerous combination of center of gravity and type results. Quite likely Lenin was an intellectually-centered Martial.

The moving-centered Martial is a formidable working machine. This is a person who can work, and work hard, for twelve to fourteen hours a day, and thrive on it. Unlike the moving-centered Mercurial, who tends toward restless and sometimes aimless movement, Martials with this center of gravity hold to goals and will literally move mountains to reach them if perhaps building a transcontinental railroad and that's what it takes. Alexander the Great was a moving-centered Martial, as was the blunt and forceful Gurdjieff. This type is a cultural ideal in the United States—the original period of colonization attracted such men and women, and the western movement attracted many more. The relatively short historical period that produced the trappers, Indian scouts, wagon train leaders, cowboys, cattlemen, and settlers of the American West created an archetypal ideal of the moving-centered Martial that has lived on in fiction and film ever since.

Martials who are centered in the instinctive center can be frightening to others because of the intensity of their energies, but as long as these energies find a useful outlet and are controlled by the Martial's sense of honor and devotion to duty, they cause little harm. Visitors to Turkey frequently find the preponderance of instinctively-centered Martials to be disconcerting because of the intensity of their stares, the prevalence of armed and uniformed military and civil police, and their wariness of strangers. It soon becomes apparent, however, that devotion to the Islamic religion, and to their families, is a strong ameliorating influence, and visitors have nothing to fear. That is, the visitors have nothing to fear as long as they respect the law and local customs. This is, after all, the country of the "Midnight Express."

Emotionally-centered Martials are also intense. The Crusades come to mind. I would not be surprised if emotionally-centered Martials were the instigators of the original campaigns to purify the Holy land, with all their attendant misdirected religious energy and lamentable bloodshed. The Spanish Inquisition also seems suspiciously like an enterprise in which emotionally-centered Martials might get caught up. And in our time, when the television screens show us marching, chanting, banner-waving enthusiasts for this cause or that religion, they may well be emotionally-centered Martials committed to some ideal or other and heading for the barricades. Ireland, a country with a strongly Martial and emotional population, has suffered much from this sort of mechanical behavior. Martials centered in the emotional function are much better off if drawn to the arts where they can invest their energy in activities such as painting or writing or acting—like James Cagney, Kevin Costner, or Kirk Douglas.

Whatever the center of gravity, Martials are at their best in the service of a higher ideal, or under the direction of a wise Saturn, or both. When the former situation applies you may see the Martial energy providing the inspired and inspiring leadership of a president such as John F. Kennedy (who suffered from a disease of the adrenals, Addison's disease). When directed by a Saturn, such as Abraham Lincoln, a Martial like Ulysses S. Grant put his warrior's energies into a higher service. Grant would have been a great general in any war; he did not have the depth and breadth of vision to be a particularly great president.

The Martial's maximum attraction is the warm, passive, sensuous Venusian. When he has finally worn himself out with strenuous activity, the Martial longs for the voluptuous embrace of a soft, nurturing Venusian. Relationships between Martials and Venusians are the most passionate of any of the maximum attractions on the enneagram. They are likely to be stormy because the two types are so different in speed, activity level, and preferences that they have difficulty understanding each other, or even wanting to. But the sexual attraction is so compelling that they are drawn to each other anyway—and then later there will be an explosion and they'll be torn apart. Two days, three at the most, and they'll be back in bed. Things go much better if the relationship is between Martial and Venusian friends of the same sex rather than a sexual relationship. Business partners, sports cronies, and colleagues can get along very well when the Venusian serves as a combination admiration society and sea anchor for the vigorous Martial and doesn't get in the way.

Martials also get along well with the other two positive types. Because they tend to be loners and independent workers, Martials are not very good managers. For one thing they tend to drive their subordinates too hard, expecting everyone to be able to keep up with their own hard-driving pace. They are not consistent or even-tempered enough to win the support of their workers. Martials are too single-minded to take all of the factors into account when trying to run a business or manage a company—they tend to lock on to one aspect of the operation and ignore the rest. Martials can, however, work very well with Saturns smart enough not to crowd them. This combination, Saturn and Martial, is among the most effective for any enterprise that requires acting upon the world. Saturns have the breadth of vision and Martials have the ability to act quickly and to continue acting until the goal is achieved. If left to themselves, Saturns tend to hesitate too long, and Martials to act too soon. Together, however, they make an unbeatable combination if the Saturns are wise enough to let the Martials know what needs to be done— and then let them do it their own way.

Martials can take orders well as long as they have the latitude to carry them out on their own. For this reason Martials can also do very well in business partnerships with Jovials. Like Saturns, Jovials can have the business and planning sense but lack the drive, energy, and endurance required to establish a successful business. Martials would prefer not to deal with planning or paperwork, but are in their element with hard work and endurance.

Martials are notorious for not getting along well with Mercurials, the other active and negative type. These two types are the fastest of all the types, but their activity is quite different. Mercurials tend to change directions frequently, and are involved in many different activities at the same time, starting a project, deviating to make a phone call, leaving to make an appointment, coming back to get a forgotten briefcase, making another phone call, and forgetting the appointment entirely. The Mercurial's short attention span and frequent deviations are nerve-wracking for Martials. Martials are persistent in their aims, single-minded in pursuing one objective until it is achieved. Furthermore, the deviousness and manipulativenesss that comes quite naturally to quick-witted Mercurials enrages the Martials' sense of honesty and fair play. And, of course, Mercurials cannot resist taking advantage of the Martial type's tunnel vision any time they get a chance to outmaneuver them, which they can do without even breathing hard. When Martials are trying to get a job done, they are totally concentrated on the effort, and the Mercurial's tendency to try to do four or five things at once drives them berserk. In brief, it's cops and robbers all the time with these two types.

Martials do somewhat better with Lunars, and in fact these two can be good friends if wise enough to take some precautions and cut each other some slack. Lunars cannot, and will not, be able to make rapid decisions and move as fast as Martials. And they won't try. In fact, the more Martials push and insist that Lunars do something, the more the Lunars will resist. But if Martials can remember to give Lunars plenty of time to make decisions, and plenty of space to be alone, they may get along famously. Martials won't be pushed, either, and are often loners, so even though the two types operate at different speeds, they have some basis for understanding each other. Since they are both negative types, they are likely to share a somewhat dim view of things— they both know for sure that the glass is half empty. So while Lunars will have nothing to do with it, and Martials plan to fill it up, they can enjoy playing "ain't it awful" in the meantime.

The Martial's chief feature is likely to be power or destructiveness, or a combination of both. If it is power, it will be of a different kind than the manipulative power of the Mercurial.

Martial power is more the sort that destroys anything that gets in its way. This may apply to many different situations. In dealing with objects, particularly if they have moving parts, Martials are likely to use more force and less attention than the situation warrants. Martials break things. They also break hearts sometimes, either through negligence and insensitivity or through their easily provoked anger. Their relationships can be destroyed by too much force just as their stuck windows can. Martials may also have the feature of lunatics. When their powerful drive and intense sex energy are directed at aims that are trivial or ignoble to the extent that they ignore the more important aspects of their lives, the Martials can become lost in this feature.

If you have a Martial in your life, you already know that it is not a calm and relaxed relationship. If you try to keep up with a Martial, you are likely to get exhausted. Furthermore, the Martial probably won't even notice your efforts, which will probably be rewarded with comments such as "Aren't you finished yet?" or "What's taking you so long? Can't you hurry it up?" Don't try to keep up. In the first place you won't be able to and will only be treated to Martial impatience. In the second place, Martials don't really want or expect you to keep up. They enjoy the work and get a lot of satisfaction from self-sufficiency. If your Martial husband is clearing land and building a cabin in the woods single-handedly on weekends, take along a deck chair, a good book, and some suntan lotion and relax. If your Martial wife is refinishing all the furniture, repainting the entire house, and sanding the floors, go on out and putter about in the garden, or better yet, go play golf so the activity and noise won't disturb you. Martials undertake their projects not out of virtue but out of necessity. They can't be still and relax, so you might as well do it for them. Somebody has to do it.

It isn't a good idea to try to convince a Martial not to do whatever she's doing. You'll just have a fight on your hands. If you disagree, and the issue is important to you, just state your case simply and calmly and clear out of the vicinity. Do not try to manipulate or use subterfuge. Martials respect directness and openness. They may not agree with you, but you will have their respect, their loyalty, and probably their consideration. The positive side of your relationship is that you can count on openness and honesty. You need never worry that the Martial is concealing anything.

If you have a Martial child, you will need to be especially vigilant when the child is young. You will probably have to get a special rate with your family doctor for stitches by the yard. Broken bones, cuts, and bruises are commonplace for this child, and probably can't be avoided. Save your energies for the really important matters, such as impressing on your little Martial that she must not run into the street without looking, or crawl out onto the roof of the house to try to reach her kite which got caught in a tree. You will never need to doubt your child's word. If he did something wrong, he will tell you. On the other hand, you may have a difficult time explaining tact and social graces to the Martial child. The best you may be able to do is impress upon her the virtues of silence as opposed to marveling over how many wrinkles her grandmother has or how fat the neighbor lady has become. You probably won't get anywhere urging the Martial to produce polite untruths. Try to find an acceptable truth for social situations and have your child practice. For instance, "Thank you for inviting me," is acceptable when leaving a party, since the Martial will not say he had a good time if he didn't. Martials are natural barbarians and need to be drilled in at least the bare minimum of manners. But don't try for more than an acceptable minimum, because anything more than that is unlikely and really not worth the effort.

The Martial type is usually admired when energies are directed toward goals that others believe to be of value, but they can be considered social outcasts or madmen when others do not understand their aims. Sometimes what others thought was lunacy at the time is in fact of enduring value. Such is the case with the art of Vincent Van Gogh. Van Gogh's life was turbulent and driven, which is not unusual for Martials, particularly before they find the cause or the leader that will channel their energies productively. Van Gogh was born in The Netherlands in 1853, the son of a clergyman. Three of his uncles were art dealers, and in his youth he worked for an art dealer for seven years but was dismissed for incompetence. In 1877 he went to Amsterdam to study theology but failed at that. He then entered an evangelical school in Brussels and became a missionary in a mining district in Belgium. Despite his intense religious feelings, he was unable to communicate his faith to the miners and their families. He lost his faith there, but found his art, taking his subjects from the coarse hard-working peasants of the region. From this period come such powerful studies of poverty as "The Potato Eaters."

He spent the winter of 1880–1881 in Brussels studying anatomy and perspective and living in poverty. He quarreled bitterly with his father over the issue of middle-class proprieties, and moved to The Hague where he had an affair with a woman of the lower class, as much to demonstrate that Christian charity should not be bound by traditional values as for the comfort of the relationship itself. In 1885–1886 he was in Antwerp, studying, living in the direst poverty yet, nearly starving to death. His health never really recovered from these years of privation and malnutrition that he endured while painting, painting, painting. No one among his friends or family or among the artistic community saw any merit or value in his work, but he continued.

Finally in 1886 he fled to his brother Theo in Paris. Theo had very little, and a family to support, but he did what he could to help. While in Paris, Van Gogh met Impressionist painters like Toulouse Lautrec, Gauguin, and Seurat. He was intensely involved in the artistic community, finding for the first time other artists whose work he understood and admired, but he had little patience with their theorizing and philosophizing. He wanted to paint, not talk about painting. Finally in 1888 he left to Arles, where the mild climate, less expensive living, and rural beauty allowed him to create the greatest of his paintings. Always he painted. Only one painting ever sold during his lifetime, and he received no encouragement from any but a very few other artists and from his brother, Theo, who continued to do his best to support him. Gauguin visited him in Arles. They had intended to live and work together, but could not get along. Van Gogh was not well, physically or psychologically, and Gauguin's presence and efforts to engage in conversation about sophisticated aesthetics only made him worse. It was during this period that the grisly incident of Van Gogh's cutting off his ear to send to a prostitute who had refused him occurred. Shortly after this he was committed to an asylum for treatment, but was unable to gain any equilibrium. His condition continued to worsen until his suicide in 1890.

There is in Van Gogh's life much that is typical of the Martial type. The intense single-mindedness of purpose, whether he was afire with religious inspiration or with artistic fervor, combined with the erratic and explosive temperament and inability to compromise or temporize are both attributes of the Martial, as are the violence and self-destruction. But it is his art that most reveals his type. Direct, almost brutal in its intensity, the energy writhes and blazes on the canvases. The paint was applied rapidly, frequently with a palette knife in thick swirls, almost flung onto the surface. The work he accomplished in barely over ten years, the sheer volume of it in addition to its brilliance, is evidence of a particular kind of genius, a Martial genius, that spared nothing, certainly not his own mind and body, in his drive for expression. Van Gogh's passionate love of light and color, of the transcendent beauty of the ordinary countryside, ordinary streets, ordinary rooms, common people are typical of the lack of pretension or sophistication of the Martial. Despite the lack of sales of his work, without the appreciation of any but a very few, he painted, day after day, week and month and year after year, until he almost literally burned himself out.

Martials may be difficult to bear, for themselves as much as for those around them, but when the work must be done—the fire put out, the sandbags filled, the battlements defended, the crops brought in—Martials step in to fulfill their destinies.

CHAPTER 15

THE JOVIAL TYPE

When considering whether someone might be a Jovial, look at the waistline. If there is one, the person is probably not a Jovial. Nothing is more typical of this type than the rounded forms of the body, particularly of the stomach. The Jovial type is large, frequently tall as well as portly or at least chubby. The Jovial's weight is carried high, which is one way to distinguish this type from the other fleshy type, the Venusian. Where the Venusian carries weight around the hips and thighs, the Jovial carries it in the chest and abdomen. Women of this type are usually large breasted and matronly looking even when young. Men can also be soft and fleshy in the shoulder, chest, and abdominal area. Jovials may, however, have quite thin legs for their bulk and thus appear out of proportion, like a ball balanced on matchsticks.

The Jovial's head is likely to be relatively large, and the hair thin. Jovial men frequently are bald, or have receding hairlines. Jovials may have difficulty with their vision and are likely to wear glasses or need contact lenses. Their skin is soft, and the contours of their faces rounded, with apple cheeks and small, round, and frequently pink noses. Jovials are likely to have high, even florid, coloring. This type perspires freely and easily becomes over-heated.

JOVIAL: The Jovial Type is passive and positive. That Jovials are positive is easily seen from their sunny nature and good humor. They have a harmonizing effect on others. That they are passive is not so easy to understand since they are very much involved with other people and with their own many projects. The passivity of Jovials is seen in their acceptance of their environment largely as it is rather than attempting to change it. The Jovial is a nurturing type which enjoys caring for people and usually has a number of dependents.

JOVIAL: The Jovial is a maternal type. Although Jovials are a passive, or feminine type, they are not currently the ideal for feminine beauty. Their fondness for rich foods and good wine combined with a tendency to carry their weight around the waist causes them to be more fleshy than willowy fashion models and movie stars. Jovials enjoy bright colors and rich fabrics and are likely to have extensive wardrobes of clothing appropriate for the many social events in which they revel. The chief feature of the jovial is likely to be vanity.

The Jovial likes bright colors and flamboyant costumes. Rembrandt, whose many self-portraits give vivid depictions of the archetypal Jovial, delighted in rich fabrics and draperies used to create costumes for his subjects or that he wore in his self-portraits. Jovial men, even when wearing conservative suits, are likely to choose a bright or contrasting colored shirt, and give full range to their penchant for startling hues and patterns in their choice of neckties. Jovial women love clothes, the more dramatic the better. Colors and textures and bright patterns delight them, and they like flowing styles that are both comfortable and good camouflage for their ample curves.

The planet thought to influence the large and colorful Jovial is the largest and most colorful of the planets—Jupiter. This distant giant is 500 million miles from the Sun with an orbit that takes twelve of our years to complete. Jupiter and its even-more-distant neighbor Saturn are very different from the four inner planets, Mercury, Venus, Earth, and Mars, which are called the terrestrial planets.

Even though it is very remote, Jupiter is brighter in our skies than any other planet except our closest neighbor, Venus. Although Jupiter is by far the largest planet in the solar system—more than twice as large as all the other planets together—it has the shortest axial rotation period: less than ten hours. This incredible speed produces enormous centrifugal force in the equatorial zone of Jupiter, which makes it bulge in the middle. This pronounced broadening of the center indicates that this planet cannot be solid in the same way that the terrestrial planets are. On the other hand, neither can Jupiter be considered only a shifting cloud mass, since some of its visual features are relatively constant.

Jupiter's most prominent markings are lines running straight across its colorful surface, appearing regular but actually composed of fine structures with brighter and fainter portions, spots, and divisions. Colorful spots are common on Jupiter, lasting for various periods of time, disappearing sometimes and then reappearing just as mysteriously. One of them, the Great Red Spct, has persisted for so many years that it is regarded as a semi-permanent feature although its color and visibility varies. The radio waves that Jupiter emits seem to be localized and to come from the zone which contains the Red Spot, although not from the Spot itself.

Jupiter has twelve satellites, more than there are planets in the solar system, although eight of them are quite small. Of the four largest satellites, two, Ganymede and Callisto, are larger than the planet Mercury while the other two, Io and Europa, are about the size of Earth's Moon. The outer satellites are very small. In fact with their erratic orbits—four go the wrong way—it may be that the junior moons are captured asteroids. Jupiter is not only the largest of our Sun's planets, but with its belts, spots, energy emissions, and retinue of satellites it is one of the most fascinating.

The gland in the human endocrine system that is thought to receive the influence of the planet Jupiter is the posterior pituitary. The two lobes of the pituitary, the posterior (which is dominant in the Jovial) and the anterior (which is dominant in the Saturn) are no larger than a medium-sized pea. Embryologically the two parts of the pituitary arise from different sources. The posterior lobe develops as an outpocketing of the hypothalamus, which is the deepest and smallest part of the brain and which integrates almost all higher functions. The anterior lobe, which meets and envelops the posterior as the fetus develops, differentiates from a structure in the roof of the mouth. The two parts of the pituitary have different cellular origins and quite different functions.

The two hormones associated with the posterior pituitary are vasopressin and oxytocin. These are produced by the hypothalamus and stored and released by the posterior pituitary. Oxytocin is associated with the smooth muscles of the inner body such as the intestines, bladder, and uterus. It also is released in nursing mothers to cause ejection of milk from the mammary glands, and is the hormone of maternal qualities. The other hormone stored and released by the posterior pituitary, vasopressin, serves as a antidiuretic, promoting water reabsorption. Vasopressin may also be involved in the control of blood pressure. Recent experiments indicate that both these hormones are involved with memory and learning. Clinical studies indicate that vasopressin improves concentration, learning, and memory. Both short-term and long-term memory were enhanced in a study with amnesia victims and elderly subjects, while long-term memory was improved in healthy subjects. Vasopressin is also involved in the development of avoidance behavior, and with the production of dopamine.

The maternal qualities of the Jovial type are among the most pronounced of the psychological characteristics of this type, which is not surprising given that the dominant gland secretes the hormones associated with childbearing. Whether the Jovial is male or female, with or without actual biological children, the tendency to protect, nurture, and feed others is strong. Jovial households have many guests, either for the parties and special occasions that Jovials are so good at organizing and presiding over or for more permanent residency. Jovials attract satellites as the planet Jupiter has done. Gregarious Jovials seem so active and involved in the lives of others that it is difficult to realize that they are a passive type. Their positive nature seems to keep them perpetually revolving in an endless round of interests and activities.

The Jovial's many interests frequently are centered in the arts. The depth and sensitivity of the Jovial mind and the creative impulses of this type produce writers, painters, musicians, and appreciative audiences and supporters for all the arts. Jovials seem to have been made to enjoy life and its many pleasures, and they seem to have a natural ability to avoid or ignore life's less pleasant aspects. It may be difficult to understand that this is a passive type, but never that this is a positive type.

Jovials can be very successful in business, particularly in businesses that involve discriminating tastes. They make excellent salespeople because they genuinely like and wish to help people. Jovials are highly motivated to succeed in business because the flamboyant extravagance that is typical of this type requires a substantial income. Jovials enjoy their possessions and they enjoy fine food and good wine. They have a hard time not buying lovely things, and frequently indulge their generous impulses, giving things away as gifts to friends and relations and inviting everyone for dinner. Where the other passive and positive type, the Venusian, would tell friends to help themselves, Jovials are more aggressive in their hospitality. Anyone spotted with an empty plate would quickly have that plate filled, and any empty glasses would soon be brimming. Jovials circulate among their guests tirelessly, urging one more helping of cake, one more drink for the road.

Jovials typically have as many different activities and pursuits as they have friends. Indeed, there may be a whole different set of friends for each interest: a writers' group for poetry, a choir for singing, a quilting circle for handcrafts, and of course the bridge club, and the children's hospital volunteers, and the Junior League, and the country club. Jovials may be involved in all of these activities, but not necessarily all at the same time. Just as the colorful features on the surface of the planet Jupiter appear and disappear mysteriously, so the interests of the Jovial type are subject to periodicity. Jovials may be intensely involved in a new interest for months, or even years. Then quite suddenly the interest wanes and the potter's wheel joins the puppet theater, the basket weaving supplies, the fencing mask, the terrarium, and the scuba diving gear that are all gathering dust in the attic. Any one of these activities may be taken up again at a later date, or it may not.

When the periodicity of the Jovial becomes too pronounced, it can result in indecisiveness, superficiality, and dilletantism. He will decide on Monday that he is going to quit his job and go into business for himself, on Tuesday that he will keep his job and write a novel in the evenings and on weekends, on Wednesday that he will take an early retirement and devote all his time to writing, and so on. Every new plan is seized upon as a firm aim—and every one changes before it is begun, remaining on the level of pipe dreams and hot air. But although it sometimes happens that the Jovial is little more than a windbag, more frequently this tendency is offset by a natural depth. Perhaps because the hormones of the posterior pituitary seem to promote learning and memory, the Jovial is frequently very good at learning languages and has well-developed verbal abilities. He can incorporate the experiences gained from his many activities into a harmonious and creative lifestyle. Many Jovials, such as Benjamin

Franklin, combine achievements in many different areas—states-manship, writing and publishing, scientific experiments and inventions, and diplomacy.

Harmonizing is one of the Jovial's greatest strengths. This type is very good at mediating disputes, arriving at mutually satis-factory agreements, reconciling differences of opinion. Jovials are frequently found in the roles of diplomats and ambassadors, smoothing the way for international agreements and treaties. Don't expect the Jovial to stay around when negotiations fail and hostilities begin, however. The Jovial has a very low tolerance for unpleasantness and negative situations, much less violence and ag-gression. The Jovial ability not to be around when the going gets tough is truly phenomenal. He will do everything in his power to keep things pleasant and civilized, but if he fails, he's out of there.

The typical weaknesses, or features, of the Jovial type are re-lated to their positive characteristics. Jovials with their natural ease of accomplishment in whatever area of interest is likely to be vain about their abilities. And an admiring circle of friends is likely to feed vanity or run the danger of no longer being invited to parties. Jovials may be very good at a number of things, but probably not quite as good as they think they are.

Jovial generosity may seem like a noble virtue, but some-times it isn't. The feature of mechanical goodness is another weakness typical of the Jovial type. In this increasingly unpleasant world, it may seem that any kind of goodness would be welcome, mechanical or not, but this is not actually so. The mechanical goodness of the Jovial is of the sort that keeps careful accounts of every favor, gift, or invitation offered. When you say to a Jovial friend, "I can't thank you enough," you may be right. The Jovial values himself very highly, and watches carefully to be sure his balance sheet of complicated accounts with friends and relations tallies out in his favor. If it doesn't, if someone has not recipro-cated for a gift or an invitation, the result may be resentment and vindictiveness.

Jovial generosity can also result in a type of power feature quite different from Martial destructive power or Mercurial ma-nipulative power. Jovial power is likely to manifest as a tendency to care for someone to the point they are overwhelmed by it, as characterized by the stereotype of the Jewish mother. This suffocating tendency to overfeed, overindulge, overprotect children and friends can make the solicitious Jovial oppressive to be around.

Characteristic abilities of the Jovial type include emotional sensitivity to people and the intellectual capacity for scholarship. Jovials make good teachers at all levels, from the ample-bosomed pre-school and kindergarten teachers who seem to have been designed to cuddle and comfort their young charges to the erudite graduate school professors whose depth of understanding and command of their disciplines can challenge the most brilliant students. Jovials are simultaneously aware of their students' needs and rigorous in their respect for the standards of their subject areas. Jovial teachers can be both kind and firm, understanding of difficulties students have but certain that it is in students' best interest to work hard and gain command of the skills or the materials being studied.

The Jovial parent also has a combination of warmth and discipline that comes from a genuine concern for the child's welfare both in the present and in the future. The Jovial's fondness for food and comfort may cause the child to be overfed, but the food will be good and nutritious, at least up until dessert. Jovial mothers will not only nurture their own children but are likely to take in the other children in the neighborhood as well, providing a place where they all like to play, have a brownie, do their homework together. The Jovial father is probably not very good at baseball, but he'll be in the yard playing catch with his child. He'll be willing to coach his son's or daughter's soccer team, making up in enthusiastic effort what he may lack in athletic ability.

Jovials also make excellent doctors and nurses. Again, the combination of the intellectual capacity required to master the rigorous training in math and science courses required for medical study and the sensitivity to people's needs that the healing professions require make Jovials well suited for these careers. Psychiatry and psychology are specialties at which Jovials excel, again because of the empathy and their genuine concern for others. And since medical careers usually pay quite well, Jovials are able to indulge themselves and their families in the luxuries they so appreciate.

Although Jovials have the intellectual capacity for research or scholarship in positions where they would be working alone, they probably would not be happy in positions where there is little interaction with others. Jovials have a need to be with people, and have little tolerance for solitude. They do not necessarily need a crowd of people—a small devoted family may ensure that their emotional needs are met. Isolation is anathema to Jovials.

Organizational ability is not the Jovial's strong suit. Jovials can be good managers because of their ability to work well with people and keep their subordinates satisfied, but they need someone else to design the flow charts and structure the work. Jovials tend to be too haphazard, and to value convenience and expediency over utility and efficiency. In other words, this is an area where it is clear that this is a passive type. Jovials will let events take their course without intervention—which is not going to result in clear organizational policies in business. Jovials hate to admit it, but they do better in middle management in companies where a Saturn handles the big picture.

Jovials do very well in politics. They are often given to intrigue, and are good in situations where horse trading and swapping favors can result in success. Their skill in effective speaking and persuasion serves them well in the political arena. At their best they can be statesmen who guide their nations skillfully— Winston Churchill and Nikita Kruschev are examples of Jovials who have guided great nations through perilous times in this century. They can fashion treaties that preserve the best interests of all concerned, and negotiate trade agreements that further the economic development of buyers and sellers alike. At worst Jovials in politics may succumb to the inducements of lobbyists, bartering the greater good for the pork-barrel benefits which will keep the smooth-talking Jovials in office.

Jovials are typically good cooks and may turn professional, becoming fine chefs or bakers. They like the restaurant business and can do very well if they stay away from the cooking sherry. They make good bartenders, too, but the Jovial fondness for food and drink can get them into trouble if habitual overindulgence leads to a problem with alcohol or to gastrointestinal disorders. It's a good idea for Jovials to be prudent in these areas because there are few creatures more miserable than Jovials on restrictive diets.

As is the case with any of the types, Jovial tendencies and interests, the careers they choose and the activities they participate in, are going to be governed by center of gravity as well as by type. The function that is dominant will interact with the characteristics of type to produce a particular set of proclivities and aversions, and these will determine lifestyle, job, hobbies, friends, mate, home, clothes—indeed, just about every minute detail of life is the result of the combination of type and center of gravity. When we look at the accomplishments of a Jovial like Benjamin Franklin, it is difficult to determine what his center of gravity might have been, except that it was almost certainly in the intellectual part of a center. His inventions and scientific experiments, and his success with the operation of printing presses suggests that he might have had his center of gravity in the intellectual part of the moving center, the king of spades. On the other hand, his diplomatic success and the breadth of political vision that made him one of the fathers of his nation suggest the intellectual part of the emotional center. Obviously not every Jovial attains the stature of a Benjamin Franklin, a Winston Churchill, a Mikhailo Lomonosov, a Rembrandt, Bach, or Beethoven, or the many other illustrious Jovials who have achieved fame in politics or the arts. Still, it is not unusual for Jovials to be very accomplished, and this frequently is the result of their operating from the higher parts of their functions.

Moving-centered Jovials may well be inventors. Perhaps their inventions will not have the significance of those of a Jovial like Thomas Edison, but they are nonetheless products of the same combination of boundless curiosity and the ability to synthesize information from different sources into new configurations and relationships. A Jovial I know has made a very successful small business, a specialty gift shop, from combining several popular items into a single product: teddy bears wearing period costumes and carrying dried flower bouquets. The Jovial's inventions may be trivial like this one, useful like a neighbor's seed planter modeled on a pastry wheel, or as earth-changing as the development of nuclear power. But whatever the importance of the things invented, the Jovial's eclectic interests and ability to synthesize ideas taken from different sources combined with the moving center's perceptions of spatial relationships are likely to produce developments in technology.

Even moving-centered Jovials may not have the excellent coordination required to be good athletes (and where Jovials do not excel they do not enjoy), but they are likely to be very good at games like chess and bridge which require the tactical ability of the moving center.

Instinctively-centered Jovials may be drawn to healthcare professions or to food-service employment. In either of these areas the Jovial pleasure in being around people combines with the concern of the instinctive center for physical well-being and comfort. Whatever their job, instinctively-centered Jovials are certain to be homebodies very attached to spouse and children, and probably a few more relatives as well. The instinctive emotions will be very strong in people who have this combination of mechanical tendencies.

Intellectually-centered Jovials are more likely to be drawn to the humanities or social sciences than to math and science. Philosophy or metaphysics, literary criticism or the history of ideas are disciplines likely to command the attention of the Jovial intellect. If the physical descriptions of Socrates are accurate, these combined with the accounts of his wandering the Agora in search of philosophical debate, almost certainly indicate an intellectually-centered Jovial on the loose in search of both ideas and companionship. Likewise, the chairmen of academic departments in colleges and universities—particularly departments of classics, languages, history, music, and philosophy—tend to include a much higher percentage of intellectually-centered Jovials than is found in the general population.

Of the Jovials I know personally, over half are emotionally-centered, and many of these are centered in the intellectual part of the emotional center, the king of hearts (the queen of hearts, the emotional part of the center, is also frequently encountered in Jovials). But whether there is some inherent tendency for this type to be emotionally-centered or not, there is definitely a tendency for emotionally-centered Jovials to be drawn to the arts. The self-portraits of many painters—Rembrandt being the most notable example—reveal Jovial countenances and Jovial paunches. And any concert goer who sits in the balcony has a bird's-eye view of all the shining Jovial bald heads of the musicians. Prolific writers of sprawling sentimental novels, Charles Dickens for example, are likely to be emotionally-centered Jovials.

Emotionally-centered Jovials might also be drawn to a religious life, although not a cloistered one. Ministers and parish priests, teaching and nursing nuns, are likely to include emotionally-centered Jovials in their numbers. The emotional center frequently is drawn to some spiritual way, and the Jovial type may express spirituality through service to others and membership in a congregation or community. Monastic discipline, however, would demand rather more asceticism than the Jovial would care to experience on a daily basis.

In their relationships with the other types, Jovials' harmonizing abilities make them popular and well-liked by almost everyone, so on the surface, at least, Jovials are able to maintain their cherished self-image as fine fellows who get along with everyone. Beneath that surface lie the preferences and aversions that are everyone's lot in human interactions. Of the other types, the Jovial's favorite is the quick, charming, child-like Mercurial. These two are maximum attractions, sharing many interests and abilities even though the Jovial is passive and positive while the Mercurial is active and negative. Both are likely to be talented performers who enjoy being in the spotlight, although in ways that complement rather than compete with each other. The quick wit and perceptiveness of the Mercurial is balanced by the greater depth and range of the Jovial. This combination is often seen in public, attending the opera or ballet, perhaps, or dining at the most elegant restaurants, the dapper, smartly dressed, trim Mercurial in attendance on the flamboyant, portly, and regal Jovial. They may be a married couple, business partners, or just good friends, but they enjoy each other's company immensely. Both are comfortable in what is basically a parent–child relationship whatever their actual connection.

Jovials also do fine with the other two negative types, Lunars and Martials. Since these types flank the Jovial on the enneagram, Jovials have 20 percent of each in their make up (the circulation and relative combinations of enneagram types will be discussed in greater detail in chapter 17, "The Enneagram") and are thus well-equipped to understand them both. Jovials do well in business partnerships with energetic Martials who can follow through on their expansive plans, work longer hours, and not have to deal directly with customers, suppliers, or others (the Martial lack of diplomacy can cause problems in business). Although Lunars would just as soon not go to all the Jovial's parties, they do seem relieved of their habitual gloominess in the presence of the Jovial cheerfulness, and of course since Jovials enjoy cheering people up Lunars are a challenge to them.

Jovials are not as drawn to the other positive types, possibly because they feel positiveness is their particular territory, possibly because Venusians and Saturns and Solars don't make appreciative audiences. The other parental type, paternal Saturns, have their own satellite system to control and little patience with someone not interested in their wise guidance, which the Jovial is not. Furthermore, the natural reserve and asceticism of Saturns does not endear itself to the outgoing and self-indulgent Jovials. Neither are vegetative Venusians likely to be amusing enough for the Jovials' fun-loving nature.

Jovials' homes reflect both their many interests and their extravagantly acquisitive tendencies. Jovials love to shop, and to shop for the pleasure of buying and owning, not just window shopping. As a result, Jovials are likely to be surrounded by a great profusion of belongings. They are great collectors, and enjoy displaying their collections for friends to admire and enjoy. Their eclectic interests may even cause Jovials to have collections

of collections, African artifacts, Turkish carpets, porcelain fig-
urines, rare books, crystal stemware, potted ferns in macramé
hanging baskets, all may crowd Jovial rooms, creating a feeling
more of claustrophobia than of comfort.

If you have a Jovial in your life, you can count yourself fortunate. The rewards of being a member of the Jovial's family or
entourage of friends are many. The Jovial is not only sympathetic
to your problems, but considers them to be her problems and will
not rest until they are solved. If you need a loan, a place to stay, a
job, the Jovial will either provide it or find someone among his
many friends who will provide it. The only payment the Jovial
ever wants is for you to be happy and perhaps just a little grateful
for his assistance. The Jovial thrives on admiration and affection,
so as long as you remember to supply these commodities, you can
count on a harmonious and extremely pleasant relationship.

The Jovial child is a joy to raise. From the placid infant coo-
ing in delight at the marvelousness of her own toes to the calm,
obedient, happy teenager surrounded by wholesome admirers
whom she helps with their homework, the young Jovial creates
harmony with the same naturalness that the young fish swims.
Like the child that's born on the Sabbath day, the Jovial is blithe
and bonny and good and gay. It is only natural for parents to indulge such a child with all the sweets and toys and clothes they
can possibly afford, but this is not the best policy. The one positive quality the Jovial child may lack is self-discipline, both in the
area of following through on projects he starts, and in the area of
overindulgence. The young Jovial is so pleased with the things
that are given to him, he makes it so pleasant to give him things,
that it is a difficult task for the parent to insist that the boy work,
either in doing chores around the house or in getting a part-time
job. After all, he does so well in school, brings home straight A's
on his report card, doesn't the boy deserve the car Dad wants to
buy him? Well, actually, his good grades come without any effort,
both because his studies are easy for him and because his teachers
enjoy having him in class. What he needs is not a car as much as
the discipline he would learn as he earned the money to buy the
car himself. The Jovial child already has many positive qualities as

a natural inheritance. If his parents can help him to learn discipline and perseverance, qualities which do not come naturally, he will have an unbeatable combination.

When this combination does occur, when the talent, intellect, and depth of the Jovial is combined with discipline and hard work, the result is sometimes a genius whose work enriches humanity. Johann Sebastian Bach was such a Jovial. Bach had musical ability as a genetic inheritance when he was born into the family of a court musician in Eisenach, Germany in 1685. He came from seven generations of musicians, and had uncles, cousins, and brothers who were organists in nearby churches. Bach came by his discipline out of necessity. His parents died within a year of each other in his 10th year, and he went to live with an older brother, earning his keep by copying music manuscripts. He was interested in the harmonic structure underlying the melodies he copied, and also studied Greek at the cloister school.

In March of 1700, the 15-year-old Bach walked 200 miles with a fellow student to attend a school for young noblemen which had a curriculum of courtly dancing, fencing, riding, feudal law, politics, and history. He was able to sight read music and supported himself by singing and playing the organ.

Although music was the area of his genius, the way he earned his living from an early age until the end of his life, and the reason he is remembered—and of course musical ability is not unusual for a Jovial—the characteristics of his type can be seen in many other areas of his life. The portraits of Bach show the typical Jovial rounded forms of the countenance. He was a man with intelligent eyes, cheerful disposition, and a kind face. Because gentlemen of that period wore wigs, there is no way to tell whether he was bald, but I bet he was. Bach never ceased creating music, but the Jovial tendency toward periodicity may have been behind the many different positions he held and the different types of music he composed. Even though his patrons let him go only unwillingly, when Bach became interested in a different way of working, he would gather up his family and go. On one occasion he was granted a one month leave of absence from Arnstadt to hear the great organist Buxtehude play, and was so enchanted he stayed away for four months, to the considerable consternation of his employer.

Bach had a large family for which he was provider and devoted husband and father. He married twice. In 1707 he married his second cousin, Maria Barbara, and shortly thereafter moved with her to Weimar where he became the court organist. The Bachs had six children at Weimar in the ten years they lived there. In 1717 Prince Leopold of Köthen appointed Bach court composer, a position which allowed him to create as he saw fit. These years produced the "Brandenburg Concerti" and the "Well-Tempered Clavier," but also grief over the death of a young son and of his wife. A year later, in 1721, he married 20-year-old Anna Magdalena. She bore him thirteen children, but seven died in infancy. All in all, Bach had twenty children, half of whom survived to adulthood.

Bach spent the last twenty-seven years of his life in Leipzig occupying one of the most famous cantorships in Germany. Whether Jovial vanity was a factor in his decision or not, he received much less pay for this position than he had received as a court musician for the nobility. The position did, however, fulfill many requirements besides that of fame. As cantor of the school his position allowed him to enroll his own sons and thus ensure that they received excellent educations—three of his sons also became musicians and composers of merit. Bach was also a teacher at the school. He would call the boys for classes at 6:00 A.M., teach several classes, and in the evening say prayers with his teenaged students at 8:00 P.M. Since Leipzig was not a court but an imperial free city, Bach was musician for the town as well. On alternate Sundays he played the organ for St. Thomas and St. Nicholas churches and provided music for two other churches as well.

Under the burden of his heavy work load, which frequently caused him to work far into the night, his eyesight gradually failed so that he was almost blind by the end of his life. He died in 1750 after suffering two strokes.

Bach loved life, his family, music, and God. His faith was such that he believed all music was a gift from God and its purpose was to glorify Him. He made no distinction between the cheerful dances and secular music and the joyful church music he composed—it was all for the glory of God.

No type is more likely to produce genius than any other, but it is about the lives of men of genius that we have the most information. Students of human types are thus able to determine with fair accuracy what type such a man as Johann Sebastian Bach might have been. In this instance there can be little doubt that he was a splendid example of the finest qualities of the Jovial type with a minimum of the weaknesses.

CHAPTER 16

THE SOLAR TYPE

The Solar is the most attractive of all the human types, with a delicate other-worldly beauty that frequently seems too refined for this coarse planet and the other humans who live on it. Quite tall, slender, and fine-boned, the Solar is gracefully proportioned with level shoulders, tapering waist, small hips, and long legs.

Solars frequently have dark hair that frames their finely chiseled features and pale, almost translucent skin. Descriptions of fairy-tale princesses—skin as white as snow, cheeks as red as blood, hair as black as ebony—seem to be descriptions of the Solar type. Their eyes are large and expressive, with long lashes and dark eyebrows. The faces are oval, sometimes heart-shaped, with well-defined cheek bones and brows. The neck is long and slender. Solars often have an androgynous appearance, the men lacking pronounced masculine characteristics and the women having a boyish, gamin charm.

Unlike the other types, Solars do not have a fixed place on the enneagram of types, and thus may combine with any of the other types and share some of the other types' physical characteristics, such as hair color or height. Still, the solar influence usually results in clear, fine skin through which the veins can be seen, large, wide-set expressive eyes, and a generally more refined appearance.

The celestial body which influences the Solar type is the Sun. The Sun is, of course, a star rather than a planet. The Solar therefore receives influences from an entirely different order of existence. In our solar system, the Sun is the origin of life. Its energy is all the energy we know on Earth, where nothing could exist without the Sun. In a very real sense the Sun is existence. It stands in relationship to the planets as a higher order, a god if you will.

A star such as the Sun is a burning sphere of gas. It gets its heat from a nuclear furnace at its core where temperatures and pressures are great enough to sustain nuclear fusion. In the Sun's core hydrogen atoms are transformed to helium, about five billion kilos of them per second, with a release of energy that works its way out to the surface. Beneath the surface, hidden from view, the energy is turbulent and interacts with solar magnetic fields to produce various patterns and sunspots.

The Sun's diameter is nearly one hundred times greater than Earth's, and ten times greater than Jupiter's. The Sun is almost entirely energy. Like fire, it has little substance. The outer areas, corona and chromosphere, are so diffuse they would be called a vacuum here on Earth. Even the next layer, the photosphere, is as rarefied as the uppermost atmosphere of Earth where spacecraft operate. As the Sun's interior is penetrated the density increases, but not until one tenth of the way to the center is it as dense as the air we breathe. Not until half way to the center is there anything as dense as water.

One of the most dramatic perceptions about the Sun to result from the many space probes and orbiting laboratories sent up in the space program, is that in a very real physical sense, we are in it. Earth, as well as the rest of the solar system, lives and moves and has its being in the Sun. Distances we talk about, such as Earth being 93 million miles from the Sun and Jupiter being 500 million miles from the Sun and so forth, are calculated in relationship to that part of the Sun that humans see. And, as noted above, even that is incredibly diffuse. What the space probes, with their cameras that took pictures of wavelengths other than those of the light spectrum our eyes register, discovered was that mater-

SOLAR: The Solar Type is active and positive. This is a childlike type, with delicate bone structure, fine skin and hair, large expressive eyes, and boundless enthusiasm. The most positive of the types, solars have few negative perceptions and therefore may not take good care of their instinctive needs. The dominant gland of the Solar is the thymus, the gland that governs growth in children and usually atrophies after puberty. The chief feature of the Solar Type is likely to be naiveté.

ial from the Sun keeps right on radiating out, permeating the entire solar system. Solar Wind blows right past the Earth (interacting with particles in its atmosphere to create visible phenomena like the Aurora Borealis) to the end of the solar system, out beyond Pluto. Out there, way out there, the Solar Wind merges with interstellar winds composed of particles streaming out from other stars in the galaxy. It is all connected—materially and energically connected.

Exactly what the nature of the connection between the celestial bodies and the endocrine glands might be has not even been hypothesized yet. Neither was the existence of Solar Wind hypothesized fifty years ago. Things become curiouser and curiouser. If there is such a connection between the great spheres whirling through space and the glands in the human body, then the gland we suppose the Sun to control is the thymus.

The thymus gland lies behind the breastbone. It is quite large in infants and continues to grow until right before puberty. It then begins to shrink until it is quite small in most older adults. This gland produces hormones known as thymosins, the action of which is not completely understood. Too much or too little thymosin in the body is believed either to cause disease or to allow diseases to be contracted. The thymus gland is also one of several locations in the body where lymphocytes are produced. These cells form an important part of the body's immune system, and the thymus is believed to be the ultimate controller of this system. As research intensifies in an attempt to bolster the immune system against the AIDS virus, we can expect to know a great deal more about this gland and its hormones.

Thymosins also seem to affect a child's growth, and to be responsible for a child's delicate skin, fine hair, and clear eyes. It is thought that in the Solar type the action of the thymus gland does not cease as early as it does in most people, so that Solars retain certain aspects of the physical delicacy and psychological innocence, or naiveté, of children.

The Solar type seems to have many of the psychological characteristics we associate with children. Solars seem to live in a fairy tale world of magical possibilities long after others have accustomed themselves to the harsher aspects of reality. They don't seem to recognize limitations, not their own, not other people's, and not even the limitations imposed by impersonal forces like weather or economic conditions. Of all the types, the Solar is least suited to life on this planet. I mentioned that of all the types Venusians seemed the most comfortable and well-suited to the Earth, perhaps because Venus is the planet most similar to Earth in many respects. Solars are the least comfortable here, and certainly it would be hard to imagine more different spheres than Earth and Sun. Solars do not feel at home here, and others do not feel comfortable around them. Solars are beautiful, but their beauty is artificial rather than sensuous. They seem like fine porcelain, or exquisite enamel work rather than flesh-and-blood humans.

The delicacy of Solars extends beyond appearance. Their health is fragile as well. In childhood Solars are likely to be sick more than other children. Many Solars die young, unable to withstand the rigors of life on our rather inhospitable planet. Their immune systems do not seem to ward off disease as effectively as the immune systems of the other types.

Not only is the instinctive function weak in Solars, but the other functions seem unbalanced as well. In each center, or type of intelligence—the instinctive, moving, intellectual, and emotional centers—the negative parts of the centers seem underdeveloped. As mentioned in discussions about the differences between positive and negative halves of centers and how they may differ in positive and negative types, one part or the other may be more developed. In the negative types (Martials, Mercurials, and Lunars) the negative halves of centers seem to be more fully developed. These types receive more impressions on the negative parts of centers. Positive types (Jovials, Venusians, Saturns, and Solars) receive more impressions on the positive parts of centers. In other words, with exactly the same impression perceived by the optic apparatus, for example, a well-dressed and attractive young woman, the positive type is likely to react by thinking, "How nicely her blouse goes with that suit," while the negative type is thinking, "Too bad she has a run in her stocking to ruin everything." But while the discrepancy between the way positive and negative types experience the world is large, with the Solar type the discrepancy seems enormous.

With Solars, the negative parts of centers are extremely un-derdeveloped. The practical result of this is that Solars are not able to estimate the negative aspects of a situation. What a person cannot, or does not, perceive does not exist as far as that person is concerned. In this way, also, Solars are like little children. The dif-ference is that children are innocent because of a lack of experi-ence while Solars are innocent because negative experiences seem not to register or be remembered in the same way they reg-ister and are remembered by other types.

In their thinking, Solars favor Utopian theories. They may be drawn to studies of metaphysics and philosophy, or they may espouse programs of social change predicated on idealistic visions. Solars embody the attitude of Don Quixote. Unable to accept, or even accurately to perceive, the real world of drudgery, coarse-ness, and brutality, Solars live in a fairy-tale world of infinite possibilities. Any vulgar barmaid could be a princess in disguise—and the Solar might marry her on that assumption. Any oppor-tunistic swindler could be the mentor who will provide eco-nomic success—and the Solar will probably buy the unseen swampland. Any charlatan peddling mystical visions could be the Avatar—and the Solar will join the cult and be a loyal follower.

In the emotional function, too, the Solar frequently fails to detect when others are insincere or selfish. It is not at all unusual for Solars to choose their friends unwisely, and to get into serious trouble because of it. They go along with gang activities and end up on the wrong side of the law (and Solars are not cunning enough not to get caught). Or they are themselves the victims of supposed friends who steal from them or cheat them in business. Solars are likely to marry unwisely, either selecting mates who brutalize them emotionally and sometimes physically, or marrying other Solars who have no idea how to live practically either.

Solars, like the Sun, seem to be almost pure energy. With this very high energy level, this type will work extremely hard, or play extremely hard, with no sense of when it is necessary to rest.

Solars can be highly focused in their aims, and intense, indeed obsessional, in their pursuit of those aims. They are not distressed when their implausible schemes do not work, at least not to the extent that others would be, and are soon engaged full tilt in the next, usually equally implausible, project.

Sometimes, to the astonishment of those who scoffed, the Solar's projects and schemes do work. Since any successful endeavor, whether in the arts, in business, in government, or wherever, is likely to be the result of prodigious efforts, the Solar's determination and hard work can pay off. Solars attempt things no one else would be foolish enough to try. They start businesses that are so ridiculous they couldn't possibly succeed, try ideas for products no one would think of buying. Teenage Mutant Ninja Turtles? How stupid can you get? I don't know, how rich can you get? This is the sort of idea that has a suspicious whiff of Solar psychology about it. And of course Solars live on this kind of success story the way they live on chocolate. For every Norma Jean who is transformed into a Marilyn Monroe (and never mind how tragic her life actually was) there are millions who know every detail and fully expect that they will experience the same magical transformation and be adored by the whole world.

The Solar can forget about time, about meals, about dressing appropriately for the weather. In the grip of enthusiasm for one of her projects, the Solar stays up until 1:00 A.M. working on the presentation she plans to give to the finance committee in the morning. Then she's up at 5:30 and out at 6:00—no time for breakfast—to get to the office by 7:00 to get the slides organized in the carousel and check out the slide projector so everything will go smoothly. It does, and the finance committee is so impressed she's given the go ahead for the project. This means she'll have to work nights and weekends to get everything coordinated. No time for lunch so she gets a Snickers bar from the candy machine. She works late—no time for dinner—and doesn't get home until after midnight.

The next day her schedule is about the same, except that it looks so sunny she doesn't wear her coat to work. It starts to rain in the afternoon and is still pouring when she goes home, so of course she gets soaked. The following day, about 4:00 in the afternoon, she collapses—high fever, pounding headache, miserable sore throat. She leaves work early and is flat on her back for the following two days. And so it goes.

One curious result of underdeveloped negative parts of centers is that Solars do not understand jokes, and frequently do not know what other people are laughing at. I remember being in a taxi in Rome with a Solar and another friend. The traffic was intense, and our driver was weaving in and out between other cars at about 60 miles per hour. "Boy," my other friend said, "this guy doesn't take hostages." We both laughed, and the Solar just looked perplexed. "But that would be a good thing, wouldn't it?" he asked, "Not to take hostages?" I explained that someone who didn't take hostages was understood to have killed everyone.

Of course, no joke is funny when it's explained, because humor doesn't work that way. We laugh when an impression falls on two parts of centers simultaneously—the momentary confusion caused by something perceived as positive and negative at the same time results in a sudden release of energy: laughter. For the Solar there is very little negative part of either the intellectual or emotional center for the impression to fall on, so they do not see when things are "funny." There is a long tradition in vaudeville and stand-up comedy in which the straight man—or frequently the dumb blonde—is the person who does not understand a situation and asks questions which the comedian can respond to with amusing lines. George Burns and Gracie Allen exploited this format for years on American radio, and many television situation comedies have milked laughs from a Solar character who does not understand what is going on.

The chief feature, or weakness, of the Solar is this naiveté. This feature does not learn from experience. Having gone out in the rain without a coat and wearing summer sandals, the Solar catches a bad cold and spends time in bed recuperating. This could happen once to anyone at the change of seasons. But it happens to the Solar over and over. Each sunny morning seems to the Solar like a guarantee of clear sunny skies all day long. Just because it has turned rainy and cold in the afternoon every day for two weeks does not make the Solar think that the same thing might happen again.

The Solar will take a short cut through streets where it is not safe to walk at night, witness a purse snatching, and take the same short cut the next night. The Solar will open a boutique selling silk blouses in a factory district, go bankrupt, and open a similar shop three blocks away. I once saw a young Solar run to get behind a car that was rolling backward down a hill with the intention of stopping it with his hands and arms. Fortunately the car had not gathered much momentum yet and another man was able to rush in and push the Solar out of the way before he was seriously hurt.

A feature like naiveté can seem harmless and even charming. It may be difficult at first to understand how this innocence can be a negative characteristic. The negativity in this case comes as a delayed reaction. It is the after effects of naiveté that can clearly be seen as negative. The Solar is frequently depicted as the romantic hero or heroine of film and fiction. Charming, beautiful, fragile, and endearing, these figures burn the candle at both ends, dance in the light of bursting shells as the enemy takes the city, and die young. The audience has a good cry at how tragic it all is and goes home to pay the babysitter and take out the trash.

As a matter of fact the Solar frequently does die young. The reason may be a weakened constitution after years of appallingly bad eating habits. It may be a serious disease that the immune system is not able to ward off. Or the reason may be suicide. It may seem a paradox that this extremely positive type would be the one most likely to commit suicide, but that is the case nonetheless.

Solars experience a sense of loneliness, a feeling of not belonging, not fitting in. Solars really don't seem to belong. In spite of the hours they spend before their mirrors trying to look perfect, in spite of the incredible amounts of energy they spend trying to achieve success in this endeavor or that, they remain different without quite knowing why. They are not comfortable here. They actually seem to be made of finer clay than other types. Another factor in the Solar's loneliness is that this type does not have a maximum attraction. There is no other type or types that the Solar is particularly drawn to. All other types have these strong affinities—which may cause them all manner of heartache and difficulty but nonetheless keep them interested in their lives. Solars don't have this, neither the joy nor the suffering that can be the result of passionate love or deep friendship. They know only emotional shallowness and mourn the lack of deeper attachments.

Solars seem most comfortable in the company of other Solars. They frequently marry each other or associate in groups devoted to fanciful pursuits such as Renaissance fairs or New Age religions or herbal healing. Indeed, it is likely that Solars find what other types might term "everyday living" or the "ordinary world" no less whimsical than the above-mentioned activities. When we consider how much we determine what is good by our understanding of what is bad, and how we recognize truth by contrasting it with falsehood or error, and how we sense what is pleasant and wholesome because of our experience with what is unpleasant and corrupt, we may get a glimpse of the Solar's predicament. A life without strong contrasts, even when those contrasts are painful, is shallow and superficial.

Because of their penchant for fantasy, and because they are usually attractive and frequently talented, Solars are drawn to the entertainment industry. Lacking a sense of belonging, Solars enjoy assuming different roles. With their high energy level and drive to succeed, they have no difficulty committing to long hours of rehearsals and demanding performance schedules—at least they have no trouble until they drive themselves beyond the limits of their endurance and turn to artificial stimulation in the form of alcohol or drugs to keep going. The entertainment industry is known for the high incidence of alcoholism, drug use, and emotional instability among its performers, but whether this is because the pressures of the work are actually greater than in other occupations or because of the high percentage of Solars in this line of work is not clear.

Whatever their occupations, Solars are ambitious, frequently seeming to be driven workaholics in their determination to achieve success. Perhaps this is their way of proving that they do belong, or perhaps they cannot conceive of anything less than the greatest accomplishments, the magical fairy-tale happily-ever-after conclusion to their endeavors.

If you have Solars in your life, you had better resign yourself to the role of caretaker and disciplinarian, even if these Solars are not children. This effort to help regulate Solars' lives is not easy, since Solars can have a strong power feature in addition to their naiveté. This means that not only do they have hare-brained ideas, but they are grimly determined to carry them out. As long as their projects are not actually life-threatening, you probably will have no alternative but to go along with them. The caretaking will consist of seeing that the Solars have nutritious meals at fairly regular intervals. They should eat plenty of protein, even though they won't want to, because their extremely rapid metabolism requires good fuel. Proteins and the complex carbohydrates, because they metabolize slower than sugars, do not provide energy fast enough for Solars because they will wait until they are famished before they even notice that they are hungry. This type would live on chocolate if they were making the choices. You will therefore need to supervise your Solars' habits of eating—and dressing warmly enough and getting enough sleep—just as you would a child's.

This necessity for seeing that the Solar's instinctive requirements are tended to can be extremely annoying. Most adults feel that other adults should take care of their own basic needs, and that it is the individual's business when and what to eat, whether or not to wear a jacket, when to go to bed, and so forth. Most people find the Solar's lack of common sense to be irritating, particularly when it results in frequent illnesses which in turn result in missing work or neglecting responsibilities. The patience and understanding that living with a Solar requires can be a heavy burden.

If you have a Solar child you can resign yourself to seeing a lot of your pediatrician, and spending a lot of sleepless nights taking temperatures, administering medications, and filling vaporizers. All children catch some colds and get some childhood illnesses, but Solars get them all—and usually have a host of allergies as well. The best training the Solar child can have is in forming good healthy habits. Instruction in proper nutrition, appropriate dress, and adequate sleep schedules needs to be undertaken intentionally and thoroughly. You cannot count on Solar children to settle into healthy instinctive rhythms on their own. Most children fall into natural patterns—they are hungry at meal times and tired at bed time. Solar children may not. They may need a great deal more parental instruction and supervision. Solars may have to be taught, and even nagged, to eat regularly just as other children have to be taught, and even nagged, to pick up their toys. It may be a good idea to keep a regular feeding schedule all through childhood and adolescence rather than relying on hunger to keep them eating sufficient quantities of the right foods at frequent intervals.

You won't be able to assume that because your child has had a painful experience falling out of the apple tree or off the fence that she won't go right back out and try the same thing again. Indeed, in many areas where most children could be expected to learn from experience, you may need to provide specific training in forming correct habits or following safe procedures. Just remember that Solars do not have the same capacity for understanding negative circumstances that others have. Because your Solar child is delicate, you may be tempted to over protect her and not require as much of her. Remember, however, that eventually she will be on her own, and that the formation of good habits of caring for herself is going to be extremely important. The Solar doesn't understand the idea of making efforts, so if at least some energy can be channeled into the continuing project of taking care of him or herself, difficulties in young adulthood may be avoided. At least it is the parents' duty to try.

It is not, unfortunately, at all difficult to find examples of Solars who achieved great things and then either died young or spent the rest of their lives in miserable circumstances. Geniuses who die in their 20s after producing prolific works are quite likely Solars. The English poet John Keats certainly had the refined sensibilities and delicate health of the Solar type, as did

Mozart, whose music is so light and ethereal that even the villains in his operas—like the Queen of the Night in "The Magic Flute"—sing arias of incredible beauty that have no tinge of negative qualities even though the character is supposed to be threatening.

In the middle years of the 20th century, a Solar film actress, Judy Garland, lived such a life, and left the legacy of dozens of films which provide a visual record of the typical Solar beauty, talent, wistfulness, and fragility. When she was born, in 1922, she was named Frances Ethel Gumm by parents who managed a movie theater in a Midwestern city. The fantasies of Hollywood were a part of her early childhood, and she and her sisters sang in the theater during intermission to entertain the audiences. A local agent took an interest in the girls and suggested that Garland would be a more romantic name than Gumm, so Judy Garland was created, a fantasy name for a fantasy creation.

One of the most interesting aspects of Judy Garland's life is how little of it there actually was outside of the films she made—the fantasy is the reality. Her childhood and early adolescence were spent in the most grueling training. Her parents moved to California where she could have the intensive education and coaching in singing and acting that would develop her talents and the best opportunities to be noticed by those in power in the entertainment industry. Her big break came with the song "You Made Me Love You" which she sang while playing the part of a young girl infatuated with Clark Gable in the film *Broadway Melody*. Her childlike wistfulness in combination with a strong and versatile singing voice made her a star. She was young, but she looked even younger. She played the part of the child, Dorothy, in *The Wizard of Oz* in 1939 when she was already 17 years old. She made twenty films during the 1940s playing child parts in many of them, such as the Hardy Boys series with Mickey Rooney and *Meet Me in St. Louis*.

Meanwhile, Judy Garland's private life, which was not at all private but was played out in the light of glaring publicity, was erratic and unhappy. She married several times. During the height of her film career in the '40s she married musician David Rose and later director Vincent Minelli. Her daughter Liza Minelli, also a Solar who became a successful film actress and singer, was born in 1947. (Liza Minelli played the part of an archetypal Solar heroine in the film *Cabaret*.) By 1949 Judy Garland was so deeply involved in the use of alcohol and barbiturates that the film studio she worked for, MGM, sent her to Boston Hospital for treatment. In 1950 she made a much-publicized suicide attempt.

During her later years the publicity about her personal problems plagued her efforts at a come-back. She had an adoring cult following, but her voice was failing and the years of hard work and chemical abuse had taken their toll. She was no longer the wide-eyed innocent child she had portrayed in films, although that fantasy child is in one sense virtually immortal. The woman who was Judy Garland lived an increasingly desperate and lonely life, going from husband to husband and country to country. She married her fifth husband three months before her death in London in 1969 from an overdose of barbiturates.

The Solar type is so different from the other six types in so many ways that it isn't clear whether this really is a separate body type. Certainly there are clear characteristics and tendencies, both physically and psychologically, which differentiate the Solar as a distinct type. But because this type does not have its own place on the enneagram and does not fit into the circulation of the enneagram, it is definitely an anomaly. It might be more accurate to consider the Solar influence to be an adjunct that may attach to any of the other types.

When I discuss the circulation of the enneagram types, which I will do in the next few chapters, it will be with the understanding that any of the classic or pure types and any of the combined types might combine with the Solar. Of course there really cannot be any such thing as a "pure" type since every healthy human being has all of the endocrine glands functioning or would not continue to live. The types are created by the relative dominance or activity of a particular gland or glands, not by the absence of the functioning of other glands.

Those individuals in whom the thymus gland evidently is more active than normal in childhood, and in whom it continues to function rather than atrophying as it does in most people, will also have another type to which the Solar influence is added in greater or lesser degree. It is possible, therefore, that a particular person might be a Solar-Lunar, or a Solar-Saturn, or a Solar-Jovial, or a Solar combined with one of the combined types such as Venus-Mercury. The Solar influence imparts a lighter and more intense energy and a more refined appearance to the characteristics of the other type, whatever it is.

When the Solar influence combines with one of the negative types, particularly with the passive negativity of the Lunar or the coarseness of the Martial, the result can be a useful balancing by the active positive energy. Both of these types, Lunars and Martials, need to lighten up and the Solar influence accomplishes exactly that. The combination of the Solar with the Mercurial type is not quite as fortuitous since the Mercurial energy is already intense, and to add the Solar intensity to the already spinning Mercurial is a bit too much.

Solars combine well with any of the other positive types, providing they are grounded solidly enough in practical reality not to be too much affected by the ding-a-ling factor of Solar naiveté. Again, the main effect is a refining of appearance and an intensifying of energy. These are attributes that Venusians certainly profit by, and the refinement of the Solar in combination with the sensuality of the Venusian can be an astonishingly beautiful combination—film stars such as Clark Gable and Elizabeth Taylor are probably such a mixture. Saturns gain a higher level of activity to counteract their sedentary ways when combined with Solar, and Jovials profit from the increased metabolic rate which diminishes some of their curves.

Perhaps the Solar influence should be seen more as a seasoning to the human stew rather than a main dish in itself.

CHAPTER 17

THE ENNEAGRAM

As you read the descriptions of the physical and psychological characteristics of the seven classic endocrine types, you quite likely were able to think of acquaintances, co-workers, friends, or family members who exemplify particular types. Perhaps you have some ideas about what your own type might be—or at least about what it probably is not. But then you may look around and think, "What about all these others?" There are classic examples of the seven human types, lots of them, and they help in beginning the process of verifying the accuracy of this system, but there are many other people who don't seem to fit any of the descriptions. If there are only seven basic types, how can this be?

To understand the bewildering variety of human beings, we need to have at least some understanding of the strange esoteric symbol that Gurdjieff used—the enneagram. As mentioned earlier, the enneagram, which is probably of Sufi origin, is currently experiencing a vogue. It is being used in systems of classifying personality traits, systems that seem little more than lists of nine items arranged at equidistant points around the outside of a circle. This popularization of the symbol makes it difficult to discuss, but since it is the symbol that best explains some of the most difficult aspects of determining type, there really is no choice.

To begin with, enclosed in the circle of the classic ennea-gram are two figures, not one. An equilateral triangle inscribes the circle, with its apex at the uppermost point. This triangle is static, without circulation. While the three points on the circum-ference of the circle which are touched by the angles of the tri-angle have significance in many of the uses to which the ennea-gram may be put in explaining esoteric ideas, they do not concern us here. We are concerned only with the other figure, a polygram, which touches the circumference of the circle at the six other points. The lines which connect these six points are seen as circulating, the movement flowing in one direction. The direction of the movement can be charted by following the nu-merical progression obtained by dividing the prime number seven into one: $1 \div 7 = .1428571428571$, etc.

If we number the nine points where the inner figures of the enneagram touch the outer circle by placing the number 9 at the top and the other numbers in their sequence around the circle clockwise, the result is the pattern seen in figure 2 (page 259). The Lunar type is at position 1. From there the circulation goes to the Venusian type at position 4, then back up to the Mercurial type back at position 2. Here the movement crosses to the Satur-nine type at position 8, drops to the Martial type at position 5, goes back up to the Jovial type at position 7, and returns to posi-tion 1, the Lunar type. The Solar type, as has already been men-tioned, is not a part of the circulation of the enneagram but can combine with any of the other types.

A particular human being may be located at any point along the continuum formed by the circulating lines of the six-pointed figure in the enneagram. That is, at birth an infant's endocrine balance may be set at exactly the point where the angles of this figure touch the circumference of the circle—and thus be a good example of one of the classic types. Or, what is much more likely, the person may be located somewhere along a line that is con-necting two types. This person would have characteristics of both of the types. The types do not combine at random, however. Each person is located at some exact point along the lines con-necting the types. One might be a Lunar-Venusian type, or a

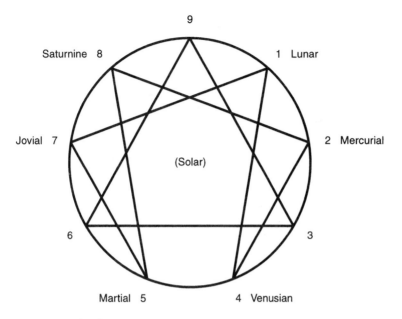

Figure 2. The classic enneagram.

Mars-Jovial type, for example, but could not be a Jovial-Mercurial because there is no connecting line between these types on the enneagram figure. To further complicate the possible combinations, the Solar type, which is not located at any specific point on the enneagram, can combine with any type or any combination of two other types. It is therefore possible that a person could be a Solar-Jovial, or a Solar-Jovial-Lunar.

When types combine, it means that the person will have some manifestations from one type and some from the other. In other words, there could be two of the endocrine glands which are equally active and thus the hormonal messages carried by the blood could be stimulating quite different responses—but not simultaneously. The psychology of such a person will therefore be more complex, and probably more baffling, than that of a classic type. When the coolness of the Lunar type is combined with the warmth of the Venusian, the result is not a lukewarm person. It is a person who will sometimes respond with cool resistance and sometimes with warm acceptance, depending on many factors both internal and external.

Of course all healthy humans have all of the endocrine glands, and so to some extent contain all of the types, just as we possess all four of the functions. The more balanced and the more aware we are able to become, the more we will recognize in ourselves all human possibilities—and all human limitations. The efforts we make to observe ourselves and others and to increase our consciousness of our actual condition can increase the ability to respond in ways that are appropriate to whatever situation we are in, rather than reacting mechanically from our type and center of gravity. But first we need to observe and understand the types as they function around us and in us.

If a person is of a classic type, located on the enneagram where the angle of the six-pointed figure touches the outer circle at, for instance, Jovial (position 7), that person responds as a Jovial 40 percent of the time. That is to say, the posterior pituitary is the most active gland and its hormones vasopressin and oxytocin are relatively more prevalent in the blood. This person also has 20 percent Martial and 20 percent Lunar responses since these are the two types to either side of Jovial on the enneagram. Therefore adrenaline would sometimes cause a flash of Martial impatience from the usually calm and harmonizing Jovial, and sometimes the Lunar's willfulness might appear. Only 5 percent of each of the four other types, Venusian, Mercurial, Saturnine, and Solar, would be included in this person's psychological makeup (figure 3, page 261).

Being aware of characteristics of the two types on either side of the dominant type can help in identifying the classic types. Both of the passive and positive types, as discussed earlier, tend to be quite large and fleshy. Thus it can be difficult to tell whether people are Jovial or Venusian until you have had an opportunity to observe them over a period of time. I once was speaking with such a woman, who was also working with this system, and asked her what type she thought she was. She said that she was certain

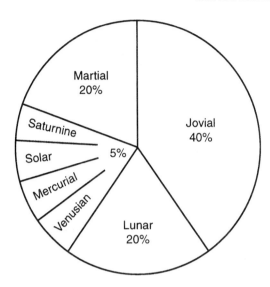

Figure 3. Proportional representation of a classic Jovial type.

that she was Venusian. I had thought perhaps she was Jovial, so I asked her how she had verified her body type. She responded that her primary verification was that she almost never experienced an adrenaline rush, no matter how dangerous or provoking a situation might be, and that if she were Jovial she would have experienced Martial reactions more frequently.

If, however, a person at the same point on the enneagram is a Solar-Jovial, he might be 30 percent Solar, 35 percent Jovial, and 10 percent each Martial and Lunar with 5 percent of the other three types (figure 4, page 262). In such an instance the two positive types, Solar and Jovial, so outweigh the negative types that they will not be as obvious. It might be quite difficult to verify whether the person is Solar-Jovial or Solar-Venusian, even for the person concerned.

Looking at the enneagram, notice that in its circulation the three passive types (Jovial, Lunar, and Venusian) follow each other. The three active types (Mercurial, Saturn, and Martial) also

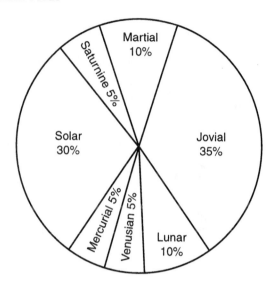

Figure 4. Proportional representation of a Solar-Jovial type.

follow each other. The fourth active type, Solar, is excluded from the enneagram circulation. A classic Lunar is therefore very passive—40 percent Lunar and 20 percent each of Jovial and Venusian means that 80 percent of this person's responses are passive and only 20 percent active. The classic Saturnine type, conversely, is very active, having only 15 percent passive responses versus 85 percent active (since the Solar is also active).

While the active and passive types follow each other, the positive and negative types alternate. The classic Lunar type, which is negative, thus has 20 percent Jovial and 20 percent Venusian from the types on either side. This means that some of the manifestations of this person come from the way positive types view the world. In other words, the intricate pattern of human types contains within it certain safeguards that should prevent extreme unbalance toward either positive or negative halves of centers, since both are needed for normal functioning. We must be able both to see the possibilities inherent in a situation and be aware of the difficulties which confront us before the pos-

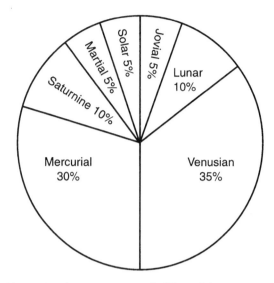

Figure 5. Proportional representation of a Venus-Mercury type.

sibilities can be realized. For this we need both positive and negative perceptions.

Most people are not classic types. That is, most people are not located on the lines of the enneagram near where they form the angles that touch the circle. Rather, the majority are situated somewhere on one of the lines connecting two types. If the point is exactly equidistant between two types, between Venusian and Mercurial for example, the result is an evenly combined type, Venus–Mercury (figure 5). The closer the point is located to one type rather than the other, the more characteristics of that type the person will have. Continuing to use the Venus–Mercury combined type as an example, a person located close to the midpoint between the two will have 35 percent Venusian, 30 percent Mercurial, and 10 percent each of Lunar and Saturn, 5 percent of the others.

The combined types are like separate types. Particularly physically, but also psychologically, they have consistent characteristics that distinguish them from either of the classic types on either side. The combined types are Lunar-Venusian, Venus-Mercury, Mercury-Saturn, Saturn-Mars, Mars-Jovial, and Jovial-Lunar. In the pages that follow I will discuss each of these in some detail, just as I did the classic types. (I find it interesting that the six classic types on the enneagram and the six combined types add up to the traditional twelve types found in so many traditions—but of course that leaves the Solar type and its combinations out of consideration.)

Before going on to discuss the combined types, however, there are some other important implications of the enneagram as it is used in this system. The value that this information about human types has—its primary value—is to help humans who wish to evolve into a higher level of being. In other words, this is an evolutionary study, not one that is concerned with success in this world. On the other hand, it is also true that the more balanced people are, the more all of their centers (or kinds of intelligence) function and work together, the more they take into account both positive and negative perceptions, the more they consider the characteristic viewpoints of all the types, the more they will be able to operate efficiently and effectively in the world. Consciousness and control of functions are developed for the purpose of strengthening the inner life, the world of the spirit. But at the same time the light of consciousness improves the functions so that people are likely to be more successful in whatever pursuits they are engaged in relating to the material world.

This idea comes up frequently in the Old and New Testaments. The story of Solomon, for example, relates how, because he asked for the gift of understanding, Solomon was granted all other gifts, such as wealth, family, and long life. And the New Testament teaches that to those who have, more shall be given, while from those who have not, even the little that they have will be taken away.

There are some very practical, and very spiritual, purposes for the information about body types and their circulation on the enneagram. When we are able to recognize types and predict their characteristic reactions, we find that this information is liberating, both as it applies to ourselves and as it helps us to understand others. Once we know that virtually all our limitations, weaknesses, and shortcomings are not things for which we can be blamed, most of us feel the lifting of a burden of guilt that we may have carried for most of our lives. If we are Lunars we cannot be outgoing and emotionally demonstrative, no matter how much others urge us to be and how much we may want to please them. If we are Saturns we cannot stop trying to control others—always for their own good—no matter how strenuously they object. If we are Venusians we cannot be aggressively ambitious, no matter how much our mothers want us to be and how much we may love our mothers.

Gradually, we also come to understand that the capacities, strengths, and abilities that we are proud of are also not our doing. If we are Lunars we cannot take credit for the painstaking attention to detail that results in accurately completed work and for which we are commended. If we are Martials we cannot take credit for our honesty and courage. If we are Jovials we have no reason to be proud of our talents and our ability to get along well with others. The more these twin illusions—guilt and pride—are diminished by an understanding of human types and how mechanically they function, the more the soul is freed to flourish. It is by separating from our mechanics, by seeing them as automatic manifestations, that we come into our true realm where we are not what we observe but what observes: where we can simply be. By understanding our own type we may come closer to that aim of the wise man, neither praise nor blame.

Once we begin to understand our own mechanicality, we can also have more compassion for others. If we are an emotionally-centered Mercurial and find it impossible to engage in repetitive tasks day after day, word processing in an isolated cubicle, or putting shingles on roofs, then we should begin to understand how hard it is for a moving-centered Martial to experience his own emotions, much less express them effectively. Once we understand how confining our own prisons are, we begin to have compassion for others who are also imprisoned in a particular way of seeing the world and reacting to it.

However painful it may be to come to these realizations—and relinquishing the illusions that we are doing things and that we can change if we wish to is very hard—they bring us closer to the truth. They bring us to a clearer understanding of what human beings actually are, and to a valuation of the inner life.

Once we begin to understand human mechanicality, we may despair because there is so little possibility of change. But there is some possibility. Gurdjieff said we have the freedom of a violin in a violin case. There's not much room to wiggle, but what room there is we can try to use, and this is where an understanding of the circulation on the enneagram is of practical use. For each person, the direction of development is toward the next type. The effort to become more balanced should be the effort to develop the positive characteristics and tendencies of the type ahead. The most useful friendships and relationships are not those of maximum attractions, although those may be the most exciting because their attributes are the opposite of our own. The most productive relationships are with those types which precede us on the enneagram circulation and whom we can use for models. These relationships are not as volatile as the strong attraction of opposites, but they can be much more valuable and much sounder over the years.

As I discuss the combined types, we will see how the weaknesses and negative features of one type can be offset very specifically by the characteristic strengths of the next type. These may not be the attributes the person most admires and would most like to have, but they are quite precisely the ones needed. The Martial, for example, may wish that she had the organizational ability and the ability to command that the Saturn has. Or she may wish for the warm and passive acceptance of the Venusian. But that's not what she needs most. What she needs is the harmonizing ability of the Jovial, to have her bluntness tempered by diplomacy and the single-minded drive to achieve goals deepened by greater awareness of other possibilities and values. And the Jovial, who may think that what he wants is the energy and drive of the Martial or the quick perceptions of the Mercurial, actually needs the coolness and detachment of the Lunar that will allow him to withdraw from the constant gregarious socializing he is caught up in and develop his considerable abilities in solitude.

Each type, then, can find remedy for their own particular weaknesses by intentionally cultivating those potentialities in themselves that are the strengths of the type they follow on the enneagram. We cannot make a silk purse out of a sow's ear, but we can make a silk purse out of an uncut piece of silk, so we might as well set to work. Or, if we have a sow's ear, we had better consider what can reasonably be made of it.

CHAPTER 18

THE COMBINED TYPES

From the discussion about the enneagram in the previous chapter, it is clear that many more people are combined types than are classic types. At birth each person will be located somewhere along the lines of the enneagram, and the lines connecting the angles have many more possible points than the angles themselves. Therefore it is clear, mathematically at least, that a large majority of people will have their type determined by being located somewhere on one of those connecting lines. When I discuss the combined types, I will again be speaking about people who fit a theoretical midpoint. Now however, this midpoint will be centered between two of the classic types rather than being one of the classic types themselves. Just as the classic types are relatively rare, however, so are combined types who are located exactly at a midpoint. Most combined types will be located closer to one or the other of the types they are between.

What this means practically is that a person located between, for instance, Mercury and Saturn will have relatively more responses governed by the anterior pituitary if located closer to Saturn and more responses governed by the thyroid gland if located close to Mercury. In the former instance we would see a person who is more organized and reflective; in the latter instance a person more perceptive and impulsive. It is useful to keep these differences in mind as you attempt to observe yourself and others.

Verifying this theory, as has been mentioned before, is an important key to understanding our mechanics—with the aim of eventually being less limited by them.

The six combined types that I will discuss are those located between Lunar and Venusian, between Venusian and Mercury, Mercury and Saturn, Saturn and Mars, Mars and Jovial, and Jovial and Lunar. I will also mention some of the combinations that occur when Solar combines with the classic types.

Lunar-Venusian

Since the Lunar type has a number of possible configurations from short and rounded to tall and thin, and the Venusian type is notoriously the chameleon of the enneagram, it is not surprising that the mixed type between them, the Lunar-Venusian, is hard to identify on the basis of appearance alone. The Lunar-Venusian can have the soft and rounded appearance that would be expected of a type midway between the partially finished look of the Lunar and the sensuous curves of the Venusian. There are many of this small and plump appearance who combine the frailness of the Lunar with the fleshiness of the Venusian. Lunar-Venusians with this physiology represent one sort of feminine ideal—not the thin, angular ideal that fashion magazines portray, but a sentimental ideal of popular songs: "The girl that I marry/ Will have to be/As soft and as sweet/As a nursery. . . ." Songs of this kind celebrate the Lunar-Venusian woman, as do hazy, out-of-focus greeting card photographs, and films about star-crossed lovers.

The Lunar-Venusian man with this combination is not, of course, the masculine ideal, but need not be lacking in very compelling masculine attraction. Film star Humphrey Bogart was of this type, and able to demonstrate his powers both to outsmart and defeat larger and more active bad guys and to attract women—most particularly his wife and frequent co-star, the beautiful Saturnine Lauren Bacall.

Some Lunar-Venusians, however, have a disconcerting tendency to look like the combined type that is their maximum attraction, the Saturn-Mars. Very frequently Lunar-Venusians are tall and relatively slender, with the pronounced jaw and cheekbones typical of the Saturn. The slenderness of the Lunar can combine with the large size of the Venusian to produce an appearance quite similar to that of the tall thin Saturn in combination with the stocky Martial. Psychologically, however, there is a world of difference. The Saturn-Mars type is among the most obviously active of all the types, and the Lunar-Venusian is among the most obviously passive.

The Lunar-Venusian, like all the combined types, is a more complex person than someone who is one of the classic types. The hormones that make up the chemistry of the blood in combined types are not clearly dominated by the secretions of a single endocrine gland. At certain times one group of hormones will be predominant; at other times another group will prevail. These secretions do not, of course, simply combine to get mixed up in a kind of hormone stew. They have their own very specific messages that they carry to the cells of the body, and very specific functions that they activate. For Lunar-Venusians this means that they will sometimes experience the coolness and consistency of the digestive, ruminative functions controlled by the pancreas while at other times they will respond with the warmth and sensuousness of the hormones of the parathyroid.

Which of these tendencies—the solitary persistence and concern with detail of the Lunar type or the warm accepting nature of the Venusian type—is going to be the more obvious in a particular person will be determined by where that person is located on the line of circulation between Lunar and Venusian on the enneagram. If the person is closer to Lunar, say 35 percent Lunar and only 30 percent Venusian (with 15 percent Jovial and 5 percent of the other four types) the Lunar tendencies will be slightly more pronounced than the Venusian tendencies. On the other hand, if the person is closer to Venusian, there will not only be more Venusian tendencies, but a correspondingly larger percentage of Mercurial traits will provide an active element not present in the previous example. But whatever the proportions may be, there are discernible qualities peculiar to Lunar-Venusians that distinguish them from other types.

This combination of types seems tough-minded and realistic, having the negative perceptions of the Lunar without the Lunar's moroseness. Lunar-Venusians are particularly well-suited for the healthcare professions, having the nurturing qualities of the Venusian when they are needed, but also having the protective armor of the Lunar so that they don't experience the burnout that occurs when too much energy is given to others. I know several Lunar-Venusians, both women and men, who have been emergency room and intensive care nurses or paramedics for years without succumbing to the stress that other types experience. If I were injured and had a choice, I would definitely want my paramedic to be a Lunar-Venusian, cool in the face of emergency but warm and concerned about my well-being.

The Lunar-Venusian type, unlike either the Lunar or the Venusian, is good at creating pleasant environments. This type seems able to strike a balance between the fussy almost sterile tidiness of the Lunar and the casual messiness of the Venusian by creating living space that is not only comfortable and inviting, but has a distinctive ambiance. The taste of the Lunar-Venusian tends to be organic. They like Maxfield Parrish prints and art nouveau design, paisley and floral prints, lace trimming, dried flower arrangements, and lots of plants in macramé hangers. They are sure of their own sense of style in clothing and interior decoration just as they are sure of who they like and who they don't like and sure of the work they want to do. The quiet certainty of the Lunar-Venusian, neither self-protective nor outgoing, passive without being weak or wishy-washy, makes this type very attractive even though they may not always be conventionally good-looking.

The moving-centered Lunar-Venusians, particularly those who are quite tall, can easily be mistaken for active types since their fondness for movement and a tendency to imitate the type to which they are most attracted, the Saturn-Mars, can be deceptive. In this type of person the passive nature is seen in the psychology, not necessarily in the activity of the moving center. This passivity is seen in an adherence to routine and a reluctance to initiate new activities. Moving-centered Lunar-Venusians may have very busy schedules of strenuous activities that they are consistent and reliable at performing, yet they take little initiative in making changes in this schedule unless outside circumstances or pressure from other people make the changes unavoidable.

The instinctively-centered Lunar-Venusian is more easily recognized as a passive type since this center of gravity reinforces the passive type's reluctance to expend unnecessary energy. This type is happy being a homebody, puttering around the garden with plants, taking the kids to the park, trying out a new recipe for spaghetti sauce.

Intellectually-centered Lunar-Venusians will appear to be more Lunar than they really are since the slowness of this center will make them seem withdrawn and timid while they ponder the response they will give. Emotionally-centered Lunar-Venusians, on the other hand, will seem more Venusian because of the interest this center of gravity has in other people and the consequent tendency to interact with more warmth.

But whatever their center of gravity, Lunar-Venusians seem the type who most need and insist upon a relationship with their maximum attraction. In many instances relationships between maximum attractions are stormy, or at the very least occasionally unhappy, because the differences in psychological makeup between opposites are so great that the two people, although strongly attracted to each other, really do not understand each other. This does not seem to occur with the Lunar-Venusian and Saturn-Mars combination. I have no idea why, but I do know that some of the most durable and genuinely happy marriages I have witnessed over considerable time are between people of these two types.

While the other types may be subject to confusion about which partners are suitable for them, and may be confused by a discrepancy between personality and essence into making disastrous choices, Lunar-Venusians do not seem to be. No matter what other types may woo or pursue them, they simply are not interested. They wait patiently until the right Saturn-Mars comes along, and then that's it. Their ability to bond permanently to this active and energetic mate, to be the calm, nurturing center to which this aggressive doer returns, is quite consistent even in this period of social chaos and the breaking up of family units. The Saturn-Mars partner seems equally devoted to the Lunar-Venusian. The Saturn-Mars type is, of course, much more active, and spends more time away from the home involved in projects and activities that do not include the passive partner. The Saturn-Mars does not, however, seem tempted into either sexual or emotional infidelity with anyone met while out adventuring.

What makes these relationships so satisfying might possibly be that they include all of the possible combinations of the enneagram types: the passive and negative Lunar is combined with the passive and positive Venusian, while the active and positive Saturn is combined with the active and negative Martial. When these two combinations in turn combine to form "one flesh" as the Biblical terminology phrases it, or, to use Plato's analogy, when the two halves of the sundered being find each other, in this particular joining of opposites there seems a completeness that is satisfying to both. This seems to be true regardless of the gender of the partners. Certainly the marriages of Saturn-Mars men to Lunar-Venusian women are those that conform to the gender stereotypes of masculine and feminine, but the marriages of Lunar-Venusian men to Saturn-Mars women also seem stable and happy—even in Hollywood, as the marriage of Humphrey Bogart and Lauren Bacall attests.

These unions may or may not produce children. If they do, the children are well cared for, but they do not become the whole focus of the household. This couple does not "stay together for the sake of the children." They are interested in their children's activities, but do not use them as an excuse for failing to live their own lives. An example of a devoted marriage between a Lunar-Venusian and a Saturn-Mars would be Britain's Royal couple, Elizabeth II and Prince Phillip. Their union has survived and seemingly remained strong through the most adverse conditions possible: the passive wife's prominent position in comparison with the active husband's relative obscurity, constant public scrutiny, the domestic problems of most of their relatives and children, etc.

But even though Lunar-Venusians seems to do well at the difficult task of forming durable relationships and marriages, they are also remarkably self-sufficient and able to tolerate being alone when they have not found a mate that suits them. (No doubt these two abilities, to live alone without much difficulty and to live in a close relationship without much difficulty, are related.) Lunar-Venusians are private and self-sufficient no matter in what situation they find themselves. One of my friends who is of this type, an intensely feminine-looking cupcake example of the type, had a career as a trucker, driving the big eighteen-wheelers. She said that she had originally gotten the training because of some feminist ideas she had and wanted to prove she could get a trucker's license. But after she started driving she found that she enjoyed it and wanted to continue. Furthermore, she said that it was her observation that a great many professional truckers were Lunar-Venusians. It does seem that this type is attracted to this business. The Lunar capacity for long periods of solitude while on the road seems to combine with the Venusian's ease with strangers, and maybe with non-existence, to make the working conditions tolerable. And the Lunar preference for late hours would mean the truck could make better time during the night when there's less traffic.

These, then, seem to be the characteristic attributes of the Lunar-Venusian combined type: a calmness and certainty of purpose and the ability to accept others without being dependent on them.

In the circulation of the enneagram, the cool, negative Lunar needs to develop the warmth and acceptance of the Venusian. The Lunar-Venusian needs to prefer the nurturing qualities of the Venusian over the Lunar tendency toward aloofness and isolation. But even more, this very passive type needs to cultivate the strengths of the next type, the active Mercurial. The Mercurial perceptiveness and ingenuity is exactly what the Lunar-Venusian type needs to counteract a tendency toward complacency and a lack of initiative. A greater sensitivity to the possibilities of situations can provide the Lunar-Venusians with a richer variety of experiences than they would have if restricted to the reactions of the two passive types.

Venus-Mercury

The Venus-Mercury type can be very attractive. The well-proportioned compact frame of the Mercurial type combines with the softened contours of the Venusian to produce meltingly beautiful women and dashingly handsome men. Film stars Elizabeth Taylor and Clark Gable, as well as many other entertainers, are examples of this combined type. The Venus-Mercury usually has thick, frequently curly dark hair and beautifully expressive eyes, long eye lashes, and Venusian sensuality in combination with Mercurial energy and fire. The amount of fleshiness or wiriness will depend on whether the person has a greater percentage of Venusian or of Mercurial, that is, on where that person is located on the line of circulation between the two classic types.

Psychologically this combined type seems to experience less inner conflict than many of the other combined types. The parathyroids and the thyroid glands seem to interact directly, the former dampening and modifying the effect of the latter. Instead of having conflicting messages delivered by the hormones in the blood stream, the Venus-Mercury experiences a continuum of a more or less active metabolic rate which produces a change in the person's external manifestations. This is not experienced as inner conflict but rather as an ebb and flow of essentially the same energy.

Although Venus-Mercuries are not necessarily plagued by inner conflict resulting from their dual natures, they can be quite baffling to others. Since this is a combination of a passive type with an active type, and indeed of the most visibly passive type with the most visibly active type, the range of behaviors Venus-Mercuries exhibit is quite startling. The two types are activated

VENUS-MERCURY: The *Venus-Mercury Combined Type includes active and passive and positive and negative elements, since this type is midway between the passive and positive Venusian and the active and negative Mercurial types. The physical characteristics of the Venus-Mercury frequently combine the tendency toward fleshiness of the Venusian with the short stature of the Mercurial. This type can be very attractive when the sensuousness of the Venusian is enlivened by Mercurial vivacity.*

by different situations—some sets of stimuli push the Venusian button and some sets of stimuli push the Mercurial button. In practice, this may mean that your laid-back, easy-going Venus-Mercury brother gets behind the wheel of a car and suddenly a Mercurial maniac takes over his body and he goes smoking down the freeway at 90 miles an hour, cutting in and out of the flow of traffic, and endangering all life forms in the area. Or the pleasant Venus-Mercury neighbor whom you've talked to over the fence while he putters about pruning his roses turns out to be the slave-driving, overbearing sales manager your daughter's boy friend complains about. It might well have been a Venus-Mercury who was the inspiration for tales of double identities—Dr. Jeckyll and Mr. Hyde, that sort of thing.

While the percentage of active or passive responses will be determined partially by whether the person in question is closer to Venusian or closer to Mercurial on the connecting line between the two, it will also be strongly affected by the person's center of gravity. Anyone centered in the emotional part of a center, for example, will seem more Mercurial because of the higher energy level of the queens of centers and the tendency of the queens to flip from the positive to the negative part without warning. In addition the dominant function will make the person seem more active or passive according to the habitual responses of that center and the speed at which it operates.

Moving-centered Venus-Mercury will seem to be much more Mercurial, and in fact may be mistaken for a classic Mercurial type because movement in itself gives the impression of being an active characteristic. Moving-centered people are usually slender, which would make the person appear more Mercurial than Venusian. In such instances it is the psychological characteristics that will reveal the Venusian element, not the physical appearance. If the person being observed is usually involved in some movement but doesn't have to be the one to choose the activity and in fact is glad to go along with any suggestions, that would indicate a Venusian element. Another indication is eye movement. The Mercurial is always looking around, noticing everything that is going on and probably some things that aren't actually going on but she suspects they might be. The Venusian is more likely to maintain a steady eye contact, and is willing to take things at face value and return a steady, open gaze.

Quite the opposite impression is presented by the instinctively-centered Venus-Mercury. Since instinctively-centered persons tend to be fleshy, this type may appear to be almost entirely Venusian on the basis of bulk alone. Again, the key is psychology, not the way the person looks. Instinctively-centered Venus-Mercury will have many more ideas and concerns about health and the health of the family, and about security, wealth, and possessions than a Venusian would have. This is the plump, comfortable neighbor who seems so easy going—until you see her out at the swap meet and realize she also runs a very profitable business in secondhand merchandise she picks up cheap by scavenging garage sales and auctions.

Intellectually-centered Venus-Mercuries can really be baffling—to the extent that we may be tempted to give up and conclude that this body-type system doesn't really cover all the possibilities and some people don't fit in anywhere. But wait a minute. What we have here is a type that is slender, perhaps even thin as intellectually-centered people have a tendency to be, and looks quite Mercurial but is so slow and deliberate that he couldn't possibly be Mercurial. On the other hand he is quite firm about his ideas and opinions and not at all suggestible or non-existent so it seems unlikely that he could be a Venusian. In brief, the intellectual center of gravity will modify the manifestations of both the Venusian element and the Mercurial element, making the former more tenacious and determined when involved with ideas and the latter slower and more deliberate.

The emotionally-centered Venus-Mercury, on the other hand, is quite obviously a Venus-Mercury since this center of gravity emphasizes both the warmth of the Venusian and the speed and high energy level of the Mercurial. With this type the changes that might confuse friends would be the shifts from the suggestible and accepting Venusian to the manipulative and suspicious Mercurial.

In their relationships with other types Venus-Mercuries frequently experience difficulties. Their enneagram-based maximum attraction, the Mars-Jovial, is not actually a suitable mate or partner. These two combined types are attracted to each other, but once in each other's vicinity they can irritate each other when the Mercurial element in one and the Martial element in the other are activated simultaneously. The relationship is likely to be brief and explosive. Since the Venusian component of this combined type is a silent partner in most instances, the Venus-Mercury may be attracted to a Jovial or a Jovial-Lunar, but their affections may not be reciprocated. The Jovial would not be interested in the Venusian aspects of the person and the Jovial-Lunar would likely be attracted to Saturns. The types which precede the Venus-Mercury on the enneagram and which therefore would theoretically be an ideal choice, Mercury-Saturns and Saturns, are also usually attracted to other types, usually either Lunars or other Saturns.

It is ironic that the type that produces the most beautiful people should be left somewhat adrift in the area of intimate relationships. There are serious difficulties in their relationships with their maximum attractions. Venus-Mercuries also have difficulties with the type they follow, or the type which follows them (since Lunar-Venusians are interested almost exclusively in Saturn-Mars).

The problems this type experiences with relationships are thus not the result of any inherent shortcomings of their own but of being located at an unfortunate place on the enneagram where the types which would theoretically be suitable mates and partners just aren't available, or are available only sporadically. It is therefore not unusual to find that Venus-Mercuries have several marriages, change partners in business ventures often, and in general experience unstable personal lives. Mercurial flightiness is not the only factor at work in this situation.

The Venus-Mercury frequently suffers from this inability to form durable relationships, and will employ a number of stratagems to overcome the difficulty. This type may become promiscuous and manipulative after having experienced several unfortunate relationships. There is a vicious circle that can operate—the Venus-Mercury who is hurt by an unfaithful partner finds it more difficult to trust the next one, and by suspicion and jealousy makes it easier for that partner to justify ending the relationship, which makes it that much harder to trust the next one, and so on. The defenses that are formed from this cycle can earn the person the reputation of being callous and cynical, a reputation that is not really deserved since the manifestations are a result of emotional pain.

The Venus-Mercury may find another channel for the energies that would otherwise be invested in a relationship. This type might develop a talent in one of the performing arts—acting or singing are good choices since the attractiveness of the type gives them an advantage as performers. Or the same energies might be put into a career in business or one of the professions. Or Venus-Mercuries may take advantage of a lack of close ties to indulge in the travel and adventure that they enjoy—the Mercurial restlessness can overcome the Venusian tendency to vegetate. Or, if it doesn't they may, as Venusians frequently do, continue to live with a parent or sibling in lieu of forming their own families.

The characteristic attributes of the Venus-Mercury combined type are attractiveness and charm. The Venusian warmth combined with the Mercurial perceptiveness and ability to entertain makes this type extremely likable. They have a tendency toward shallowness which may contribute to the difficulty people of this type sometimes have making commitments to long-term relationships, or in finding partners willing to make such commitments.

In the enneagram circulation, the non-existent, vegetative Venusian needs to develop the perceptiveness and quickness of the Mercurial type. In the Venus-Mercury type, it is the Mercurial characteristics of activity that should be preferred over the Venusian tendency to sloth. Even more important is the reach forward to cultivate the Saturnine qualities of thoughtfulness and organizational ability and control. These are exactly the characteristics the Venus-Mercury needs to mitigate a tendency toward superficiality and aimlessness.

Mercury-Saturn

In appearance the Mercury-Saturn is the most elegant of the types. This combined type has the Mercurial's wiry slenderness and the Saturn's long bones. The result is a tall, slim body, beautifully sculpted with delicate but prominent bones. Mercury-Saturn fashion models, both male and female, are currently much in demand for fashion shows and fashion magazines, not only because this type is currently in vogue but because clothing looks best when draped on a body almost devoid of flesh and certainly devoid of fat. Formal gowns and tuxedos were designed with this type in mind.

In addition to being tall and slender, Mercury-Saturns are usually dark with black hair and dark brown eyes. The men frequently have the Mercurial mustache. The type frequently has a regal bearing, is aloof, a bit haughty—the very embodiment of aristocratic style. There is even something of the sinister about the appearance of many Mercury-Saturns. These are the archetypal villains of silent films, twirling their mustaches as they tie the heroine to the railroad tracks, the bad guys of thousands of Westerns on film and television. This is Iago, or the Cassius of Shakespeare's *Julius Ceasar* who "has a lean and hungry look . . . such men are dangerous."[1] This is Count Dracula. The women fare a bit better but seldom play the ingénue. Innocence is simply not a characteristic attributed to Mercury-Saturns of either gender. The parts played by Mercury-Saturn actresses are more likely to be those of home-breakers and fallen women, wicked witches or cruel stepmothers.

The depiction of this type in drama and film is a bit harsh, but may stem from perceptions about the Mercury-Saturn psychology. Combining the quick perceptions of the Mercurial with the ability to organize and control of the Saturn might indeed

---

[1]Wm. Shakespeare, *Julius Caesar* in *Shakespeare Arranged for Modern Reading*, Frank W. Cady and Van H. Cartmell, eds. (New York: Doubleday, 1936), p. 781.

produce a master criminal. Usually it does not, but this type does tend to include schemers whose projects and plans are kept secret lest they meet with opposition or competition before they are put into effect. On the other hand, this elegant type is also frequently portrayed positively—consider the roles played by Cary Grant, Gregory Peck, David Niven, and other actors of this type who have played heros.

But whatever the appearance and the stereotypes associated with the type, Mercury-Saturns seem consistently to be very kind and considerate. They combine the Mercurial's powers of observation, a perceptiveness that causes them to be aware of what others are experiencing, with the Saturn's paternal concern with the well-being of others. The result of this combination is that when Mercury-Saturns are aware of someone in need of help, they will offer that help. The offer may be diffident or dominating, depending on whether it is being tendered by the Mercurial or the Saturnine part of the person, but it will be genuine, and genuinely kind.

Mercury-Saturns experience the tension between the erratic, impulsive Mercurial and the organized and controlled Saturn—and are not always successful in reconciling these two aspects of their nature. When a person of this combined type is able to combine the best of the Mercurial characteristics—perceptiveness and an abundance of ideas—with the strengths of the Saturn type—thoughtfulness and organizational ability—the combination can produce remarkable achievements.

Peter the Great, the amazing monarch who single-handedly forged the Russian nation and dragged it by force into the world of modern Europe, was of this type. His great height and strength would suggest this type, and his range of interests and accomplishments certainly seems to confirm it. The more we examine the details of his life and rule, the more characteristics of this type we see. He had an inexhaustible flow of ideas and schemes and the Machiavellian deviousness to survive the court intrigues, the plots and insurrections, that surrounded him. He even had the Mercurial love of disguise, pretending, when he traveled to the capitals of Europe to learn what he could of their technologies, to be an ordinary soldier or craftsman. Along with this amazing range of interests and abilities, he had the Saturn's ability to organize, to control and dominate, so that he was able to delegate authority to trusted generals and ministers and thus create a government that transformed Russia. (And of course it must have helped considerably that he was the maximum attraction of the heavily Jovial-Lunar population that he ruled.)

But while there are examples, like Peter the Great, of Mercury-Saturns who have achieved great things, it is also true that in the psychology of many Mercury-Saturns the ability to organize and coordinate is not consistent enough to keep the Mercurial restlessness and enthusiasm for new ideas from scuttling schemes before they are fully realized. As a result, the Mercury-Saturn is liable to self-deprecation as the severe Saturnine element judges the childlike Mercurial for its flightiness and irresponsibility. This makes the Mercurial tendencies all the more likely to rebel against the controlling Saturn, and the whole cycle of internal struggle repeats itself.

As is true of all the combined types, the psychology of the particular person of the type will be determined by the proportion of each type, that is, by where the person is located on the line connecting the two types on the enneagram. The greater the proportion of Mercurial, the more obviously active the person will be, with the kinetic restlessness, the quickly changing ideas, the negative perceptions of that active and negative type. The greater the proportion of Saturn, the more the external manifestations will be controlled until all factors in a situation have been considered, evaluated, organized, and pondered. These people will doubt themselves and others to the extent that the Mercurial elements are activated, and trust their own ability to do what is right for all concerned to the extent the positive Saturnine element is dominant.

The instinctively-centered Mercury-Saturn is likely to be particularly forbidding and unapproachable. The aloof dignity of this combined type is formidable when it is combined with instinctive energy since the instinctive center is wary and self-protective and does not like to be observed—and certainly does not want to be touched, or even spoken to, by anyone who is not a close friend. This is definitely not a cuddly and inviting type, although it is certainly an intriguing one that stimulates others to speculate about what might be behind that icy facade.

Moving-centered people of this combined type seem more Mercurial than Saturnine, except for their height. Much more open and demonstrative than instinctively-centered Mercury-Saturns, they are nonetheless also subject to the obvious mood shifts of the Mercurial part as well as alternating between the compulsive, erratic movements of the Mercurial and the controlled immobility of the Saturn. It is, in fact, by observing the moving-centered Mercury-Saturn that we can get an inkling of the kind of inner conflict this type must be experiencing.

The slowness of the intellectual center makes Mercury-Saturns with this center of gravity seem more Saturnine. The Mercurial element causes a greater variety of ideas and a tendency for the many ideas to cancel each other out in inner dialogues in which each set of possibilities squabbles with (and criticizes) other possible concepts and theories until the moment for action has passed. The Mercurial's tendency toward indecision because of a lack of trust in their abilities can combine with the Saturnine tendency to procrastinate while waiting for more information. The result can be a deadlock that effectively immobilizes the person.

When the Mercury-Saturn is emotionally-centered, the tendency toward aloofness is mitigated since the emotional mind is primarily concerned with and interested in other people. This center of gravity can also cause the Mercury-Saturn to develop a highly refined aesthetic sensitivity which will extend the elegance of the type by creating environments of exquisite taste, and clothing of distinctive style.

In their relationships with the other types, Mercury-Saturns seem to demonstrate quite a broad range of affinities, while they also have the capacity to be loners. Their maximum attraction, the Jovial-Lunar, is very frequently the type that the Mercury-Saturn marries. The relationship can be fragile, however, either ending in divorce or going through periods of separation and reconciliation—possibly because the Lunar element in the partner would react with distaste to the manipulative tendencies of this type. The most durable relationship for the Mercury-Saturn seems to be the next type on the enneagram, the Saturn, or the Saturn-Mars. The more Saturnine elements they have in common, and the less of the two active negative elements to cause friction, the better the relationship is likely to be. As was mentioned when the Saturnine type was discussed, Saturns very frequently marry other Saturns. In this instance, the unstable Mercurial elements profit from the steadying influence of the Martial consistency and directness while the two partners enjoy a similar level of active energy.

Sometimes the Mercury-Saturn forms a stable relationship with the combined type which follows it, the Venus-Mercury. In this case it would be the Mercury-Saturn partner who would be the leader or guide, providing a model for the ability to organize and to control manifestations that the Venus-Mercury lacks.

The same combinations that work well in marriage are likely to be good for business partnerships for the eclectic Mercury-Saturn. They can also do well in business with Mars-Jovials. For that matter, there are really no types with which this type could not work with effectively if it suited the purpose and fell in with current plans. This type rarely follows a single career throughout their working days. It is much more usual for them to be involved in a series of endeavors—importing Oriental carpets, operating a painting and wallpapering contracting business, selling electronic equipment, opening a consulting firm, starting a landscaping service. It is not that these business endeavors all fail—some of them may be very successful—but once the challenges have been met and the possibilities realized, the Mercurial restlessness makes these people look around for a new challenge and new possibilities.

The characteristics of the Mercury-Saturn, then, result from the combination of two types that are quite different in their psychology, even though they are both active types. Mercury-Saturns can lose so much energy in the effort to reconcile the disparate elements of their being that they are unable to hold to a steady course of action—and being an active type, outwardly directed action is important. It is necessary for people of this type, wherever they may be located between Mercury and Saturn on the enneagram, to develop their Saturnine qualities of self-discipline and to diminish their Mercurial tendency to ride off in all directions. It is also useful for them to reach beyond to the openness, honesty, and fixed purpose of the Martial type, because it is exactly the Martial ability to pursue a single aim to completion that could cut through the labyrinthine inner complexities and conflicts of the Mercury-Saturn.

Saturn-Mars

The Saturn-Mars type is the rugged "doer" of the enneagram. Tall and muscular, the men of this type, and the women, too, are the favored type of Americans. Since this type is the cultural ideal in the United States, and since the movie industry is located primarily in the United States, images of this type have become familiar all over the world as the archetypal hero in the guise of frontiersman, cowboy, lawman, Texas Ranger. Actors such as John Wayne, Clint Eastwood, Charlton Heston, Paul Newman, and many others have ridden to fame almost on the strength of their type alone. Of few words but great deeds, the Saturn-Mars male has dominated hero roles.

The Saturn-Mars female is also a strongly preferred type in the United States. Long-legged and slender, frequently with long blond sun-streaked hair, this is the California girl, tan and athletic. Kathryn Hepburn typified the Saturn-Mars woman for a previous generation as Glenn Close, Meryll Streep, and Julia Roberts do for this one—and so, in a stylized version, does Barbie.

It is not hard to understand why this type has dominated the imagination of Americans and why the attributes of the Saturn-Mars were exactly the qualities needed to conquer a continent, tame a wilderness, guide wagon trains to California, and in general reduce an unspoiled Eden to a polluted wasteland. American Indians, largely a Venusian population, thought them quite mad in their lack of sensitivity to the natural environment. But sensitivity is not one of the characteristics of this type. The Saturn-Mars is a combined type between two of the most active types on the enneagram in terms of an orientation toward acting upon the environment rather than being acted upon by it. Even the Mercurial type, which is also active, is not as confrontational in their approach to the world but work indirectly through manipulation and subterfuge and are therefore more aware of the operation of external factors. The Saturn-Mars, on the other hand, sees the external world—and to a certain extent the internal world as well—as the raw material from which something else can be made.

The Saturnine type is characterized by virtual immobility while all possible relevant information, opinions, precedents, and theories are taken into account and pondered before any course of action is decided upon. Saturns, therefore, act relatively seldom since by the time they make their considered decisions the situation will have changed to a degree that they need to start over and consider a new situation. Martials do not have this problem. The first plausible suggestion or the first hint of an injustice occurring is the one they act on, and continue to act on until the project is complete no matter how ill-advised it may actually be.

The Saturn-Mars type combines the careful thought processes of the Saturn with the Martial ability to swing into action and to see the action through to the completion of whatever process was initiated. An entire art form, the Western movie, has been structured on the tensions inherent in the Saturn-Mars psychology. Not only are the actors who play the parts of the Western heroes of this type, but the stories are built from the contrast

SATURN-MARS: Both the Saturn Type and the Martial Type are active, so the Saturn-Mars Combined Type is doubly active. This type includes both positive and negative elements from the positive Saturn and the negative Martial. Physically this type will be taller and thinner than the typical Martial, but more solidly built than the typical Saturn. The intense energy of the Martial enlivens the sedentary Saturn to produce both organizational ability and goal-oriented activity.

between Saturnine and Martial temperaments. During the first half of the narrative there are grave doubts about the hero's ability. Is the hero really a coward and afraid to act? Is he a drunk too far gone to shoot straight? Have years of peaceful domestic life made him too soft to stand up to the bad guys? The other characters aren't sure, while the hero is in his Saturnine pondering stage, whether he has what it takes or not. And many times the hero isn't sure either. His ability to act is compromised by his need for more information, a better plan, more security for the helpless townspeople who need protection.

But suddenly, wham, bam, something happens. The villain insults the schoolmarm. The bad guy torments the little kid. The Indians attack an isolated homestead. Whatever. And the "whatever" is the stimulus that evokes the Martial part of the hero. And watch out, bad guys! The daring plan that the Saturnine element had been working out is put into action by the fearless Martial (frequently a Marshall—James Arness playing Marshall Matt Dillon). Guns blazing, horse shot out from under him, the hero proceeds on foot across the burning sands of the desert, never giving up until the bad guys are brought to justice.

This ritualistic celebration of the Saturn-Mars characteristics has achieved a curious ethical status in the political attitudes of the United States. Unlike the British, whose more Saturnine approach will tolerate the inactivity of continued deliberation, Americans will deliberate only to a certain point, a clearly delineated incident of some sort, and then they feel compelled to act—no matter how stupid the course of action actually is.

With the Saturn's ability for strategy and the Martial's ability as a warrior, it is not surprising that the Saturn-Mars often chooses a military career or that they make excellent officers. General Charles DeGaulle of France, General (and later President—Americans like to elect Saturns to their presidency) Dwight D. Eisenhower, and General Charles MacArthur are all Saturn-Mars military men who served in World War II.

If the male Saturn-Mars is a formidable doer, the female is no less so. Her sphere of action is likely to be the home, the school, the community, and she is a largely self-appointed guardian of public and private morality. Women politicians, such as Margaret Thatcher, are frequently of this type, as are lady missionaries and those who demonstrate for worthy causes. The Saturn-Mars certainty that the world needs to be changed for its own good operates in the women without the blazing six guns, but with no less forceful activity. Since this type is a masculine type regardless of the sex of the person, there is a tendency toward lesbianism in the women, and regardless of their sexual orientation many leading feminists, such as Germaine Greer, are Saturn-Mars women.

The moving-centered Saturn-Mars has great endurance. The most physically powerful of all the types, people with this combination virtually have to work steadily from dawn to dark and then on into the night to dispel their amazing amount of physical energy. Agricultural work or similar kinds of hard physical labor will attract this type, and if they are in managerial or supervisory positions they will be that much more effective because in addition to their planning and organizing abilities they will work right alongside their laborers, setting the pace and demonstrating how the work should be done. This type will probably be athletic. Most of the physical education teachers I have known are moving-centered Saturn-Mars men and women, and many professional athletes are of this type, particularly basketball and football players and track competitors.

The instinctively-centered Saturn-Mars would be interested in financial success and economic theory and investment strategies. This person would be very concerned with family obligations and would enjoy providing the finest home in the best neighborhood. This type is also interested in health regimens and is knowledgeable about dietary requirements, exercise, skin care, and all the factors involved in staying healthy. The instinctively-centered Saturn-Mars parent is likely to be a firm disciplinarian whose children will receive a lot of guidance in all areas of their development.

The intellectually-centered Saturn-Mars will probably be involved in some practical application of ideas and theories. Geology, archeology, marine biology—any area of the sciences where the theory and academic work is balanced by vigorous field work—would attract the person with this combination of dominant function and endocrine type. If their interest is in the social sciences, they might be case workers or parole officers. If they are psychologists they will be actively involved in some part of the therapeutic community. Whatever the ideas the intellectual center is drawn to, this type will translate them into action.

The emotionally-centered Saturn-Mars will almost certainly be involved with other people in some capacity in which their activities are being directed. Teachers, coaches, therapists, personnel directors, tour guides, recreational leaders, counselors—all of these occupations might attract the emotionally-centered Saturn-Mars. The combination of a concern with other people and a compulsion for doing makes this type well suited for those situations in which groups of people need to be organized, supervised, managed, and in general told what to do and when to do it. The success of the Saturn-Mars in these leadership roles occurs because they do indeed lead—they are always the hardest workers and the hardest players no matter what the activity, and their energy is infectious.

In their relationship with other types, the Saturn-Mars is a magnet who attracts the passive types who have a significant amount of Lunar, and particularly Lunar-Venusians, who have little interest at all in any other type than the Saturn-Mars. Jovial-Lunars are also strongly drawn to the Saturn-Mars man or woman, and in marriage relationships this combination is frequently very durable. In business partnerships and other work collaborations the division of labor according to natural inclinations works out very well, with the Saturn-Mars handling the organizing and doing and the passive types attending to the details. These very active doers also combine well with other active types, with the occasional exception of Mercurials who may be a bit too erratic for the organized and direct style of the Saturn-Mars. Mercury-Saturns provide a good balance for them, however. The Mars-Jovial is usually too headstrong to be directed effectively, but these two types can be good business colleagues.

Remembering that in the direction of circulation of the enneagram each type needs to develop the strengths of the type ahead in order to overcome its own inherent weaknesses, we can see that the overly ponderous and thoughtful Saturn needs to develop the Martial's ability to act. In the Saturn-Mars type this balance is achieved and the members of this type need to try to develop the strengths of the next type as well. The depth and diplomacy of the Jovial are characteristics much needed by the tirelessly active Saturn-Mars. The ability to relax occasionally and appreciate the pleasures of life is also something the Saturn-Mars would do well to develop.

Mars-Jovial

The Mars-Jovial, like the Venus-Mercury, combines active and passive, positive and negative elements. In this combined type the combination has considerable forcefulness. There's a genre of jokes on the theme of what the result might be if creatures of different species were related. One of them asks, "What would you get if you crossed a parrot with a tiger?" The answer: "I don't know, but when it talks, you listen." Combining the Jovial ability with language and ideas and the Martial high-powered negative energy and drive gives much the same result.

Mars-Jovials have a very predictable appearance. They are hefty, combining the bulk of the Jovial with the sturdy frame and powerful musculature of the Martial. Although not as fleshy as Jovials, the Mars-Jovials typically have thick waists and carry their weight in the chest and abdomen. The women of this type will be large-breasted and heavy; they have borne the children and cooked the food, scrubbed the floors and tilled the fields of Central Europe since time immemorial, and still do.

The psychological makeup of the Mars-Jovial backs up the Jovials' interest in people with the Martials' concern for fighting for the right as they understand it. The result is a person who has definite notions about what other people ought to be doing and how they ought to be doing it. This type is drawn to teaching, particularly teaching children. With the Jovial vanity assuring that their understanding is the right one, and the Martial power ready to back this right understanding with firm discipline, the Mars-Jovial teacher enters the classroom determined to mold the available young people into the shape they should have or, failing that, to make them very sorry for their recalcitrance. Walk into the teachers' lounge in any elementary or secondary school and you will find a dozen or so Mars-Jovials of both sexes taking a brief break from their efforts to set their students on the right path.

Dictators of this century, and probably any century, provide examples of the Mars-Jovial combination. Joseph Stalin is probably the most obvious example, but Benito Mussolini was also of this type (and so is Boris Yeltsin—Russian politicians, whether dictators or not, run heavily to the Mars-Jovial type). In these tyrants we can see how the Jovial affability produces the charisma that inspires followers to place them in positions of power. Later we see the single-minded ruthlessness of the Martials in their elimination of anyone who opposes them. Military leaders and captains of industry also abound in this combined type. The Mars-Jovial is not necessarily the type best suited to command, but is probably the type which most desires to control others.

Given this tendency of the Mars-Jovial to attempt to attain power over others, it is not surprising that this type frequently has difficulty in relationships. The maximum attraction of the Mars-Jovial is the only other enneagram combined type which contains both active and passive elements, the Venus-Mercury. These types are drawn to each other, but when together they experience a constant game of Russian roulette. Things go well as long as the Jovial is manifesting in the Mars-Jovial while the Mercurial element is in control of the Venus-Mercury. And the situation is pleasant, even passionate, when the Martial and Venusian elements combine. But when the two members of this couple find the Martial squared off against the Mercurial, there will be trouble. And the Jovial and Venusian elements aren't all that fond of each other, either. The Mars-Jovial and the Venus-Mercury find each other attractive, but their relationships, partnerships, and other associations are likely to be stormy and brief. It is not advisable for them to marry each other.

MARS-JOVIAL: The Mars-Jovial Combined Type is midway between the active and negative Martial and the passive and positive Jovial, and thus has all four elements. This combined type, which has both the muscular build of the Martial and the fleshiness of the Jovial, is the most solidly built of all the types. The combination of Martial power with Jovial vanity also produces a psychological forcefulness that enforces the physical strength.

The Mars-Jovial is frequently one combined type off in its maximum attraction, being extremely susceptible to the charms of the passive Lunar-Venusian. Unfortunately, as was mentioned when that type was discussed, the Lunar-Venusian is a type very seldom wavering from its choice of Saturn-Mars as a mate. Thus the almost irresistible force of the Mars-Jovial's passion meets the immovable object of the Lunar-Venusians' certainty that they are not interested, and the result is considerable pain because Mars-Jovials really are helpless in the grip of their own passions.

It is because of this helplessness to control their own powerful sexual and emotional energies that Mars-Jovials seldom find the type that would be the best mate, the combined type one place ahead on the enneagram, the Jovial-Lunar. Having the Jovial element in common, these two can understand each other well, particularly since they also share the negative perceptions of the Martial and Lunar elements. Probably the most important factor, however is the calming effect the Lunar has on the Martial's intense energies. When Mars-Jovials have the good fortune to find a Jovial-Lunar mate or partner, there is a good chance the relationship will endure—at least until the more active partner is caught in the grips of strong attraction to someone who is not suitable but after whom they can't resist chasing. Even if Mars-Jovials do find a durable but unexciting relationship with Jovials or Jovial-Lunars, they are at risk for an affair with one of the types on the other side of the enneagram.

The inner world of the Mars-Jovial, like that of the Mercury-Saturn, is one of inevitable conflict as the psychological tensions between negative and positive, active and passive are unavoidable. The Jovial need for warm, close relationships will be thwarted by the Martial temper and impatience. The Martial tendency to be constantly active, working strenuously on projects until they are completed, will conflict with the Jovial love of comfort. The Martial in the role of warrior, fighting for what he believes to be right, will have difficulty giving way to the Jovial diplomat who can understand the claims of both sides of a controversy.

Mars-Jovials can often be seen caught in the dilemmas these conflicts cause. Driven by the need for companionship, the Mars-Jovial host will invite friends for dinner, then become involved in an impossibly difficult five course menu which includes appetizers that require hours of preparation, a delicate soup that must simmer all day and then be served with croutons and condiments that need attention at the last moment, Beef Wellington with its layers of paté and pastry crust, a crisp salad of vegetable rosettes, and an impossibly time-consuming dessert that must be served flambé. Of course things will go wrong, the Martial temper will flare, the host will spend most of his time in the kitchen, and everyone else will have a fine time while the Jovial part suffers with longing to be part of the party instead of producing it. Nor does he have a much better time when invited to dinner at someone else's house. He'll be out in the kitchen there, too, either taking over or explaining how things should have been done as opposed to how they are being done. If he hadn't brought such a superb wine he probably wouldn't be invited again.

The complexity and conflict that are typical of anyone who is of a combined type are intensified in the Mars-Jovial because the basic needs and tendencies of the two types that are going to manifest in the psychology and in the actions of the same person are so strongly opposed. The Martial's outspoken bluntness cannot coexist with the Jovial's harmonizing diplomacy. The Martial's commitment to duty and honor cannot coexist with the Jovial's devotion to ease and comfort. Whichever part of the Mars-Jovial makes a choice, the other part will berate him for it or complain about it. If this type is difficult for others to get along with, and it is, it is no less difficult for themselves to bear.

We can hear this conflict in the music of Beethoven. This Mars-Jovial composer gave us not only some of the world's most beautiful music, but music that is an unmistakable illustration of the psychology of his type. The contrast of bombastic Martial passages with deeply moving and delicately melodic movements give Beethoven's symphonies, concerti, and sonatas the unmistakable drama and intensity that is characteristic of his work. The suffering and loneliness of this great composer's personal life, and the prolific production typical of the tremendous energy of this type are also indications that he was a Mars-Jovial.

The scale and intensity of Beethoven's music is only one expression of the scale which Mars-Jovials prefer. For this type bigger is better. More is better. Louder is better. More expensive is better. Anything which displays the importance of its owner the most dramatically is better. Mars-Jovials will drive the biggest car their means allow: a Rolls-Royce would be best, but Mercedes is acceptable. One of the American luxury cars, a Cadillac or Lincoln Continental, might be preferred for ideological reasons. Mars-Jovials will have big houses, new if possible, but big at all costs and in the best neighborhood possible. A luxurious apartment might do, if it were in an exclusive area. A country estate would of course be better than either a house or an apartment.

Catherine the Great, the obscure provincial German princess who became one of the most powerful monarchs the world has ever known in her adopted Russia, is an example of the strange combination of characteristics that fight for control in the Mars-Jovial. Catherine's Jovial love of languages and study engendered her beliefs in enlightened liberalism, but her Martial autocratic tendencies were what actually controlled her huge realm. To view the Mars-Jovial love of excess, one need only visit her palace at Tsarskaye-Selo, one of the most grandiose architectural creations the world has ever seen. Although Catherine was quite short, she had the bulk of the Mars-Jovial, particularly as she aged. And she certainly had the sexual drive typical of her type, consorting with twenty or more favorites during her thirty-four-year reign.

In brief, then, moderation, restraint, and understatement are not concepts that this type is equipped to understand. The combination of power and vanity inherent in the features of Mars-Jovials compels them to display their possessions, position, and themselves in whatever ways they imagine will impress others. Of course the effect actually made on other people is likely to be the opposite, but this type seldom can understand why and only redoubles the efforts to impress by an even greater display of things or accomplishments. Perhaps because of inner conflict and dissatisfaction as the Martial tendencies conflict with the Jovial preferences, this type thinks they will only be acceptable if they can impress others.

The characteristics of the Mars-Jovial are the result of the energy of the Martial type combined with the depth of understanding of the Jovial. Right development for persons of this type would be the emphasis of their Jovial qualities and the diminishing of their Martial characteristics. The positive and passive qualities of kindness, generosity, and the ability to be a harmonizing influence need to take precedence over the Martial drive and ambition. In addition, the Mars-Jovial needs to cultivate the strengths of the next type on the enneagram circulation—the Lunar. To balance the intense involvement with other people, the Mars-Jovial would profit greatly from the Lunar's capacity for cool detachment and the ability to tolerate, and even enjoy, solitude.

Jovial-Lunar

One virtual certainty about the appearance of the Jovial-Lunar is that the men will be bald. I have known very few exceptions. Aside from that the appearance of this combined type will be most affected by whether the person is closer to Jovial, and thus has the rounded contours typical of that type, or closer to Lunar and exhibits the characteristic frail and indistinct build of the Lunar type. Jovial-Lunar women are often pleasingly plump, very soft and feminine looking without appearing overweight as the Jovial frequently does. The men may be more slender, but typically have a small potbelly and spindly legs.

The Jovial-Lunar is one of the combined types that experience an inner conflict because of the marked contrast in the characteristics of the two types that are combined in a single person. Even though both the Jovial and the Lunar are passive types, the warm, generous, expansive, and gregarious Jovial tendencies conflict with the cool, careful, solitary Lunar propensities and produce people who are confusing to themselves no less than they are to others. This type is likely to be very conservative in their choices of clothing, cars, furniture, and other possessions. Neutral tones of tans or grays mixed with an occasional light blue or a darker shade, solid colors rather than patterns, and conventional styles or practical models are typical of Jovial-Lunar taste.

In the back of the closet, however, there may be a bright, splashy floral print dress that the Jovial-Lunar woman has never worn, or a half-filled rack of colorfully patterned ties that the Jovial-Lunar man bought but never put on. The Jovial part will make purchases that the Lunar part would never wear or use. One Jovial-Lunar friend who after many years finally began to wear bright neckties on occasion, explained to me that for a long time he would put one on, look in the mirror, and think, "Everyone will look at me." Then he would take the colorful tie off, put on a plain dark tie, and go out.

This contrast between the preferences of the two types can also be seen in social interactions. The Jovial part will accept an invitation to a party, but once at the party the Lunar part of the person is likely to react negatively to being around so many people and either sit in a corner all evening or leave early. Or the Jovial-Lunar may invite friends over to the house for dinner, but prepare a meager and bland meal.

Friends and acquaintances are frequently baffled by this type's seeming emotional availability on some occasions, contrasted with the cool withdrawal they may encounter when they try to reciprocate at another time. On the first occasion the Jovial-Lunar would have been manifesting from the Jovial part and being open, warm, and convivial. But when peole who have experienced this friendliness attempt to make similar overtures at a future time, they may meet with a cool rebuff and wonder what they did wrong to so alienate their former friend. Of course, they did nothing except encounter their Jovial-Lunar friend operating as a Jovial on one occasion and as a Lunar on another.

Of all the types, the Jovial-Lunar is the most likely to be talented and accomplished in many fields, and particularly in music and the other arts. A very high percentage of professional musicians are Jovial-Lunars. Poets and other writers are also likely to be Jovial-Lunars. The greatest writer the world has ever produced, William Shakespeare, was of this type. The combination of the Jovial depth of understanding and the Lunar ability to tolerate solitude is an ideal combination for the development of an artist. Talent, which most Jovials seem to possess, is not enough by itself to produce a mature and disciplined artist. Great persistence, patience, and attention to the details of developing an art form are also required. It is here that the components of the Jovial-Lunar type are seen to be the perfect combination for a serious artist.

This combination, depth of insight and understanding combined with perseverance and attention to detail, is hard to beat in just about any undertaking, so it is not surprising that Jovial-Lunars can be successful in whatever they undertake. They can do very well in business, particularly small businesses where the owner must be able to manage the financial and bookkeeping aspects while being effective in product development and sales as well. Jovial-Lunars can also be good administrators in large corporations where again, they need to wear more than one hat, having the people skills of the Jovial combined with the patience and detail-oriented psychology of the Lunar. The social-services field is also one where Jovial-Lunars excel, since these jobs—case workers, counselors, parole officers, therapists—require an ability to interact almost constantly with people while still having enough detachment not to burn out when constantly exposed to human misery.

The Jovial-Lunar is a self-sufficient type which seems to be able to form durable relationships or live alone without undue suffering. They do not seem set in their ways as far as a particular preferred type for relationships is concerned, and seem more interested in a partner with whom they share common interests than with one who is a maximum attraction. In general, it seems that the stronger the Jovial element the more likely the Jovial-Lunar will be attracted to partners with a strong Mercurial element. And the stronger the Lunar element, the more likely the attraction will be toward a partner with a lot of Saturnine characteristics. It is also not unusual for Jovial-Lunars to marry the combined type which they precede on the enneagram circulation, the Mars-Jovial. They share Jovial characteristics and thus have a foundation for understanding each other while the Mars and Lunar aspects tend to balance each other.

When not in a close relationship, Jovial-Lunars have an almost monkish ability to live alone—monkish, but within the confines of a community, not in complete isolation. It seems that the Jovial part is satisfied by interaction with many people and so doesn't require a close relationship with one other person. In men, this type also has a tendency to homosexuality which, combined with the natural conservatism and conventionality of the type, frequently produces a person who prefers celibacy to the difficulties of sexual alliances which are not approved by society.

The center of gravity of the particular Jovial-Lunar will determine how the inclinations of this endocrine type will work themselves out in the areas of work and other activities. The instinctively-centered person of this type will be the most likely to need a family, and will quite likely be a devoted homebody and a good parent since the maternal qualities of Jovials of both sexes dispose them to have children and enjoy spending time with young people. The Jovial-Lunar who has an instinctive center of gravity may not have many interests outside the home and may be quite content with children, a hobby or two, a good stereo system with which to enjoy music, and a backyard barbecue.

With a center of gravity in the moving center, the Jovial-Lunar will be more self-sufficient and likely to remain single, or to terminate any relationship that interferes with independence. Moving-centered Jovial-Lunars may be harder to identify than others of this type because of the more fully developed musculature typical of moving-centered people, but not typical of either Jovials or Lunars. They frequently look more like Martials, but observation over time will determine that they are much more passive than the Martial type.

When Jovial-Lunars are intellectually-centered, they can be excellent scholars. The Jovial depth combined with the Lunar fondness for detail makes this type enjoy a life of research, writing, and teaching at the university level. Even when they do not choose an academic life, people of this type will usually be well read and experts, of amateur status at least, in one or more fields of inquiry.

Emotionally-centered Jovial-Lunars are also quite common, and are particularly drawn to the arts and to childcare. Teachers in pre-schools and kindergartens are frequently of this type and can be very nurturing and patient with their small charges. If they can move beyond the Lunar coolness to develop some of the warm accepting nature of the Venusian, so much the better.

Solar Combinations

The Solar type is not located on the enneagram circulation and therefore can combine with any of the classic or combined types. This can make recognizing the enneagram type very difficult. The Solar element is unmistakable because of the quite different and much faster vibrations of Solar energy. This produces people of more refined and delicate appearance, as children are more refined and delicate than adults. The texture of the skin and hair is much finer, the skeletal structure lighter, and of course the Solar type is the most positive of all the types and a very active type. All of these are the attributes of children, so it is by this childlike quality that we can recognize the presence of a Solar element in a person.

When these Solar qualities combine with the characteristics of other types they can mask them, making it very hard to recognize the underlying enneagram type. The Solar-Lunar, for example, combines the Solar's active and positive attributes with the Lunar's passive and negative qualities to produce people who are both idealistic and practical, visionaries who can attend to the details of making their dreams into actualities. Solar naiveté is balanced by Lunar negative perceptions and ability to foresee the problems which will arise before a given aim can be achieved. The Solar intensity is backed up by Lunar perseverance, and the result can be a frail-seeming, fragile-appearing person whose drive and accomplishments can seem almost miraculous, someone who looks like a butterfly and operates like a pile driver.

When the Solar combines with either of the active negative types to produce a Solar-Mercury or a Solar-Martial, the energy level is almost frightening. It can, in fact, endanger the health of a person having either of these combinations. People with this type combination may suffer from illnesses, particularly allergies, or from chronic fatigue syndrome. They burn out because they have more energy than they can control and are unable to rest well enough to replenish their strength. Solar-Mercurials and Solar-Mercury-Saturns are particularly likely to suffer from ill-health after making excessive energy expenditures in their youth. The Solar-Martial will be a little more sturdy because of the strength of the Martial type, but the Martial destructiveness can combine with Solar naiveté in ways that cause them to need all the strength they can muster.

When the Solar combines with one of the positive types on the enneagram circulation (Venusian, Saturn, or Jovial) the result can be a person whose negative perceptions can be deficient. While on the surface this sounds as if it would be useful, as if it would prevent negativity and depression and create the positive thinking that supposedly makes friends and influences people and ensures success, this isn't really the case. Because people who cannot see the negative aspects of situations are unable to make intelligent choices, they frequently experience more problems than those who are more balanced. Certainly it is true that negative types who are aware only of negative aspects in situations will have problems, but being too positive is also a drawback.

Solar-Jovials may be a bit flighty, social butterflies who are charming and fun but who lack common sense. They may be extremely self-indulgent, willing to go along with any scheme presented as long is it sounds easy, comfortable, and fun. They get involved in all manner of get-rich-quick schemes from pyramid clubs selling plastic jewelry to real estate ventures in malarial swamps. They may be unable to be serious about such realities of life as showing up for work on the days when the sun is shining and they'd rather be at the beach, or paying for the merchandise

SOLAR-LUNAR: When the active and positive Solar combines with the passive and negative Lunar Type, the Solar-Lunar Combined Type has the psychological extremes of either type reduced. The Solar tendency toward naiveté is offset by the negative perceptions of the Lunar, and the Lunar tendency to morose introspection is offset by the light energy and positive perceptions of the Solar. Since both the Lunar and Solar Types are small-boned and delicate, however, the Lunar-Solar is slender and fragile, and needs to be careful with nutrition and the expenditure of energy.

they've charged on their credit cards. True, they think the best of everyone, but that includes people who may not be the best—they may attract the unscrupulous who take full advantage of the Jovial generosity combined with Solar naiveté. And they also may leave dreadful messes for other people to clean up.

Solar-Venusians are a little better off, since the inactivity of the Venusian profits from the active energy of the Solar, and the natural earthiness, or coarseness, of the Venusian is lightened and refined by being combined with Solar characteristics. The warmth and receptivity of the Venusian, and the sensuousness, can counteract the Solar's feeling of isolation and loneliness. Still, the Solar-Venusian is certainly gullible and easily influenced.

Of the three positive types, the most fortuitous combination is the Solar-Saturn. Even though the Saturn is also an active type, it brings a certain weight and seriousness that the Solar lacks, as well as an ability to plan and organize which can offset the Solar inability to calculate for difficulties. Solar-Saturns, and particulary the triple active Solar-Saturn-Mars, are among the most formidable types in terms of accomplishing their goals. And no goal is too vast for their vision. This is a type that builds empires, like Donald Trump, or creates magnificent art on a heroic scale, like the architect of the Parthenon. Solar-Saturns tire other people out.

The combined types, particularly if they have quite a bit of Solar in their makeup, can be difficult to recognize—for people who are trying to observe themselves as well as for others. But the fact that determining a person's type can be very difficult in no way invalidates the theory of types. The very difficulty can be an advantage, since we have a strong tendency to stop observing those things which we think we know because we have labels for them. In this sense being of a combined type can cause continued observation while being an easily identified example of one of the classic types can cause observation to cease. And it is the continued observation that is of value, not the facile ability to recognize types. The observation of human types is a tool that can be used to develop greater awareness. It is not an end in itself.

CHAPTER 19

CONCLUSION

I have several times mentioned that the material in this book, the classification of human types, is merely a guide to the beginning steps of a much larger and more significant process. The use of this information is crucial. Although it may have some usefulness in the way we function in the world, our successes and failures in our personal relationships, our accumulation of wealth and prestige and so forth, that material usefulness is not the point. There are thousands, perhaps millions, of self-help books that address these matters far more effectively.

The point here is to get a clear fix on the actual nature of human beings in order to separate out the elements that are mechanical and arrive at some understanding of what else might be there. In other words, this is an effort to see if there is something else or if behaviorists like B. F. Skinner are correct in saying that we are only stimulus-response mechanisms and nothing else.

Much of the greatest literature and art that humanity has produced deals, metaphorically or directly, with realms of the human spirit. The great religious works do so. The greatest literature and philosophy does so. This study of human types makes no effort to do so, but it has meaning only in relationship to this higher understanding. Human beings have the potential to live in two worlds simultaneously, and the understanding of this possibility was much more common in prior times than it is now. One of the most dire difficulties of modern times is that people have become oblivious of this potential and are convinced that the material world is all that there is. From this misapprehension, this alienation from our own birthright of greater awareness, come the evils of the modern world. Indeed, this is the nature of evil, and always has been. Evil is the absence of consciousness, which is not to say that evil is passive. The material world, the body, the senses, are tremendously active and forceful. When they are not governed by a higher understanding, they lay waste all that is good and true and beautiful, leaving a destruction not only of the spirit but of the material world itself.

The understanding of human types is a necessary beginning in the development of consciousness because of the accumulation of artificial and illusory elements in the dreams we dream about ourselves. A very basic distinction that the Fourth Way system describes is the division between personality and essence. What I have described here are the components of a person's essence, the type of being that person was born to be. Each human arrives in the world with a certain genetic endowment and with four types of intelligence—the lower centers with which to function in the world. One of these functions will be the one that person uses most, the center of gravity. This brand new squalling person is also of a particular endocrine type since one of the endocrine glands will be more active than the others. Rodney Collin presents the theory that these glands are influenced by the planets and other bodies nearest the Earth:

> If we imagine a set of seven photographic light-meters, each sensitive to the light of a different planet, and made to register once and for all the reading recorded at the moment they are brought out of the darkroom, we get some picture of this "setting" of the human machine at birth. In another figure, we may imagine a safe with a combination lock of seven rollers, all in continuous movement at different speeds. At one particular moment, the moment of birth, the lock is "set." The combination registered at that moment will thereafter

provide the permanent key to the safe, the only one which will enable it to be opened and its contents examined.[1]

These metaphors describe the Fourth Way understanding of how the human types are determined by the planets affecting the glands.

These two sets of schematics describing the human machine, the description of the four lower functions and the classification of the seven body types, are separate but related, just as the circulatory system and the digestive system are separate but related in the body. These are the components of a person's essence. It takes long and careful observation to be certain which manifestations come from which sources. Not only are the elements that make up a person's essence complex and sometimes quite confusing, but they are usually obscured by the development of personality. It takes a very long time to separate those characteristics and manifestations that are a part of personality from those that are a part of a person's essence.

The essence of a person is that with which a person is born, what that person essentially is, and the personality is what that person learns. This seems like a tidy and easily grasped distinction, but the practical reality is much more complex. It is in the essence of all humans to learn, and to be changed by what they learn. The actual configuration of the brain cells, the neurons, is altered by the language learned in the first few years. So an actual part of essence has been molded to a particular form that it will have throughout the person's life. The language learned, and many other aspects of a child's early experiences, such as family and culture, penetrate the essence and modify it. Such very basic matters as food preferences, for example, whether the carbohydrate staple is bread or rice or potatoes, will remain as strong preferences of essence throughout the person's life.

---

[1] Rodney Collin, *The Theory of Celestial Influence* (London: Vincent Stuart, 1954), p. 146.

As a child grows, however, the formation of personality includes many elements that are not assimilated by essence but which form a protective barrier around it. The personality protects a child's essence from painful or unpleasant experiences. The young essence is very sensitive to negativity and learns to avoid it with responses that deflect it. A child who is ridiculed for crying may learn to act tough, and even may be a bully who terrorizes other children rather than suffer the taunts received for being sensitive. A child who is naturally rambunctious may be so severely punished for breaking things that she becomes very cautious and restrained in her movements. In these instances the personality forms a protective shell around the essence, and may eventually stifle the continued growth of essence. It sometimes takes years of observation and work for essence to emerge from the stultifying pressures of a thick shell of personality. It may be very difficult for someone just beginning this work to be sure of what he or she is observing, whether a particular manifestation is coming from essence or from personality. This is where the description of essence types is useful—it provides a basic description of what specific patterns to look for in essence.

It takes a lot of observations over a long period of time to gather enough objective material to arrive at any conclusions about any one tendency. Imagine that a man just entering the work observes that when he is around people he does not know well, he will take out a book or pick up a magazine and begin reading. Does this indicate that he is intellectually-centered and therefore more attracted to words and ideas than to people? Or is he a Lunar type and using the book as a way of protecting his privacy? Or is he perhaps an emotionally-centered Jovial whose essence would delight in meeting new people but who was so badly treated when he was a child that he has a deep fear of people and is using the book as a barrier against them? Or, as has been suggested before, did this man observe this behavior because it is not at all typical of his mechanics, because it is unusual for him not to begin socializing immediately when with new acquaintances—and thus caused him to be a bit more aware of his actions? It may take many, many observations of himself in different situations with different people before this man is at all certain where his behavior originates. Gradually, however, certain patterns will emerge that point quite clearly to characteristics which are in essence and which can be classified as coming from a particular function and a specific body type.

Personality is weakened by this work. The more observations are made, the more divided attention is sustained, the more the manifestations of center of gravity and type are recorded, the stronger essence becomes. And it is only from a strong and healthy essence that development is possible.

The main problem that we face in our attempt to observe ourselves is that we simply forget our aim to do so. The "I's" that are constantly generated in the different parts of our makeup continue to be stimulated by the impressions around us and within us. These old habitual associations are so strong that they reestablish themselves the moment concentrated efforts to be present and to observe ourselves cease. This is the nature of our sleep: we have the aim to be more conscious, but we forget it. It is too hard. It takes too much effort. We don't have the energy. Personality, which is artificial, nonetheless thrives on the illusion of being real. Its existence depends upon avoiding the present, because in the present we can experience our actual condition by dividing our attention between what we are doing and ourselves doing it.

Many great writers about the human condition have commented on our avoidance of the present. Here is such a passage from Pascal:

> We never keep to the present. We recall the past; we anticipate the future as if we found it too slow in coming and were trying to hurry it up, or we recall the past as if to stay its too rapid flight. We are so unwise that we wander about in times that do not belong to us, and do not think of the only one that does: so vain that we dream of times that *are not* and blindly flee the only one that is. The fact is that the present usually hurts. We thrust it out of sight because it distresses us, and if

we find it enjoyable, we are sorry to see it slip away. We try to give it the support of the future, and think how we are going to arrange things over which we have no control for a time we can never be sure of reaching.

Let each of us examine his thoughts: he will find them wholly concerned with the past or the future. We almost never think of the present, and if we do think of it, it is only to see what light it throws on our plans for the future. The present is never our end. The past and present are our means, the future alone our end. *Thus we never actually live*, but hope to live, and since we are always planning how to be happy, it is inevitable that we should never be so.[2]

We never actually live. This is our condition when we are not conscious of what is going on in the present moment. If we are not present to our lives, we are not living them. We are dreaming them. Memories of the past and plans for the future are ways to avoid seeing ourselves as we really are.

When we do begin the effort to observe, to divide our attention between observing ourselves and taking in impressions from our surroundings, we encounter another obstacle: the desire to change that which we see. Our first reaction to glimpses of reality is to be repelled, even horrified, by it. When we start to see just a little bit of our actual condition, how we act and what we say and the effect we have on others, we want to be different than we are. But that is neither possible nor desirable. If we want to live our lives and not die without having lived, we will have to bear whatever the light of consciousness reveals. That's what there is.

There's a teaching story from one of the esoteric traditions, Sufi or perhaps Zen, that tells about a criminal who wanted to

---

[2]Blaise Pascal, *Pensées* (Chicago: University of Chicago Press, 1952), Great Books of the Western World Vol. 33, p. 203.

change his life. The man was a master thief, a safe cracker who was so adept he had never been caught. But he was sickened by his life of crime and the harm it did. Nonetheless, he could not stop. In desperation he went to a perfect master and begged him to accept him as his student and to help him stop robbing safes. The master agreed to accept him as a student, but told him that he must continue breaking into homes and stealing money. The thief was anguished at this requirement, but so desperate he agreed to do whatever the master directed. The master insisted that he continue cracking safes, but that he observe himself as he did it.

Several months went by during which the thief followed his teacher's instructions as best he could. Then he could stand it no longer and went back to the master to beg him to help him stop. The more he saw the more he wanted to stop. But the master was adamant. He said that the thief must continue, and must make more efforts to observe every bit of the process that went on when he broke into a safe. More time passed and again the thief returned to his teacher to beg for help in giving up his robbery. The teacher asked him how well he was able to observe himself, and the man explained that he could see much of the process, could watch himself slip into the house in the dark, locate the safe, and begin feeling the combination with his fingers, but could not always continue observing as the door opened.

The master nodded and sent him out to steal more, and to watch until he could see every step, every detail of the whole process.

The next time the two met the thief had achieved consciousness and was himself a master.

Most of us, hearing this story, want to know if he stopped robbing safes. We have considerable difficulty entertaining the possibility that it doesn't matter whether he did or not. We are so conditioned to evaluate everything in terms of its relationship to the exterior, material world—the world that the greatest writers tell us is illusion, the shadows on the wall of Plato's cave, Maya— that we find it very hard to value consciousness itself as opposed to what it is we are conscious of.

That, however, is the purpose of this system of classifying human types. We are the safe we are trying to crack, and we are trying to watch ourselves do it. The point is the watching. If we are watching, then we exist. If we are not watching, then it doesn't matter whether we crack safes or what we do.

BIBLIOGRAPHY

Asimov, Isaac. *The Human Brain: Its Capacities and Functions*. New York: Penguin, 1994.

Bennett, J. G. *Enneagram Studies*. York Beach, ME: Samuel Weiser, 1983.

———. *Gurdjieff: A Very Great Enigma*. York Beach, ME: Samuel Weiser, 1984.

Bentley, J. Kelly. *The New Solar System*. Cambridge, MA: Cambridge University Press, 1981.

Berman, Louis. *The Glands Regulating Personality*. Garden City, NY: Garden City Publishing Co., 1928.

Burton, Robert E. *Self-Remembering*. York Beach, ME: Samuel Weiser, 1995.

Carroll, Lewis. *Complete Works*. New York: Vintage Books, 1976.

Carter, Charles. *The Principles of Astrology*. Wheaton, IL: Theosophical Publishing House, 1971.

Collin, Rodney. *The Theory of Celestial Influence*. London: Vincent Stuart, 1954.

———. *The Theory of Conscious Harmony*. London: Watkins, 1976.

Crowley, Aleister. *The Book of Thoth*. York Beach, ME: Samuel Weiser, 1978.

Cunningham, Bill. *Child Development*. New York: HarperCollins, 1993.

D'Agostino, Joseph D. *Tarot: The Path to Wisdom*. York Beach, ME: Samuel Weiser, 1994.

De Ropp, Robert S. *The Master Game*. New York: Delacorte Press, 1968.

Donovan, Bernard T. *Hormones and Human Behaviour*. Cambridge: Cambridge University Press, 1985.

Douglas, Alfred. *The Tarot: The Origin, Meaning, and Uses of the Cards*. London: Gollancz, 1972.

Fortune, Dion. *The Mystical Qabalah*. York Beach, ME: Samuel Weiser, 1984.

Franklin, Benjamin. *The Autobiography of Benjamin Franklin*. Kenneth Silverman, ed. New York: Penguin Classics, 1986.

Frazier, Kendrick. *Solar System*. Alexandria, VA: Time-Life Books, 1985.

Friedlander, Joel. *Body Types*, 2nd ed. New York: Inner Journey Books, 1993.

Gad, Irene. *Tarot and Individuation: Correspondence with Cabala and Alchemy*. York Beach: ME: Nicolas-Hays, 1994.

Gallagher, Winifred. "How We Become What We Are." *The Atlantic Monthly* 274, no. 3 (September 1994):38–55.

Gardner, Howard. *Frames of Mind: The Theory of Multiple Intelligences*. New York: Basic Books, 1985.

Goodman, Linda. *Linda Goodman's Sun Signs*. New York: Bantam Books, 1968.

Greene, Liz, and Howard Sasportas. *The Inner Planets: Building Blocks of Personal Reality*. York Beach, ME: Samuel Weiser, 1993.

Grimal, Pierre, ed. *Larousse World Mythology*. New York: Putnam, 1965.

Gurdjieff, George I. *Life Is Real Only Then When "I Am."* New York: E. P. Dutton, 1975.

———. *Meetings with Remarkable Men*. New York: E. P. Dutton, 1963.

———. *Views from the Real World*. New York: E. P. Dutton, 1973.

Hadley, Mac E. *Endocrinology*. Englewood Cliffs, NJ: Prentice-Hall, 1984.

Hamilton, Edith. *Mythology*. Boston: Little, Brown, 1942.

The Holy Bible. Revised Standard Version. New York: Nelson and Sons, 1951.

Jung, C. G. *Memories, Dreams, Reflections*. Richard and Clara Winston, trans. New York: Vintage Books, 1989.

———. *The Essential Jung*. Princeton: Princeton University Press, 1983.

MacLeish, Archibald. *New and Collected Poems*. Boston: Houghton Mifflin, 1976.

Morgon, Brian L., and Roberta Morgan. *Hormones: How They Affect Behavior, Growth, Metabolism, and Relationships*. Tucson, AZ: Body Press, 1989.

Mouravieff, Boris. *Gnosis I: The Exoteric Cycle*. S. A. Wissa, trans. Exeter, England: Wheatons, Ltd., 1989.

Myers, Isabel Briggs, and Peter B. Myers. *Gifts Differing*. Palo Alto, CA: Consulting Psychologists Press, 1980.

Ouspensky, Peter D. *The Fourth Way*. New York: Alfred A. Knopf, 1959.

———. *In Search of the Miraculous*. New York: Harcourt, Brace, 1949.

———. *A New Model of the Universe*. New York: Vintage Books, 1971.

———. *The Psychology of Man's Possible Evolution*, 2nd ed. New York: Alfred A. Knopf, 1974.

———. *Tertium Organum*. Nicholas Bessaraboff and Claude Bragdon, trans. New York: Alfred A. Knopf, 1968.

Palmer, Helen. *The Enneagram: Understanding Yourself and the Others in Your Life*. San Francisco: HarperSanFrancisco, 1988.

Pascal, Blaise. *Pensées*. The Great Books of the Western World. Vol. 33. Chicago: University of Chicago Press, 1952.

Piaget, Jean. *The Child and Reality*. New York: Grossman, 1973.

Preiss, Byron. *The Planets*. New York: Bantam Books, 1985.

Read, Piers Paul. *Alive! The Story of the Andes Survivors*. New York: J. B. Lippincott, 1974.

Rilke, Ranier Maria. *The Duino Elegies*. Stephen Garmey and Jay Wilson, trans. New York: Harper & Row, 1972.

———. *The Notebooks of Matte Laurids Brigge*. Stephen Mitchel, trans. New York: Vintage/Random House, 1990.

Ryan, Peter. *Solar System*. New York: Viking Press, 1979.

Scholem, Gershom G. *Major Trends in Jewish Mysticism*. New York: Schocken Books, 1941.

Seymour, Percy. *Astrology: The Evidence of Science*. London: Arkana, 1990.

Shakespeare, *Hamlet, Prince of Denmark* in *Shakespeare Arranged for Modern Reading*, Frank W. Cady and Van H. Cartmell, eds. New York: Doubleday, 1936.

Sheldon, W. H., S. S. Stevens, and W. B. Tucker. *The Varieties of Human Physique*. New York: Harper & Row, 1940.

Speeth, Kathleen Riordan. *The Gurdjieff Work*. Los Angeles: J. P. Tarcher, 1989.

Sun Bear and Wabun Wind. *The Medicine Wheel*. Englewood Cliffs, NJ: Prentice Hall, 1986.

Webb, James. *The Harmonious Circle: The Lives and Works of G. I. Gurdjieff, P. D. Ouspensky, and their Followers*. New York: G. P. Putnam's Sons, 1980.

Wills, Garry. "Dishonest Abe." *Time* 140, no. 14 (October 5, 1992): 41.

INDEX

THE FELLOWSHIP OF FRIENDS

The Fellowship of Friends, a Fourth Way School in the tradition of Gurdjieff and Ouspensky, was founded by Robert Earl Burton. The Fellowship's main location is at Apollo, a community in the foothills of California's Sierra Nevada mountains. Teaching centers are maintained in major cities throughout the world, some of which are listed below:

Ahmedabad	Milan
Amsterdam	Moscow
Athens	New York
Berlin	Palo Alto
Brussels	Paris
Buenos Aires	Rome
Copenhagen	Sacramento
Dublin	San Francisco
Edinburgh	Saõ Paulo
Florence	St. Petersburg
Frankfurt	Sydney
London	Taipei
Los Angeles	Tel Aviv
Madrid	Tokyo
Mexico City	Toronto

For more information on the Fellowship, or details of membership, please call or write for the Fellowship center nearest you:

The Fellowship of Friends
Post Office Box 100
Oregon House, California 95962
(916) 692-2244

Susan Zannos has been a lifelong student of the Fourth Way. She was born in Minnesota, grew up in Iowa, has worked in Lithuania, and now lives in California. She was trained at the State University of Iowa, and Arizona State, completed graduate work in education at the University of Washington, and has taught English at the college level for many years. She says that her real education came as a student of Robert Burton and the Fourth Way at the Fellowship of Friends. She has written all her life, with poetry, fiction, and travel articles published in various literary magazines including *Transitions Abroad, Greek Accent, The Athenian, East Sider,* and *Northwest,* and is the author of *Trust the Liar* (Walker & Co., 1989).